Wireless PC-Based Services

D1245069

R. Scott Lewis

PH
PTR

Prentice Hall/PTR

Upper Saddle River, NJ 07458

ISBN 0-13-041664-9

90000

9 780130 416643

Library of Congress Cataloging-in-Publication Data

Lewis, R. Scott.
    Wireless PC-based services : how to design, build and program systems using the latest
Internet standards and organizational techniques / R. Scott Lewis.
        p. cm.
    Includes bibliographical references and index.
    ISBN 0–13–041664–9
    1. Wireless communication systems.   2. Computer networks.   I. Title.

TK5103.2 .L47 2001
004.6--dc21

                                                                        2001035312

Production Editor: Rose Kernan
Acquisitions Editor: Mike Meehan
Editorial Assistant: Linda Ramagnano
Marketing Manager: Dan DePasquale
Manufacturing Buyer: Maura Zaldivar
Cover Designer: Talar Aqasyan
Cover Design Director: Jerry Votta
Composition: Pine Tree Composition

 © 2001 Prentice Hall PTR
Prentice-Hall, Inc.
Upper Saddle River, NJ 07458

The publisher offers discounts on this book when ordered in bulk quantities. For more information
contact: Corporate Sales Department, Prentice Hall PTR, One Lake Street, Upper Saddle River, NJ
07458. Phone: 800-382-3419; Fax: 201-236-7141; E-mail: corpsales@prenhall.com
Intel is not affiliated with this book

Printed in the United States of America

10 9 8 7 6 5 4 3 2 1

ISBN 0-13-041664-9

Prentice-Hall International (UK)Limited, *London*
Prentice-Hall of Australia Pty. Limited, *Sydney*
Prentice-Hall Canada Inc., *Toronto*
Prentice-Hall Hispanoamericana, S.A., *Mexico*
Prentice-Hall of India Private Limited, *New Delhi*
Prentice-Hall of Japan, Inc., *Tokyo*
Pearson Education Asia Pte. Ltd.
Editora Prentice-Hall do Brasil, Ltda., *Rio de Janeiro*

Contents

Foreword

In this world there are dancers and there are critics. This book is dedicated to my daughter Samantha Noelle Lewis, one of the dancers.

ACKNOWLEDGMENTS

The author wishes to thank the many people kind enough to devote time and energy in helping me with this book. I would like to acknowledge my supervisors at Ericsson Messaging Systems, Inc.—Mr. Borje Lundwall, Mr. Paul Nussbaum, Mr. Per Lindblad and Mr. Bryan Scallon—for supporting my development efforts. In addition, I'd like to thank Mr. Ake Gufstafson for assisting in the development of the S.100 aspects of the book; Mr. Sverker Mellhage for being a pal, and a damn good developer who likes to get his hands dirty in MQSeries code, among other things; Mr. David Oren for helping me with IMAP and various audio issues; Mr. Bo Svensson and Mr. Peter Scallante for encouraging the use of DNS, LDAP, SNMP in all the applications; Mr. Barry Wernick for input on the hardware trends and directions; and lastly, Ms. Nathalie Plaziac for advice on the IEEE and various video technologies and for just being a good friend and professional.

ENDORSEMENTS . . . .

Rajnish Prasad
Senior I/T Achitect at IBM

"Mr. Lewis' book is always the first wireless book that I pick up when I need to find a thorough treatment of all phases of wireless systems. It covers a wide variety of topics ranging from protocols to devices, networks, and applications, each with a clear and concise treatment. It will quickly become the standard reference for wireless solutions designers and architects."

Chris Harding
Directory Program Manager at The Open Group

"It (the book) presents a forward-looking vision of wireless services, in which Directory will play a key role, and helps us to understand more clearly what that role should be."

Gregory Gorman
Director, Wireless and Mobile Program, The Open Group

"Excellent overview of the protocols and technologies that are required to implement wireless data solutions."

Peter Becker
Director of Applications, the New York City Transit Authority

"Scott Lewis, with his insightful advice, guidance and depth of knowledge was an essential asset in our implementation of MQSeries. His book was at the side of our team the entire time and made for great reference. It was a pleasure working with him."

Thomas E. Deegan
Chief Executive Officer at GloveOp Financial Services

"Scott has produced an extremely, well-written, organized and informative book touching upon a wide array of technologies and techniques. This book has the breadth and depth to provide the necessary theory and reference information critical to the understanding of today's fast moving wireless industry."

Nathalie Plaziac
PhD in Electrical Engineering at Motorola

"With these brilliant descriptions of possible service available to the wireless industry, Scott clearly takes his place as a leading developer in the wireless space. He shows that there is no end to the number of services that can be created for a mobile phone."

Chris Deminis
Marketing Manager, Roche Pharmaceuticals

"Scott's knowledgeable approach to technology and his penetrating insights have influenced and accelerated our product development. He's inspired and challenged every member of the teams that he's worked with, resulting in even more cutting edge ideas."

Greg Antonsen

Chief of Staff, New York City Department of Sanitation

"With clear and brilliant descriptions, Scott shows time and again that there is no end to the number of services that can be created for a mobile phone, explores all the routes a message may travel in the wireless domain, and proves why he is a leading developer in the field."

Aldo Fortini

Director of Sales, Focal Communication

"Scott Lewis is the peerless inventor of such wireless service extenders as the unified inbox for microbrowsers, text-to-speech-to-language conversion, and handwriting-to-speech-to-language conversion. Instructive, provocative, always enlightening, he is truly an asset to the field."

Charlie Call

Personal Development Manager at IBM

"Very impressive book on wireless service."

ABOUT THE AUTHOR . . . .

I would like to offer a brief synopsis of my twenty years of experience with value-added services so that you may gain a better understanding of the evolution of wireless communications and services.

Let me start with some trivia I learned along the way. When I first arrived at Ericsson in 1995, the company wanted me to determine if we should pay or dispute a voice mail patent. I researched the subject of voice mail, which interested me since I had just finished a graduate level Computers and Law class at Columbia. I knew I needed to find some prior material that might make the patent null and void, so I began by looking at other patents. To my surprise, I found the patent cited *Muzac* (electronic music with messages played over the radio). At first, I found this quite peculiar until I came across the book, *The Development and Practice of Electronic Music* at my public library, of all places. In this scholarly work, they explained how to digitally record prompts, music, and voices for the purpose of playing them back over many different mediums, including the phone. But, the book was mainly about the creation of Moog synthesizer.

Furthermore, the book was printed in 1975 and the voice mail patent was issued in 1977. I felt we should seek to invalidate the patent, given what was found. However, since it was not Ericsson's policy to dispute patents and there was a slight leap in logic between the book and the patent, we decided to pay the royalty. The patent I am referring to was U.S. Patent No. 4,124,773, titled, "Audio Storage and Distribution System," filed 26 Nov 76. My main reason for mentioning this here has to do with the fact that Rob Elkins, holder of the patent, warned other integrators that his organization would pursue more litigation in the future.

Therefore, I suggest you see the subsection titled, "Legal Strategies for Software Companies" before proceeding with any further development. When I started my career in value-added services, I began in 1985 with computer systems, PBX, and voice messaging, among other things, as a VAR (Value-Added Reseller) for NYNEX, a RBOC (Regional Bell Operating Company). I felt the two most difficult parts of the job were dimensioning the systems to determine the system price tag and installation. Technically, attaching the mini-computer system to the PSTN (Public Switched Network) or PBXs (Private Branch Exchange) after it was sold was not trivial. I must have been capable because we sold two systems, one to the Federal Reserve Bank of New York, and another to the United Nations. They were two very selective customers.

To this day, these are still the most perplexing problems faced by VARs and OEMs (Original Equipment Manufacturers) of messaging equipment, especially since the world is moving to packet switching.

Infotext and Audiotext

Later, I got involved with IVR applications for the same RBOC. We were both a value-added reseller of equipment and a service provider. As service providers, the RBOCs would do the billing and collection for the entrepreneurs who wished to provide Infotext or Audiotext services by way of a 540 or 970—exchange phone number. These included everything from horoscopes and celebrity messages to selling tickets.

VATC (Voice Activated Telephony Control)

In 1990, I joined a development team responsible for creating a service titled *Voice-Dialing*. This was at a time when the RBOCs began to build labs to compete with Bell Labs and Bellcore. We made history when we replaced the ordinary dial tone with a speaker-dependent voice recognizer in a PSTN.

VoiceDialing resided in a VATC (Voice-Activated Telephony Control) architectural framework, which had a fault tolerant mini-computer(s) on the back end for storing the speaker-dependent templates (recordings) used in the pattern recognition process, and a networked, custom-designed rack of PCs built to withstand an earthquake. Each PC contained specially built recognizer cards, dual Ethernet cards, and a

T1 network interface card. Everything was proprietary except the local area network and the database. The most interesting interface was that to PSTN, since a whole new protocol was needed for tighter coupling. The protocol was NFA (Network Facilities Access). In other words, dial tone was replaced with a prompt and a speaker-dependent recognizer.

Callability

After VoiceDialing, it was possible to create many new services. One such service was *Callability*, which allowed the subscriber to remote call forward their phone from an 800 number. This was an IVR service that manipulated the databases of a #5ESS, DMS-100, DMS-10, and AXE. These were all fixed line telephone switches.

MXE (Multimedia Message Exchange)

In 1995, I joined the development team of the MXE (Multimedia Messaging System for wireless communications), an Ericsson product. The forte of the MXE was protocol conversion (i.e., Internet to PLMN) among other things like voice mail, e-mail, and fax mail.

IPMS (Internet Protocol Messaging System)

At the end of 1997, we prototyped a new system based entirely on the Internet standards (a.k.a. off-the-shelf). This initiative was counter-intuitive, since the current system architecture had some strength over the Internet architecture. However, the new Internet architecture prevailed, since it was much easier to introduce new features. Time to market a new messaging feature took precedence.

Therefore, we sacrificed things like the performance of our old system in favor of getting new features like those found in a new operating system or off-the-shelf e-mail server software. Our costs do not matter to our customers unless they impact the price substantially.

First Unified InBox

At the end of 1998, we had prototyped the unified InBox for wireless communications, which just so happened to be another first and the documentation is forthcoming in this book. However, we learned more from the business perspective than the technological, because our industrialization process lacked a means of getting press releases to the public by way of a media campaign. As a result, Lucent made the announcement first.

My point is, you need to coordinate prototyping, public relations and industrialization efforts by way of a good process. One such process is included within this book.

The Open Group

I had the opportunity to participate in The Open Group Wireless Task Force. This activity allowed me to experience what is necessary to change or influence various standards bodies. After working with them, it became clear that the standards for wireless were out of control, but I will discuss this later in the book.

Managerial Perspective

Throughout my career, I have worked in a management capacity, managing various products, developing the processes necessary to insure quality, and dealing with the human side of development. This is my reason for adding the managerial twist to this book. Use it as you may. Incorporate it into a business plan or use it to establish your own processes and practices.

Preface

TECHNOLOGICAL AND BUSINESS CONVERGENCE . . . .

Predicting the next big convergence of technology and business is simplified by contrasting the past as shown in Figure P-1 to the present shown in Figure P-2.

Convergence

Digitization is breaking down walls, as portrayed in Figure P-2.

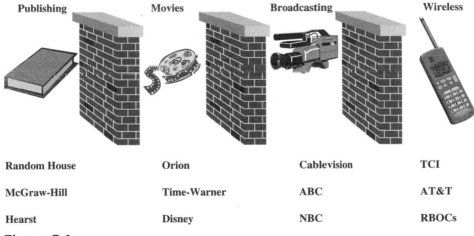

Publishing	Movies	Broadcasting	Wireless
Random House	Orion	Cablevision	TCI
McGraw-Hill	Time-Warner	ABC	AT&T
Hearst	Disney	NBC	RBOCs

Figure P-1
The medium was the message.

Figure P-2
The message is the message.

Rate of Bandwidth Convergence

The convergence of bandwidth between network, computer buses, and wireless networks is shown in Figure P-3. The baseline is that of a networked PC of late 1980s/early 1990s vintage, in which the most pressing application was compressed video conferencing. It is anticipated that the enterprise will see a 11 Mbps 802.11 server by 1999, and the commercial launch of 2 Mbps 3G (third-generation) technology in PLMN as early as 2001.[1]

Rate of Consumer Convergence

I believe that wireless service will mimic the growth rate of on-line services, but with a five-year lag. The lag is primarily due to bandwidth constraints that exist in the networks of the 1990s. The newer wireless technologies have bandwidths comparable to the fixed networks that on-line services have today. For my estimation of ubiquitous wireless services compared with the percentage of TV households and computer households, see Figure P-4.

[1]Cellular, p. 5.

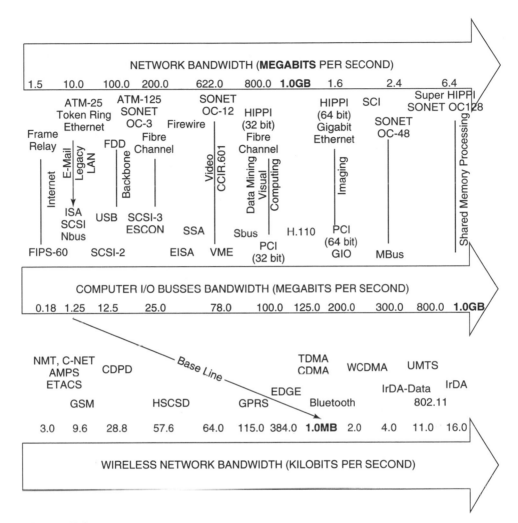

Figure P-3
Comparison of wireless, network and computer I/O buses.

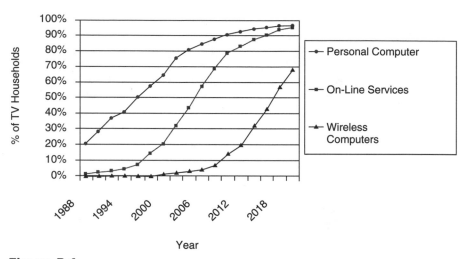

Figure P-4
Infrastructure driving consumer convergence.

Source: Forbes ASAP, Braxton Analysis with addition of five-year lag for wireless.

1 Introduction

PURPOSE OF BOOK . . . .

Convergence of the Internet with wireless information systems is neither well documented nor well understood. This book attempts to explain the basics on how to programmatically interface a PC to the technologies listed below for the purpose of facilitating services between them:

- Analog Cellular Telephony
- Digital Cellular Telephony
- 3G (Third Generation) Digital Cellular Telephony
- Enterprise Wireless
- Internodal Wireless Messaging
- Internet
- Wide Area Paging
- Personal Communication Services
- Global Positioning Systems

Furthermore, the book concentrates on services that unify the aforementioned network types.

Tech Talk

NOTE: There is some overlap with the fixed network standards (i.e., SS7), but an effort was made to concentrate on the wireless networks.

For example, a service under Windows NT is explained that performs text-to-speech conversion for the purpose of retrieving a voice, fax, or e-mail message from your mobile terminal.

Last, the Internet Protocol suite was used to interconnect the various components and services, since it provides a vendor-neutral architectural framework, among other things.

Hence, it should be possible to use these same services on other platforms (e.g., LINUX) besides Windows NT.

AUDIENCE ....

This book is for the developer, entrepreneur, VAR, OEM, or technical-savvy manager.

A distinction between VAR and OEM is needed in order to clarify what is meant by integration as opposed to development.

Original Equipment Manufacturer

The maker of the equipment is marketed by another vendor, usually under the name of the reseller. The OEM may manufacture only certain components, or it may build complete computers, which are then often configured with software and/or other hardware by the reseller.[1]

Value Added Reseller

Typically, VARs are organizations that package standard products with software solutions for a specified industry. VARs include business partners ranging in size from providers of specialty turnkey solutions to larger system integrators.[2]

Typically, the OEM is a specialist that is responsible for developing a product, whereas the VAR is a manager responsible for integrating the product into the customers' facilities.

The operative word is "integration"—where does the integration by the OEM stop and where does it begin for a VAR?

For argument's sake, let's take the example of a unified messaging system. Here are the basic off-the-shelf components for unified messaging:

- PC-Based Voice and Fax Processing System (i.e., Intel processor, Ethernet port, Dialogic D/12x and Fax/120 Boards,etc.) as the platform
- Computer Telephony (CT) Application Generators for creating telephone answering interface

---

[1]Newton, pg 695.
[2]Newton, pg 1052.

- Electronic Mail Message Server Software for message storage
- Web Server Software for browsing messages

Integration of these components was once difficult. An expert was needed in each of these fields: PC hardware, software, and networking for both Internet and Public Switched Telephone Network.

Now, however, the assembly is easier since the software is intelligent and user-friendly and getting easier by the day. No longer is a computer scientist needed to build a state machine for handling the incoming calls. Today, ordinary users with little to no expertise can create a new service just by reading the online help within a CT (computer telephony) application generator and, before long, they have a service.

Therefore, having made this distinction, successful VARs must be quick at identifying applications to turn up in their system, whereas successful OEMs must focus on creating a specific component while not losing sight of the bigger picture the VAR contends with. The forte of the OEM will determine the components they build. What this means is that the OEM will have specialized talents in one field or another.

What distinguishes one OEM from other OEMs are state-of-the-art advances, for example, being the first company to fax at 56Kbps or implementing some new standard of compression.

An OEM requires talented employees who really understand the technology. As soon as a company loses its talent, it is in jeopardy of becoming a VAR.

Quick Managerial Commentary

Avert the shift from OEM to VAR by way of proactive human resources intervention. Consider a new retention policy (e.g., try using better raises) or try hiring someone new.

However, don't be so quick to think you'll be able to find a replacement. According to Grady Booch, "Hyperproductive developers constitute less than about 1 or 2% of the entire development population." Furthermore, "hyperproductive developers are, on the average, 4 to 10 times more productive than the average developer."

If the company wishes to remain an OEM, it had better focus on keeping its talent.

OEMs have the potential to sell products directly to the consumer, the government, or to VARs or operators. They are not precluded from selling services pertaining to their component.

VARS only have the potential to sell product to the consumer or the government. They typically don't have the talent to sell to OEMs.

PREREQUISITES . . . .

The author assumes a basic knowledge of object-oriented concepts. Experience in both C and an object-oriented programming language is helpful.

NEXT ISSUE . . . .

Thought has been given to create another book geared for especially for ISPs (Internet service providers) and wireless operators, since their requirements are far more rigid as far as reliability and availability goes. In addition, subject areas such as voice recognition, speech-to-text, and language conversion were examined and are deemed within scope.

MODELING AND TERMINOLOGY . . . .

The terms used in this book are in accordance with the Unified Modeling Language 1.3. This is important when a question arises pertaining to a definition, notation, or semantics used heretofore, since the UML gives you a standard way to write a system's blueprints, covering conceptual things such as classes written in a specific programming language, database schemes, and reusable software components.

This was done intentionally so the author could focus on the business of wireless PC-based services.

Tech Talk

PRINCIPLE: Many organizations lack a documented process for development. The UML language and Rational Unified Process provide that infrastructure. Using them raises the quality, capability, and maturity of any development team. Use them today in place of making your own.

The necessary documentation is available free on the Internet at www.rational.com.

2 Wireless Services Overview

CONSUMER PERSPECTIVE . . . .

Bringing computing power to a wireless handset opens an extensive new consumer market for information access. This market is very different from the traditional desktop or even laptop market because the subscriber has a different set of needs and expectations.

Ease of Use

Despite the fact that using a desktop computer has become progressively easier over the last five years, a wireless computing device must be dramatically easier to use than even the simplest desktop computer. People who have no desktop computing experience use these devices. Furthermore, they will often be used in a dynamic environment where the use is engaged in multiple activities. Subscribers won't be focused on their handset the way they are when they sitting in front of a desktop computer. Therefore, the device must be extremely simple and easy to use. Application built for these devices must therefore present the best possible user interface for quick and simple usage. There can be no installation scripts, complicated menu structure, application errors, general protection faults or complicated key sequences such as ctrl-alt-del, or alt-shift-F6.

Market Size

The growth and size of the wireless subscriber market has been phenomenal. According to Global Mobile magazine, there are more than 200 million wireless subscribers in the world today. According to Nokia, there will be more than one billion wireless subscribers by the year 2005. The wireless market is enormous: it can afford and will demand optimized solutions.

Price Sensitivity

Even with today's sub-$1000 computers, a price difference of $50 between two models is not considered significant. However, a difference of $50 between two handsets is very significant, especially after years of subsidized handset pricing by the service provider. Market studies have shown that a mass-market handset must be priced under $14 to be competitive. A solution must add significant value at a low cost to be effective in this market.

Usage Patterns

Subscribers expect wireless data access to perform like the rest of their handset: the service should be instantly available, easy to use and designed to be used for a few minutes at a time. Hourglass icons telling subscribers to wait will not be acceptable.

Essential Tasks

As soon as professionals step out of the office, information needs and desires change. Wireless Internet subscribers will not want to use their handset to "surf the Internet." They will have small, specific tasks that need to be accomplished quickly. Subscribers will want to scan e-mail rather than read it all, or see just the top stock quotes of interest. Receiving timely traffic alerts on the handset will be essential, whereas the same information may not be as valuable at the desktop. The best applications will give the user a comprehensive, personalized summary of important information and will allow them to easily drill down for more detailed information.

The Network is Different

Wireless data networks present a more constrained communication environment compared to wired networks. Because of fundamental limitations of power, available spectrum and mobility, wireless data networks tend to have:

- Less bandwidth
- More latency
- Less connection stability
- Less predictable availability

Furthermore, as bandwidth increases, the handset's power consumption also increases, which further taxes the already limited battery life of a mobile device. Therefore, even as wireless networks improve their ability to deliver higher bandwidth, the power availability at the handset will still limit the effective throughput of data to and from the device. A wireless data solution must be able to overcome these network limitations and still deliver a satisfactory user experience.

The Device is Different

Similarly, mass-market handheld wireless devices present a more constrained computing environment compared to desktop computers. Because of fundamental limitations of battery life and form factor, mass-market handheld devices tend to have:

- Less powerful CPUs
- Less memory (ROM and RAM)
- Restricted power consumption
- Smaller displays
- Different input devices (e.g., a phone keypad, voice input, etc.)

Because of these limitations, the user interface of a wireless handset is fundamentally different than that of a desktop computer. The limited screen size and lack of a mouse requires a different user interface metaphor than the traditional desktop GUI.

These conditions are not likely to change dramatically in the near future. The most popular wireless handsets have been designed to be lightweight and fit comfortably in the palm of the hand. Furthermore, consumers desire handsets with longer battery life, which will always limit available bandwidth, and the power consumption of the CPU, memory and display. Because there will be a performance gap between the very best desktop computers and the very best handheld device, the method used to deliver wireless data to devices will have to effectively address this gap. As this gap changes over time, standards will have to continually evolve to keep pace with available functionality and market needs. The functionality is delivered by way of consumer services.The services expected are shown in Table 2.1.

Tech Talk

The services at the top of the table are ranked higher than those on the bottom according to the survey.

Table 2.1 Consumer Services[a]

Entertainment	Infotainment	Transactional	Outcasts
Big Event	Language Dictionary	Banking	Gambling
Sports	Weather	Phone Book	Grocery Store
Free Time	Travel	Remote Control	
Jokes	City Navigator	Ring Tone	
Sunrise	News	E-Mail	
Biorhythm	Stock Info	Pizza Order	
	Stock Portfolio		

[a]Source: *"The Demand for Mobile Value-Added Services—Study of Smart Messaging, Case Study," Nokia; 1998.*

Additional Characteristics

The following is a list of desirable characteristics a service might have:

- The personal component of the services seem to be very important.
- The most valued services enable a wide range of mass customization.
- The most desired services are those that are mobility-related.
- The most valued services are tied to timely information.
- Communication-related services such as e-mail and Unified Messaging may be popular.

Tech Talk

Mere entertainment services have a generally low demand. However, this may not be the case for adolescent age users.

- Instant messaging of active friends.
- Simple person-to-person messaging.
- Voice and fax mail notifications.
- Unified messaging.
- Internet e-mail.
- Prepayment.
- Over the air activation.

- Ring tones.
- Chat.
- Information services.
- Types of information services.
- Success factors for information services.
- Simplicity.
- Timeliness.
- Customization.
- Localization.
- Mobile phone jamming.
- Information services market structure.
- Shout mail for streaming voice messages to animated graphic electronic greeting cards, or e-cards, from any telephone or cell phone.

Handheld Computers

The two current platforms dominating this part of the market are the PalmPilot and handheld computers based on Windows CE. Both support modem communications and both support wireless communications with specific networks. The Palm VII, as shown in Figure 2-1, has a built-in wireless modem that operates with the BellSouth Wireless Data network. The Palm unit currently uses the Palm OS, but Java may be an option in the future.

Companies such as Telxon and Symbol Technologies that supply handheld systems for vertical markets such as warehousing have their own handheld systems traditionally based on MS-DOS. These companies are now migrating to the Windows CE and PalmPilot platforms.[1]

Smart Phones

The advantage of a smart phone is that by definition it comes with a communications channel built in. There are two types.

One type has a computing platform that supports a variety of applications. Examples include the Nokia 9000 product family (which flips open to reveal a complete, though tiny, keyboard) and the Qualcomm pdQ CDMA Digital Smart Phone based on the PalmPilot platform. WinCE will also start appearing in smart phones.

[1] www.networkcomputing.com/netdesign/1017mobile.html

Figure 2-1
Handheld computer.

The other type includes a microbrowser for accessing Web content. An example is the PocketNet phone from AT&T Wireless Services, as shown in Figure 2-2. Web access is via a gateway operated by the cellular carrier and Web content must be formatted specifically for the platform. In the future, these types of phones will use a standard set of communications and scripting protocols called Wireless Application Protocol (WAP). By 2000, a good percentage of cell phones sold will come with WAP browsers built in. As for operating systems, many will be based on these three platforms: the EPOC operating system from Symbian, the Windows CE from Microsoft, or even 3COM's Palm OS.

Figure 2-2
Smart phone.

Messaging Devices

The last type of platform is gathering increasing attention. These are small messaging devices about the size of an alphanumeric pager. Examples include the PageWriter 2500 from Motorola and the RIM Inter@ctive pager from Research in Motion (see Figure 2-3). These devices operate on two-way paging networks or wireless WANs such as BellSouth Wireless Data or ARDIS. Service includes e-mail intelligently forwarded from corporate e-mail systems or from the Internet and select Web content.

Wireless Network Appliances

A wireless network appliance is a computer peripheral that enables Internet access and specialized home or business use. It generally has one function and does it very well. Network appliances comprise hardware and software in one package, so they are easy to install—just plug the appliance into a wall and they require very little maintenance. Wireless network appliances include network-attached disks, cameras and displays, set-top boxes and Web browsers, handheld and portable devices, application gateways, and special purpose servers, such as Web and files servers. The difference is, these appliances come with the hardware and software together instead of the general-purpose servers of the past. General-purpose servers tend to get burdened by trying to run too many applications at one time. If one fails, the whole server has to be shut down to be serviced.

Furthermore, Jini from Sun Microsystems attempts to enable "spontaneous networking" of hardware and software; plug a new device into the network and it can participate. The aim of Jini is to allow people to use networked devices and services as simply as they currently use a telephone.

Figure 2-3
Messaging device.

ENTERPRISE PERSPECTIVE . . . .

- Corporate e-mail.
- Affinity programs.
- Mobile banking.
- Electronic commerce.
- Customer service.
- Vehicle positioning.
- Smart automobiles.
- Remote vehicle diagnostics.
- Customer service and sales.
- Ad-hoc stolen vehicle tracking.
- Rental car fleets.
- Job dispatch.
- Remote point of sale.
- Over the air.
- Remote monitoring such as meter reading.
- Web browsing.
- Document sharing/collaborative working.
- Audio.
- Still images.
- Moving images.
- Home automation.
- Voice store and forward.
- Text-to-speech.
- Voice recognition.
- Out-dial notification.
- Fax store and forward.
- Fax synthesis.
- Newer features.
- Internet access.
- Voice over the internet.

More Services

- Mobile trade services (securities).
- Credit card service (check account balance, member information).
- Life insurance account services (account information, money transfer).
- Airline services (online reservations, mileage account checks, etc.).
- Travel services (u.s. travel bureau, hotel online reservations, railway/ subway transit guidance, discount ticket search).
- Concert ticket reservations (searching concerts, telephone booking, online booking).
- Sales (online book sales).
- News/information (headline news, sports news, web news, horseracing info., Music news, technology news, business).
- Database services (recipe db, telephone directory, dictionary, restaurant guide).
- Entertainment (network games, character delivery, karaoke, surfing, fm radio station info., Web picture delivery, horoscope, fortune-telling).
- Auto-attendant.
- Voice mail.
- Voice messaging.
- Audiotex.
- Pay-per-call.
- Automated order entry.
- Call center.

EXAMPLE INFORMATION SOURCES . . . .

Table 2.2 shows a list of websites that provide information. These sites may be exploited by SMS, paging, e-mail among other wireless services. One component of the service would be an HTML provisioning interface used to establish subscriber accounts.

Table 2.2 Information Providers

Information Provider	Features
Money.com	www.money.com/rtq 50 free quotes per day No e-mail alerts to news/movements Delayed portfolio tracking News search available
Fox Market Wire	www.foxmarketwire.com 50 free quotes per day E-mail alerts for news/movement Real-time portfolio tracking News search
Free Real Time	www.freerealtime.com Unlimited free quotes No e-mail alerts for news/movement Real-time portfolio tracking News search
InfoSpace	www.in-114.infospace.com 50 free quotes per day No e-mail alerts for news/movement No portfolio tracking News search
Quote Central	www.quotecentral.com 100 free quotes per day E-mail alerts for news/movements Delayed portfolio tracking News search
ThomsonRTQ	www.Thomsonrtq.com 50 free quotes per day E-mail alerts Delayed portfolio tracking News search
Wall Street City	www.wallstreetcity.com Unlimited free quotes E-mail alerts Delayed portfolio tracking News search

PRODUCER PERSPECTIVE ·

Producers include wireless network operators or producers of a service.

Wireless Distinction

Audible service and visual services from a wireless perspective presents many challenges to the wireless service providers, application developers and handset manufacturers. While the obvious limitations are rooted in the nature of wireless devices and data networks, there are also fundamental differences that are important to understand. The next few subsections outline the challenges that must be overcome to make wireless Internet access appealing to the average wireless subscriber.

Kinds of Services for the Service Provider

- Trending.
- Operational reports.
- Service level agreements.
- Quality of service.
- Root cause analysis.
- Backup.
- Upgrades.
- Monitoring.
- Overall system health.
- Performance indices.
- Optimize resources utilitazation.
- Preventive management.
- Proactive management.
- Self configuring.
- Adaptive routing & load sharing.
- Load control.
- Self tests.
- Simple network management.
- Remote access.
- Gateways.
- Zero cost of ownership initiative.

i-Mode Service

i-mode service was launched by NTT DoCoMo of Japan. It began with 106 application alliance partners, 870 voluntary i-mode web sites, 5 i-mode search engines to provide service to hundreds of thousands of customers. i-mode services uses a subset of HTML and HTTP protocol. The service possibilities are shown in Table 2.3.

Table 2.3   *i-mode Service Possibilities*

E-mail	Transaction	Information	Web Access
Short text mail	Database	Entertainment	
Personal (Pacific) Digital Cellular (PDC)-Protocol			
Voice (PDC)			

3 Wireless Standards

EVOLUTION OF STANDARDS . . . .

Guglielmo Marconi first demonstrated the possibilities of radio communication in the mid-1890s.[1]

In 1901, he managed to send a radio message across the Atlantic Ocean, and by 1918, he had sent a signal all the way from England to Australia.

The early uses were for telegraph messages—signals made up of the dots and dashes of Morse code—but as early as 1906, Reginald Fessenden was able to transmit the human voice successfully by radio.

As early as 1903, the first international wireless conference was held in Berlin to discuss the use and reservation of radio frequencies for various purposes. In 1912, the Radio Act addressed radio-spectrum allocation in the United .States. The main concern was the emerging radio broadcasting industry. During the 1920s and 1930s, the radio receiver came into everybody's home, as a new and fairly bulky piece of furniture.

As early as 1946, AT&T obtained approval from the U.S. Federal Communications Commission (FCC) to operate the first commercial or mobile telephone service. Those early systems used a wide-area architecture, one in which a single base site atop a high building managed fewer than a dozen radio channels, connecting subscribers to the public-switched telephone network (PSTN). The 6-channel central radio at the base site transmitted tremendous RF power to the horizon about 100km away.

To deal with the power problem, AT&T was quick to come up with a solution to the first part of the challenge. As early as 1947, Bell Laboratories presented the crucial cellular concept, which showed how frequencies could be reused.

Briefly, the idea was to divide the area to be covered into smaller areas–cells–each with its own base station, using a number of frequencies corre-

---

[1]Meurling, pg 15.

17

sponding to the traffic expected within the cell. In adjacent cells, other frequencies would have to be used, in order not to risk interference. But in more remote cells, the same frequencies as those in the first cell could be reused.

The cellular concept includes the "handoff" function—that is, the switchover from one cell to another for a call in progress when a car crosses a cell's boundary.

As the area covered by a cell is limited compared with the total coverage of a system, transmitters in the cell use much less power. This also true, of course, of the transmitters in vehicles—less power to be transmitted means less battery capacity to carry around.

AT&T presented Bell Labs' proposal for a cellular system to the FCC, but because the critical technology for implementing the handoff feature was not yet available, the matter rested.

Twenty-one years later, the FCC reserved the spectrum for land mobile ("private") radio.

FM radio was another enabling technology which emerged during World War II. In countries like the United States, the mobile telephone system offered 11 channels of FM-based mobile phone service in the 40-MHz band. Two improved systems (IMTS-MJ and MK) followed, occupying 11 and 12 radio channels in the 152-MHz and 454-MHz bands, respectively.

As FM radio technologies were refined, radio channels got narrower. The earliest mobile phones needed 120 kHz of spectrum to transmit a 3-kHz voice circuit. By the early 1960s, the requirement had dropped to 10–30 kHz.

Trunking freed mobile equipment from the constraint of dedicating a single channel to each user. A frequency-agile radio could search for idle channels among a catalog of frequencies, rather than wait for its own assigned channel to be freed.

The earliest wide-area mobile phone systems used no trunking techniques at all. Later systems employed manual trunking, in which subscribers searched for open channels until they found one with no live traffic. Still later, systems flagged any free channels with a tone, for which mobile phones could search ahead of a subscriber's wish to make a call.

Even with narrow 30-kHz channels and the best automatic trunking schemes, IMTS service was often abysmal. The largest systems were usually oversubscribed, and blocking was typically 20 percent. Blocking during the busy hours was so high as to render some systems useless. Tariffs were also high.

Bad as the service was, people were still willing to wait for the privilege of becoming subscribers—five times the number of subscribers total in the largest systems. Radio channels were simply too fallible to accommodate the traffic offered. Private dispatched module radio (PMR) systems with 11 or 12 channels could cope with far more traffic than could a mobile radio system offering PSTN interconnection, because typical phone connections lasted two to three minutes as opposed to seconds for connections in a dispatched scenario.

Efforts to secure more spectrums for mobile telephony and PMR fell on the deaf ears of the FCC, which saw spectrum for broadcast services as more socially responsible. But the political winds began to shift in favor of mobile telephony and PMR in 1968, when the commission agreed to hand over television's UHF channels 70–83 (the 800-MHz band) to land mobile use. Then, in 1970, the FCC set aside 75 MHz for common carrier ("public") cellular systems.

The first cellular system came about as the result of the 1971 allocation of non-wireline, as well as wireline, carriers' access to the 75 MHz allocated for common carrier cellular systems. A wireline carrier is the traditional telephone company (Bell Companies and independents like MCI). *Nonwireline carrier* as the term given to prospective new operators of cellular networks (i.e., paging or radiotelephony companies).

Furthermore, Bell Laboratories proposed the cellular concept as the advanced mobile phone system (AMPS) architecture in 1971. They proceeded to replace the single base station with multiple low-powered copies of the fixed infrastructure distributed over the coverage area on sites placed closer to the ground. Each cell site was a copy of the trunked radio installation with its traffic channels being run by a trunking controller over a dedicated control channel.

The cellular concept added a spatial dimension to the simple trunking model. The low-profile, low-power cell sites were linked through a central switching and control function. It was the old wide-area network redeployed on a grand scale.

Reusing each cell's area of coverage invited frequency reuse. Cells using the same set of radio channels could avoid mutual interference if they were a sufficient distance apart. Interference among cells is proportional not to the distance between them, but to the ratio of that distance to their radius. Since a cell's radius is proportional to the transmitter power, system designers have great leeway in determining the number of radio channels available to subscribers. More radio channels can be added to a system simply by decreasing transmit power per cell, by making the cells smaller, and by filling in vacated coverage areas with new cells.

Cellular systems started to spring up all over the world in the early 1980s in a crazy quilt of incompatible signaling schemes deployed in different frequency bands. Each was a variation on the AMPS model that appeared in the Western Hemisphere, Australia, and parts of Asia. Some of the other simple FM systems were NMT-450 and NMT-900 in Scandinavia, Eastern Europe, and parts of Asia; C-Nets in Germany, Portugal, and South Africa; RMT in Italy; RC-2000 in France; TACS in the United Kingdom and elsewhere; and the MCSL1 and JTACS systems in Japan.

BACKGROUND . . . .

This section briefly describes most of the standards applicable for wireless electronic communications. It emphasizes how the standards have an impact on bandwidth utilization for voice, data, and video services. Scenarios are used to assist in understanding the key concepts involved in interfacing the various network types. The focus is on the newer standards.

The following features distinguish the different types of PLMN (public mobile network) from one another:

- Radio access techniques (e.g., TDMA, FDMA, or CDMA).
- Access network design residing in the MSC or the networks themselves.
- Functionality distribution (e.g., channel selection by network or mobile).

PC-Based Server

The concept of a PCBS (PC-based server) was used for the purpose of explaining access to the wireless systems. The PCBS is a PC computer with interfaces to a wireless network moving forward.

ANALOG CELLULAR TELEPHONY . . . .

Analog cellular telephony networks are characterized by analog control and traffic channels. Both voice (commonly 3 kHz) and data are frequency-modulated on a carrier.

Analog wireless network standards are

- NMT–Nordic mobile telephony,
- AMPS–Advanced mobile phone systems, and
- TACS–Total access communications system. Table 3.1 provides an in-depth overview of the analog standards.

Most analog and digital phones can lock on to these network types using a complex scanning algorithm of narrowband FM radio frequencies:

Table 3.1 Analog Cellular Telephony Standards

Standard	NMT 450	AMPS	TACS	NMT 900
System start	1981	1984	1985	1986
Frequency-band uplink	453–457.5MHz	824–849MHz	890–915MHz	890–915 MHz
Frequency-band downlink	462–467.5 MHz	869–894 MHz	935–960 MHz	935–960 band MHz
Channel capacity	180/359	832	1000	999/1999
Bearer	2400–9600 bits/s	2400–9600 bits/s	2400–9600 bits/s	2400–9600 bits/s

- 850 MHz AMPS
- 850 MHz IS-136
- 1900 MHz IS-136

Five Basic Parts

Figure 3-1 shows how cellular systems may be divided conceptually into five parts: radios, switching systems, databases, processing centers, and external networks. However, multiple parts will be realized into a single physical entity–for example, a database combined with a switching system.

The mobile connection of cellular subscribers and fixed telecommunications networks are realized with radios. The MS (mobile station) is usually a small handset. Its corresponding BTS (base transceiver station) works through a BSC (base station controller). Together, the BTS and BSC are called BS (base station). The switching function is a combination of computing platforms and transmission facilities that route user information and signaling among nodes through the mobile network. The functional entity is called the MSC (mobile switching center). The center, its attached base stations, and any inter-working functions to terrestrial networks or other kinds of networks are collectively called a mobile switching center and an interworking function. This function communicates with mobile stations over an air interface.

Several types of databases are queried by network entities while providing services to mobile subscribers. Location registers manage mobility and are unique to mobile networks. The home location register (HLR) permanently stores subscriber data relative to network intelligence, while the visitor location register (VLR) maintains temporary working copies of active subscribers in the network.

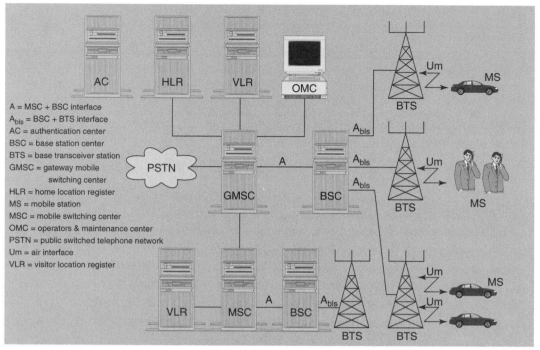

Figure 3-1
Cellular system.[2]

Furthermore, peripheral computing platforms enhance the profitability of mobile networks. The authentication center (AC) performs functions that validate a mobile station's identity. Voice-announcement systems and message centers are other functions.

The mobile station is divided into two physical parts, whereas TIA/EIA-41 networks see the mobile station as a single entity, in which the subscriber's MIN (mobile identification number) resides in the terminal.

GSM separates the subscribers' identities and their personal record—for example, quick dialing numbers–from the terminal. The terminal hardware is called the ME (mobile equipment); a subscriber's identity is contained within a SIM (subscriber identity module). The SIM is a small computer embedded in a plastic carrier that, when inserted into the mobile equipment, makes the equivalent of the mobile station defined in IS-41 networks, which is explained later in this section.

[2]Oliphant.

The fact that GSM segregates the subscriber records from the handset affects the fixed network in many ways, particularly within the databases. For example, mobility management is confined to the identity module in which the authentication algorithms are stored. The module makes international roaming among the GSM networks on different bands as simple as moving it from one handset to another. The subscriber identity module encourages more handset sales than would be expected in IS-41 network, because a single subscription may be moved among different handsets—perhaps between a small handset for voice communications and a larger smart phone for retrieving e-mail.

A mobile station consists of the hardware components listed in Table 3.2:[3]

Roaming has two types of standard interfaces (one for GSM and another that spans TIA-136 and IS-95).

The moment the user registers on a visiting system, an IS-41 (the inter-network signaling protocol) data message is sent back to the phone's home location register. Mobile radio networks use packet-switched common-channel communications protocols among their databases. IS-41 allows X.25 and SS7 communications protocols, but most networks are SS7 based. IS-41 authentication relies on the cellular-authentication and voice-encryption (CAVE) algorithms.

Even more, mobile radio networks add extra message types between nodes. These additions are called MAP (mobile application part) messages.

Short-message service (SMS) is by way of an out-of-band signaling channel, even for analog networks. This holds true for MWI (message-waiting indicators). The remaining services use the voice channel, just as they do in the PSTN.

Table 3.3 shows how a cellular phone receives service.

AMPS are notable mobile network standards specified by the U.S. consortium TIA/EIA/ANSI. The air interface standard is referred to as EIA/TIA-553. The stan-

Table 3.2 MS Hardware Components

DSP	Display
Memory	Manual input
RF section	Substrates
SIM card	Connectors
External and internal packaging assembly	Power management and batteries

[3]http://www.the-arc-group.com

Table 3.3 *Analog Cellular Phone Service Channels*

Mobile Equipment Sessions	Channel Type	PCBS Applications
1	Out-of-band signaling (SS7)	SMS, MWI, etc.
2	In-band signaling (DTMF)	Voice, Fax, Outbound Notification, Text Messaging.

dard was expanded to contain a wider frequency band, E-AMPS. AMPS networks are found in the Americas, in Australia, and in Asia.

A PCBS can indirectly support the analog cellular telephony standard for data communications, called American mobile phone service (AMPS), which means users can get reliable circuit-switched data connections, provided that the network has a cellular-protocol modem pool (e.g., Mobidem series from Ericsson mobile data business unit).

NMT was specified by the Nordic telecommunications administration and was the first commercially operated public mobile network. Two variants exist: NMT 450 and NMT 900. The numbers relate to the frequency bands used. NMT has been implemented in Europe, the Middle East, and Asia.

TACS is a modified version of AMPS, but its frequency band is somewhat higher. The modification was made with the British market in view, because that is where the standard was operational. TACS also received a wider frequency band, in turn making it ETACS. ETACS is spread around the world.

A PCBS indirectly supports the analog cellular telephony standard for data communication, called Extended Total Access Communications Systems (ETACS), which means users can get reliable circuit-switched data connections, again provided that the network has a cellular-protocol modem pool.

Speeds

A data-communication user can obtain uncompressed speeds of 9.6 Kbps, or 14.4 Kbps with good radio conditions. One drawback to achieving high performance, however, is that both sides of the connection require cellular-enhanced modems.

If one side uses a conventional landline modem, both connection reliability and throughput can suffer.

Digital cellular systems address connection stability and are explained in the remainder of the section.

SIGNALING SYSTEM NO. 7 AND WIRELESS . . . . . .

The Common Channel Signaling System No. 7 (SS7) was initially developed to manage call connections and disconnections. It has expanded to provide many other service functions for both fixed and wireless networks (such as "800" call features, SMS, call forwarding, and database administration). The SS7 specification is based on the ISO seven-layer model, is ISDN compatible, and is suitable for use over a satellite link. It introduced packet-switched networks for carrying call-signaling messages and is used in both the PSTN and the PLMN.

Figure 3-2 shows one signaling channel with two exchanges, A and B. The data link level is a full duplex, a 64-Kbps (Europe) or a 56-Kbps (North America) link dedicated to signaling, depending upon the error-encoding format.

Figure 3-3 shows a subset of an SS7 network that handles the routing of long-distance calls, along with a great deal of other traffic. The network is fully connected for reliability. It has two interconnected duplicated STPs. The regional STPs are augmented by area STPs. Either switching signal points (SSP) or end exchange offices are the termination points of the circuit-switched connections.

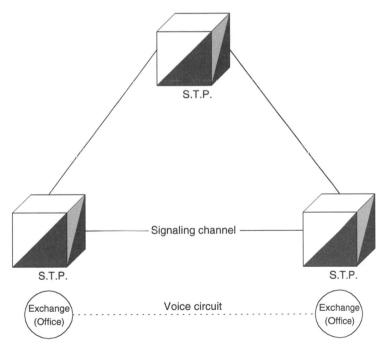

Figure 3-2
Portion of a CCS network.

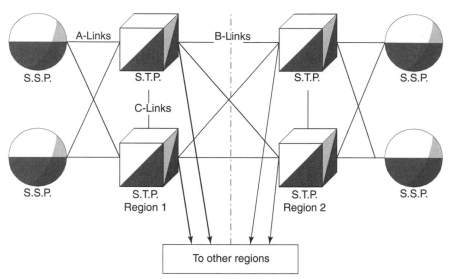

Figure 3-3
CCS network.

User Part

The user part comes in several varieties, each one corresponding to higher layer protocols that enable user functions (possibly on dissimilar machines) to communicate
with one another. Examples of user parts include a telephone user part for basic telephone service, a data user part for circuit-switched data service, an operations and
maintenance user part, and an ISDN (integrated service digital network) user part for
providing combined voice, data, and video services. The user part makes use of the
network delivery services provided by the message transfer part.

Message Transfer Part

As indicated in Figure 3-4, the message transfer part covers the lower three OSI levels. The data link level is a full-duplex 64-Kbps link dedicated to signaling. Because
the system may have to handle the needs of many thousands of callers simultaneously, it is most important that this link be error free. This level ensures that blocks of
data are delivered in the correct order, are not transmitted at a rate too high for the receiver, and data are not duplicated. The extensive nature of this control feature is also
shown in Figure 3-4. The upper levels of the protocol manage the actual data transfers
through the interfaces and the switching systems.

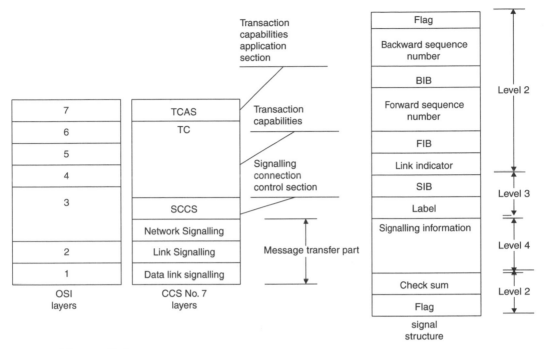

Figure 3-4
CCS No. 7 signaling.

Portable SS7 Stacks

PCBS typically supports the C7 node architecture by way of an interface card (i.e., Adax Inc.), which means that the PCBS software requires the following characteristics:

- Each PCBS is divided into different parts and then layered.
- Each part generates messages relating to its own functions.
- The PCBS supports both types of messages (circuit related and non–circuit related).
- PCBS messages are packed into a standard format called SU (signal units), by the MTP (message transfer part) and then sent over the signaling network.

Terminology

- Circuit-associated signaling (CAS)—Register and line signaling to establish calls and connections.
- Circuit-oriented signaling (ISUP, TUP)—Common channel signaling to establish calls and connections.
- Connection-oriented signaling (TCAP, SCOC)—Calls and messages along an established virtual connection.
- Connectionless signaling (SCLC, CBDS)—Calls and messages addressed by a number.
- DQPSK, OQPSK—Differential/offset quadrature phase-shift keying.
- FDD—Frequency division duplexing.
- GMSK—Gaussian minimum-shift keying.
- PCS—Personal communication system.
- UTRA—Universal mobile telecommunication system (UMTS) terrestrial radio access.

Intelligent Networks

Intelligent networks are equated to the standard IS-41. A PCBS needs special C7 stacks to communicate with these types of wireless networks. This section explains the variations.

Wireless networks vary by region. Tables 3.4–3.11 prepare the developer for what is necessary in the specified regions.

Table 3.4 *ITU Europe and Non-North America*

Layer	Application Parts (SMS & Text messaging)	User Parts
Application Part	EMAP (Blue Book)	ITU-T Blue ISUP
TCAP	ITU-T White TCAP	
SCCP	ITU-T Blue SCCP	
MTP-L3	ITU-T Blue MTP	

Table 3.5 BTNR Europe and Non-North America

Layer	Application Parts (SMS & Text messaging)	User Parts
Application Part	EMAP	BTNR 167
TCAP	ITU-T Blue TCAP	
SCCP	ITU-T Blue SCCP	
MTP-L3	ITU-T Blue MTP	

Table 3.6 Japan

Layer	Application Parts (SMS & Text messaging)	User Parts
Application Part	EMAP	Not used
TCAP	ITU-T Blue TCAP	
SCCP	ITU-T Blue SCCP	
MTP-L3	ITU-T Blue MTP	

Table 3.7 PCS North America

Layer	Application Parts (SMS & Text messaging)	User Parts
Application Part	EMAP	Not used
TCAP	ITU-T White TCAP	
SCCP	ANSI SCCP	
MTP-L3	ANSI MTP	

Table 3.8 ITU Non-North America

Layer	Application Parts (SMS & Text messaging)	User Parts
Application Part	ANSI IS41.B	ITU-T Blue ISUP
TCAP	ANSI TCAP	
SCCP	ITU-T Blue SCCP	
MTP-L3	ITU-T Blue MTP	

Table 3.9 ANSI North America and Japan

Layer	Application Parts (SMS & Text messaging)	User Parts
Application Part	ANSI IS41.B	ANSI ISUP
TCAP	ANSI TCAP	
SCCP	ANSI SCCP	
MTP-L3	ANSI MTP	

XML Derivatives For SS7

Derivatives of XML are taking center stage in the effort to force open the formerly closed world of circuit-based switches in the telephone company's central office.

The advent of tools that leverage Web-scripting languages could presage what hardware designers hope will be the eventual demise of the complex and burdensome SS7 protocol.

Call Policy Markup Language (CPML) takes a fresh approach to converged voice-and-data networks that could open a new market avenue for third-party software. CPML may also challenge the business model by which carriers and OEMs alike develop and deploy voice features on an increasingly IP-based network.

Furthermore, CPML develops open interfaces between PBXs and IP networks. VoIP (Voice-over IP) is a key driver for the programmable switch model, although the effort entails a variety of market incentives for melding circuit and packet backbones. Advocates of CPML describe it as a standard metalanguage that is used to create Web pages, which network switching elements use to present the appropriate switch action for given customers.

Table 3.10 Proprietary Mix

Layer	Application Parts (SMS & Text messaging)	User Parts
Application Part	VAP or TMC	BTNR 167
TCAP	ITU-T Blue TCAP	
SCCP	ITU-T Blue SCCP	
MTP-L3	ITU-T Blue MTP	

Table 3.11 *SS7 Acronyms*

Parts	Acronyms	Description
User	TUP	Telephone user part—generates messages relating to telephony. CCITT Blue Book rec. Q.721-Q.725.
	TUP+	An enhanced version of the TUP to cater for some ISDN functions.
	ISUP	Integrated services digital network user part—the full ISDN User Part. It generates messages related to ISDN services. ITU-T (formerly CCITT) Blue Book rec. Q.730 and Q.761–Q.764.
Application	OMAP	Operation and maintenance application part—allows the telecommunications administration access to the signaling network for operation and maintenance purposes.
	MAP	Mobile applications part—manages the mobile communications network. CCITT Blue Book (1988) rec. Q.701–Q.707.
	EMAP	EMAP provides use in both mixed stacks and ITU stacks on top of the ITU white paper TCAP.
	TCAP	Transactional capabilities application part—allows applications other than telephony and ISDN to make use of the signaling network. For example, such applications might involve the use of OMAP and MAP.
	ISP	Intermediate services part—provides services to the TCAP and MTP.
	SCCP	Signaling connection control part—provides services to the TCAP and MTP. CCITT Blue Book (1988) Q.711–Q.714.

Moves to an open scripting language could augment rather than replace the open protocols, such as IP device control and MGCP (merged gateway control protocol), that link the circuit and packet worlds.

Nortel has been a key driver of the emerging MGCP standard. CPML is from telco switchmaker Digital Telecommunications. Lucent, meanwhile, has promoted its SoftSwitch program. This software is geared for reprogrammable packet switches. The Full Circle developers' kit seeks to open up interfaces to Lucent's switches. Excel Switching Inc.'s PPL (Programmable Protocol Language) consists of two components: the PPL environment and the PPL tool. Together, they provide the ability to create and download multiple custom protocols on a per-channel basis to their proprietary platforms, giving the user full control over call processing. Lucent now owns Excel, so it can be expected that either SoftSwitch or PPL will be phased out as part of that acquisition.

But the idea of programming new voice features onto a network from a remote Web browser also poses a threat to some carriers' and switch makers' business models. OEMs working directly on developing ASIC-based (application specific integrated circuit) switches may be intimidated by the concept of a true virtual switch controller that has advanced features for voice calls downloaded into generic hardware.

A fully open virtual switch would halt product differentiation in its tracks. Even those who advocate open software models say carriers may want to write their own software applications in order to keep a tight hold on both security and stability features.

An HTML-like approach to creating a programmable network is the latest concept to emerge for future switches. Three (3) alternatives to the true virtual switch have been identified.

Protocol-based systems such as MGCP allow flexible interfaces between circuit and packet systems, but they require the definition of a gateway controller, which may impede the creation of embedded systems that can handle multiple switching and routing tasks in next-generation networks. In that model, the switch becomes little more than a rules engine, shuttling all intelligent processing of packets and time-division multiplexed channels to the gateway controller. The gateway could introduce a choke point of delay into the network, unless the definition of open switch primitives could speed the execution of controller-based instructions.

Some companies promote the use of high-level languages to program call features as an alternative to protocol engines. C and C++ have many proponents. Tachion and Castle Networks (now part of Siemens' Unisphere Solutions) advocate Java and JavaBeans. Java's portability carries many advantages, though developers are far from identifying a Java virtual machine for telephony applications. A tiered-driver model similar to the I^2O approach in servers might work for Java processors, though vendors are far from proving it can be done. (See www.intel.com for more information on I^2O.)

The third method of markup-language scripting is SIP and H.323. The Internet Engineering Task Force's IPTel working group has been discussing such an approach for a few months, and a team from Columbia University submitted the first formal proposal for a call processing language framework.

Open Model SS7 Model

Digital Telecommunications has defined an extensible service policy architecture, in which all network elements communicate through open high-level APIs, such as those defined by the Parlay Consortium. All management functions are Web-based, and the extensible service policy architecture uses real-time search engines to access a Web page that describes the service logic and interprets the Web-page data into switch functions. CPML translates advanced voice switching and calling applications into switch functions, independent of the switch hardware architecture.

In this architecture, any piece of network hardware, whether ATM switch, IP router, or circuit switch, is a general service switch element—a level of abstraction still not possible within SS7. A service logic element is any CPML page, database, or configuration directory that would be used in call processing.

The service agent can be any software module for a switching element acting as a proxy to either protocols or open Parlay APIs. The service portal is a Web site that performs all organizing and indexing of service logic elements. It embeds search engines, call-policy servers, application servers, billing event managers, an SNMP agent, and a CPML interpreter.

AMATEUR PACKET RADIO . . . .

This section is about the marriage of PC technology and amateur packet radio communications (see Figure 3-5). Amateur radio operators have enjoyed using digital communications techniques for years. They started with Morse code and now employ packet radio. With the expansion of privileges available to entry-level ham operators through the new Novice class license, operators of all ages may use radio waves for computer communications.

Hardware

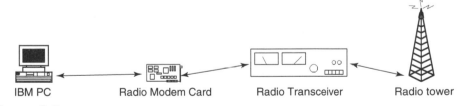

IBM PC   Radio Modem Card   Radio Transceiver   Radio tower

Figure 3-5
Hardware for amateur packet radio.

CSMA

The amateur community has adopted a standard system to determine who has access to the communications channel at any given time. Since the presence or absence of a carrier determines whether the channel is available, this system is called carrier sense, multiple access (CSMA). Ethernet was based on this technology. For completeness, what follows is a review of how CSMA works. Figure 3-6 illustrates a CSMA network. In the figure, station 1 is transmitting to station 3 and station 4 is transmitting to station 5. Now, let us suppose that station 2 wants to transmit data to station 1. Station 2 checks to see if the channel is idle. Since the channel is in use, station 2 does not transmit, but continues to monitor the channel. When the channel is clear, station 2 begins transmitting. There still is the possibility for a problem. For example, suppose that two stations have data to send, so both are waiting for the channel to clear. When the channel clears, both begin transmitting at exactly the same time. They therefore cannot detect each other. As a result, both transmissions are garbled. Fortunately, there is a way to resolve this situation. When the expected acknowledgment is not received, a timer in each station generates a short, random delay before trying to send the transmission again. The random delay does not guarantee that the connection will complete, but it helps to ensure that the two stations will retry at different times so that one can seize the channel and the other can detect its presence.

With several stations sharing the same path, it is mandatory that each transmission carry both the sender's and the receiver's identification, called the address. The AX.25 protocol provides for this requirement.

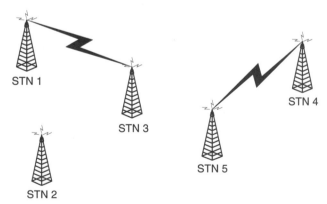

Figure 3-6
CSMA stations share a single channel.

AX.25

The AX.25 protocol is a modified version of X.25 for amateur radio. V1 and V2 represent the versions of the Vancouver protocols, and they are incompatible with X.25A. In amateur radio, the longest callsign consists of five letters and a single numeral, or at least six characters. In addition, another position is called the secondary station identification (SSID). This is a number between decimal zero and 15 that is appended to the end of each callsign. This additional identifier is needed because each amateur operator is issued only one callsign, but can conceivably operate many stations. For example, K9EI might run a bulletin-board system and a digital repeater in addition to a regular terminal system. It would be confusing if all of them used the same callsign. By assigning a unique SSID to each callsign, confusion is avoided.

The terminal is usually SSID zero. Internally, it is identified as K9EI-0, but on the screen, callsigns with an SSID of zero are displayed without the SSID characters. The bulletin-board system might be designated K9EI-1, while the digital repeater would be given another SSID, for a total of 16 unique combinations.

Information Packet

The information packet contains an information field which may or may not contain PID bits, a control field, an error-correction field, and so on. When two stations are connected in error-correction mode, the frames are numbered so that the packet can be tracked. It is also possible to transmit an information packet that is not error checked. Such a transmission, which can be equated to AMTOR Mode B, is usually used to send a short piece of information through the data network to any monitoring station. Since there is no connection between the stations, there is no way for the transmitting station to know whether the information is properly received. This type of transmission can be used for a rough form of round-table conversation, in which all the stations are receiving each other quite clearly and do not need the advantages of error checking. This type of packet is also used for multicast, or beacon, transmissions (see Figure 3-7).

START FLAG 01111110	ADDRESS 112-560 BITS	CONTROL 8 BITS	INFO. NO MORE THAN		CRC 16 BITS	STOP FLAG 01111110
			PID 8 BITS	2048 BITS		

*Depends on the number of digipeaters used.

Figure 3-7
Information and unnumbered information (UI) frames.

Supervisory Packet

The supervisory packet contains the same fields as an information packet except that there is no information field. The supervisory packet transmits no information from station to station, but it does help to control and supervise the path between the two connected stations. The frame type being sent is declared in the control field of each packet (see Figure 3-8).

Table 3.12 shows the common AX.25 abbreviations for the various types of frames.

DIGITAL CELLULAR TELEPHONY . . . .

Digital cellular telephony networks are primarily characterized by their digital traffic channels, which means that the speech they carry is coded. However, they can include both analog and digital control channels.

Examples of such systems include

- GSM—Global system for mobile communication,
- PCS—Personal communications services (IS-95, IS-136, and others),
- D-AMPS—Digital AMPS, referred to earlier as ADC, American digital cellular, and
- PDC—personal (Pacific) digital cellular, referred to earlier as JDC, Japanese digital cellular.

This subsection discusses wireless services primarily from the digital cellular perspective for each of the various radio access techniques. Understanding these techniques is necessary in determining the message text limitations. The limitations include message size and message throughput to end user, among other things.

START FLAG 01111110	ADDRESS 112-560 BITS	CONTROL 8 BITS	CRC 16 BITS	STOP FLAG 01111110

*Depends on the number of digipeaters used.

Figure 3-8
Supervisory and unnumbered frames.

Table 3.12 Common AX.25 Acronyms

AX25 Term	Descriptions
DISC	The disconnect mode is used as a response indicating an ACK for unnumbered frame commands.
DM	The disconnect mode is used as a response to any frame other than an SABM while disconnected
FRMR	Frame reject is issued when a received frame passes the CRC check, but cannot be processed. This means that a protocol error has occurred.
PID	The protocol identification bits identify exactly what version of AX.25 is being used.
REJ	The reject frame requests the retransmission of information frames that are received out of sequence.
RNR	Receive not ready indicates that the station is temporarily busy. For example, the buffer might be full.
RR	Receive ready acknowledges reception of information frames and includes the frame number.
SABM	The set asynchronous balance mode is the connect command.
UA	The unnumbered acknowledge is a response indicating an ACK for unnumbered frame commands.
UI	The unnumbered information frame is used for transmission of information when no connection exists.

D-Amps

D-AMPS is a version of AMPS that has been extended to employ digital traffic channels. One 30-kHz channel has capacity for three traffic channels at full coding rate using TDMA as the access technique.

The extended standard, referred to as IS-54, thus enables D-AMPS to include both analog and digital traffic channels in the same network or the same cell. Users of such a mobile network experience the best GoS (grade of service) if their mobile device can shift between analog and digital traffic channels even during handoff.

Dual Bands

The extension of D-AMPS to include a digital, physical control channel that occupies one time slot has since been specified in IS-136 rev. 0. In much the same way as in GSM, logical control channels are mapped onto the time slot. The two older standards are covered. Hence, a D-AMPS network is in accordance with IS-136 rev. 0 which contains both analog and digital traffic control channels. Following an additional extension, with IS-136 rev. A, D-AMPS is currently specified for 1900 MHz and is referred to as 1900-AMPS. Mobiles that use 1900 MHz need not be capable of handling analog channels, but they should be able to use both the 800- and 1900-MHz bands (dual band).

D-AMPS for data communications is a generic term for one of the forthcoming standards supported either directly or indirectly by the most PCBSs (by way of protocol conversion). Table 3.13 shows the applications that may run concurrently on a typical digital network.

Tech Talk

Be aware that there are country-specific variants to the generally accepted standards.

Table 3.13   *Digital Cellular Phone Channels*

Mobile Phone Session	Chn	Channel Type	Application	Numbering Plan
1	d	Out-of-band signaling (SS7), data services	SMS, MWI, etc. *NOTE: This interface is also used for text messaging.*	X.121 *NOTE:* Text messaging to mobile phones is the special case in which E.164 is used.
	b	Circuit-switched voice-signaling, bearer service	Voice, fax, or text messaging	E.164/E.163
	b	Circuit-switched data-signaling, bearer service	ISDN applications	E.164/E.163

X Series

CCITT Recommendation X25, which has a close relation to frame relay, defines a packet-switching network interface rather than the complete network. Therefore, any device that matches this requirement can be connected to an X25 network. The protocol at each X25 node error checks each received frame, makes the necessary corrections, and retransmits the packet to the next node, which may or may not be the final destination.

The node also makes a backward acknowledgement through the network to confirm that it has received the packet. X25 operate as high as 2.048 Mbps.

The point codes of X.121 (i.e., 0000-99999-01) have been around since X.25, and they will remain until the death of the intelligent network. Most wireless networks do not embrace the intelligent-network system. They do, however, embrace SS7, which uses the aforementioned point codes. The X.121 supports multiple connections to one physical device.

The E.164 (i.e., 9995551212) number plan is what most people throughout the world are familiar with. Phone numbers range from 1 to 21 digits in this numbering plan.

GSM

Group Speciale Mobile (GSM) represents a pan-European development backed up with ETSI standards. It also has been referred to as global system for mobile.

Both the traffic and control channels of a GSM system are digital. The aggregate frequencies are used to identify the system (900, 1800, and 1900 MHz). The corresponding standards are GSM 900, GSM 1800, and GSM 1900, respectively. High-density areas use GSM 1900; that is why GSM 1900 makes extensive use of microcells within umbrella cells and the output power from its terminals and its base stations is low. GSM networks are found all over the world.

Compression

The first digital wireless networks used pulse-code modulation without compression; one voice channel used 64 Kbps of bandwidth (8000 eight-bit samples per second). Bandwidth is limited, so sophisticated voice-coding techniques were implemented. Typically, each speech channel is sampled at 8 kHz and quantized to a resolution of 13 bits/Kbps. The vocoders are designed around high-speed DSPs (digital signal processors) and use a form of regular pulse excitation-long term prediction-linear predictive coder, hereafter referred to as RPE-LTP. The algorithms for RPE-LTP attempt to model the human vocal chords in order to produce realistic synthetic speech with the minimum of memory. Given the 13.4-Kbps rate of GSM, the maximum compression attainable is 4.78 to 1. But, since most architectures compress

20-ms PCM frames containing 160 bytes, or 80 words, into 17-word GSM blocks, the actual compression is 80 to 17, or 4.71 to 1.

What's more, a provision was made for an extra digital data channel with a capacity of 9.6 Kbps. The speech CODEC operates at 13 Kbits/s.

In fact, Windows NT has a GSM 6.10 version of the CODEC installed. This subject is explained completely later and is useful for things like GSM on the Net.

Authentication

GSM-based authentication is based on an A3/A8 scheme that resides entirely in the SIM. Operators can have their own implementations of SIM-based authentication.

TDMA

Time-division multiple access (TDMA) yields a threefold increase in capacity over analog. The Telecommunications Industry Association (TIA) has released two TDMA digital cellular standards:

- IS-135 (TDMA services, asynchronous data and fax), and
- IS-130 (TDMA radio interface, radio link protocol).

These are techniques in which each frequency channel is divided into several time slots, each corresponding to a voice channel.

The roaming ability of TDMA (IS-136)/AMPS provides seamless service for customers, as the technology supports dual-band, dual-mode roaming, allowing traffic across 800- and 1900-MHz frequency bands on both analog and digital networks.

Value-added services are another important aspect of international roaming. Together with the ANSI-41 WIN (wireless intelligent network) standard, the TDMA (IS-136) network allows mobile users to continue using their services as they roam into other networks. Such portable services include SMS (short message service), data, fax, and automatic delivery of voice-mail messages, as well as wireless office services.

Deployment of products and services based on TDMA and the Universal Wireless Communications Consortium (UWCC) promotes ANSI-41. This organization is responsible for the coordination of international roaming agreements.

CDMA and WCDMA

Code division multiple access promises an even greater increase in capacity, but has not been proven by field trials. The TIA specification for CDMA is IS-95 (data services option standard for wideband spread spectrum digital cellular systems). Engineers estimate changing from FDMA to TDMA allows a provider to increase channel capacity by a factor of 7.5. CDMA reports improvements ranging from 25 to 40 percent in channel capacity, but under a controlled environment. In less controlled environments, the improvements are less favorable-only by a factor of 6 to 8.

Wideband CDMA has two modes (FDD and TDD-see Table 3.14). In the first mode, a physical channel is a unique frequency code assignment. A user requiring service capable of handling a high data rate could be assigned multiple physical channels. The uplink accommodates different information streams on the in-phase and quadrature branches of a channel, which means an uplink channel corresponds to a specific carrier frequency, a spreading code, and a relative phase (0 or $\pi/2$ radians). A 10-ms frame structure resides under the assigned spreading code. Each 10-ms frame is divided into 16 slots of 625-ms duration, each of which corresponds to one power control period. (There are 1600 power control adjustments per second.)

The downlink frame structure in the frequency-division duplexing mode is identical to the uplink structure, in which user and signaling information are time multiplexed within the 625-ms slots. The spreading codes in both the uplink and downlink directions have spreading factors that vary from 4 to 256, where the spreading factor is inversely proportional to the required data rate. When the bitrate to be transmitted in one downlink channel exceeds the maximum allowed, several parallel connections can be established using the same spreading factor.

The time-division duplexing mode has a 10-ms frame structure composed of 16 slots, each 625-ms long. Multiple switching points can be set within the 10-ms frames to accommodate asymmetric uplink and downlink circuits. Each 625-ms slot is spread with a unique code. Two or more 625-ms bursts can be accommodated in each slot, distinguished by its own spreading code. Handoff between second-generation (GSM) and third-generation (UTRA) systems is supported. With UTRA, quadrature phase-shift keying (QPSK) replaces GSM's Gaussian minimum-shift keying (GMSK) modulation.

Table 3.14   W-CDMA/UTRA Specification Summary

Characteristic—Mode	Frequency-division duplexing (FDD)	Time-division duplexing (TDD)
Dynamic channel allocation (DCA)	No	Yes
Spectrum allocation	2 x 60 licensed	35 MHz, licensed and unlicensed
Carrier spacing	5 MHz on 200-KHz raster	
Spreading factors	42-56	4-16
Power control	0.25-dB steps over 80-dB range	
Synthesizers in mobile station	Dual	Single

Furthermore, IS-95 and CDMA use the IS-41 reference model for roaming, as does TDMA.

iDEN

iDEN is a spectrally efficient, fully digital system. It combines TDMA and M16QAM technology to achieve up to a 6:1 increase in capacity in a single 25-kHz RF channel. The iDEN system provides both fast access and wide-area coverage. iDEN is a proprietary system created by Motorola.[4]

PDC

PDC was specified by RCR in Japan, in cooperation with eleven manufacturers, three of which were non-Japanese enterprises. The air interface is open and similar to that of D-AMPS, while the network architecture and services are more like GSM. It is only available in Asia.

PHS

In addition, the Personal Handy Phone System (PHS) is used in Japan. Both GSM and PHS support enhanced data service functions. Both are incompatible with the TDMA and CDMA systems planned for North American operators.

Summary

Table 3.15 provides a summary of the second-generation digital cellular systems and standards.

CDPD

Cellular digital packet data uses idle capacity in the cellular voice network to transmit packet data. End-user software breaks data files into standard Internet protocol packets before transmission. Data rates are typically given as 19.2 Kbps, but the overhead brings it down to about 10 Kbps; hence, short bursty file transfers are best suited to CDPD. This is what has made CDPD successful in vertical markets, like public

---

[4]http://www.motorola.com/iden.htm

Table 3.15 *Second-Generation Digital Cellular Systems*

	GSM (MHz)	TIA/EIA-136	IS-95 (MHz)	PDC (MHz)
Band	GSM-900	Cellular (a.k.a. D-AMPS)		
Uplink	935–960	869–894		940–956 MHz
Downlink	890–915	824–849		810–826
Band	GSM-1800			
Uplink	1805–1880			
Downlink	1710–1785			
Band	GSM-1900	PCS		
Uplink	1930–1990	1930–1990	1429–1453	
Downlink	1850–1910	1850–1910	1477–1501	
Channel spacing, kHz	200	1250		25
Min. no. of chn.	125	832	20	1600
User per channel	8	3	< 63	3
Multiple-access technology	FDMA/TDMA		FDMA/CDMA	FDMA/TDMA
Duplex mode	FDD			
Modulation	GMSK	$\pi/4$-DQPSK	OQPSK (uplink) QPSK (downlink)	$\pi/4$-DQPSK

safety, utilities, and transaction processing. This technology is good for companies that have local or regional requirements. Channels are full duplex. The strategy of most carriers is to move from CDPD to GPRS.

PROTOCOLS AND INTERFACES . . . .

A mobile computer is connected to a digital cellular telephone using a simple serial connection rather than an external modem, and uses the familiar "AT" commands implemented in most conventional landline modems.

Speed

Users are able to move data and faxes at 9.6 Kbps, and up to 14.4 Kbps with compression, for GSM, TDMA, CDPD, and CDMA. Details for PHS will be provided later.

Higher rates on digital cellular service are also supported, provided that the network supports the concept of channel aggregation for higher data rates. TDMA allows three channels to be combined for user data rates of 28.8 Kbps.

Compatibility

Both TDMA and CDMA digital cellular service are designed to coexist with AMPS, so that a single cell can support both analog and digital service.

Data Channel Aggregation

Concatenation of up to eight time slots works well for video applications, as shown in Figure 3-9. This technique can be used for n x 9.6 Kbps or n x 14.4 Kbps. The concatenation technique is referred to as HSCSD (high-speed circuit switched data).

MOBILE SWITCHING CENTER MODEM POOLS . . . .

Figure 3-10 shows a modem pool in a mobile switching center (a.k.a., PCBS). A PCBS may support text messaging over a 56-Kbps redundant SS7 link. The interfaces are typically V.35 and X.21. Additionally, a converter is needed to make the split of a DS0A (56 Kbps) circuit from an E1.

A PCBS can support a direct PRI interface from the network hub into both the PLMN and the ISDN networks.

CELLULAR MODEMS . . . .

Cell modems are similar to ordinary modems—they allow users to send and receive data over cellular telephone links. The difference is that they include special protocols for dealing with cellular connections, which are noisier and less reliable than wired links. For example, cellular V.34 modems do not even come close to matching the speed or the reliability of their landline counterparts.

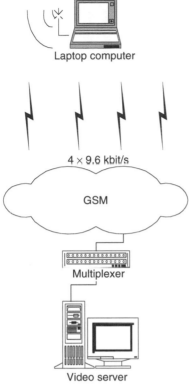

Figure 3-9
Data channel aggregation.

Cellular Protocols

Here are two cellular protocols used by wireless modem manufacturers:

- ETC—Enhanced throughput cellular, and
- MNP10EC—Microcom networking protocol 10 enhanced cellular.

Two-Way Graphics and Text Transfer

A throughput test was used to determine how quickly an identical pair of modems could transfer two-way graphics and text. Since few cellular modem calls are placed to other cellular phones, the setup used one modem as a cellular device and the other

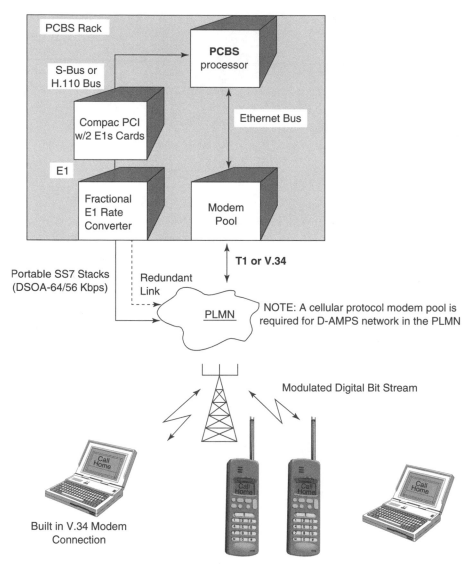

Figure 3-10
PCBS for text messaging and data communications.

as a landline device. The simulation included a 4500 RF channel emulator, a 6000 wireless communications analyzer, a Series II network emulator, a Gemini dual terminal emulator, and a 240A voiceband subscriber loop emulator. It also included a micro-TAC cellular phone, not to mention the modems.

Notably, modems using ETC (US Robotics, Xircom) error correction fared better than those using MNP10EC. Furthermore, the average data rates for all of the motion tests hovered between 2 and 3 Kbps, with throughput under some conditions dropping below the 1-Kbps mark. Plan accordingly. The results are forthcoming.

Stationary Scenario

Figure 3-11 contains the results of the stationary test of cellular modems.[5]

Impairment Scenario

Three important tests (rural, suburban, urban) at 55 mph demonstrated the effect that driving has on data transfer. The results appear in Figure 3-12.

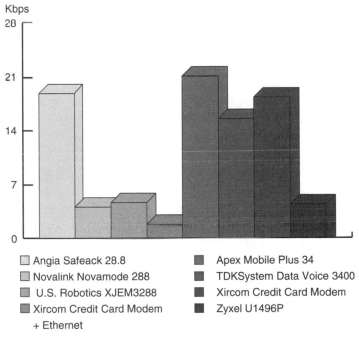

□ Angia Safeack 28.8   ■ Apex Mobile Plus 34
□ Novalink Novamode 288   ■ TDKSystem Data Voice 3400
■ U.S. Robotics XJEM3288   ■ Xircom Credit Card Modem
■ Xircom Credit Card Modem   ■ Zyxel U1496P
  + Ethernet

Figure 3-11
Results of stationary test of cellular modems.

[5]Newman, David.

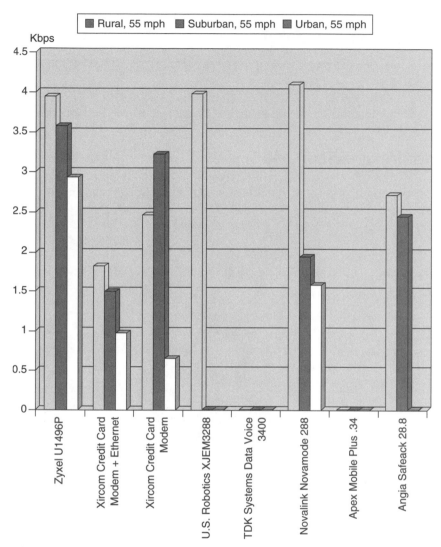

Figure 3-12
Results of driving test on data transfer.

PERSONAL COMMUNICATION SERVICES ....

A personal communication service (PCS) system can be either analog or digital and use either cellular or a combination of cellular and cordless techniques. Digital access can be based on either TDMA or IS-95 (CDMA). PCS mainly specifies a service interface. PCS utilize a personal communications network (PCN), also known as a digital cellular system (DCS).

Apart from the operating frequency, which is a band between 1.8 and 1.990 GHz, the PCN developing system is compatible with the specifications for GSM 900, but supports cells that are less than about a 7-km radius. This concept forms one of the UK's commitments to PCN.

In addition, PCN uses less power and is less expensive than the current cellular technology, and it permits the use of inexpensive pocket telephones, which have very long battery lives. PCN will have more features in the years to come.

Services

PCS incorporates a broad range of individualized telecommunication services that let people or devices communicate, irrespective of where they are located. The logical link between PCS and text messaging becomes apparent by examination of the services that PCS offers. The services for the PCBS are as follows:

- Personal number assigned to individuals rather than to telephones.
- Call completion, regardless of location ("find me").
- Calls to PCS customers can be paid for by the called party. This provides much greater control over incoming calls.
- Caller identification.
- Text messaging exception or rejection (deleted, but not read, text message).

PCS can both find and complete a call to a person regardless of location, but the person has the choice of accepting or rejecting the call or message. The user may also send the call or message somewhere else.

CORDLESS SYSTEMS . . . .

Cellular systems are not the only means of providing mobile telephony. Cordless systems can be used to build logical networks, but they are primarily employed in private networks and, increasingly, as a PSTN access method. The appellation "cordless" has its origin in the technique that made it possible for subscribers to connect a small base station to their telephones, thereby attaining a limited degree of mobility (within a radius of a few kilometers). CT-1 denotes cordless telephony, first-generation. CT-3 is based on DECT, which uses TDMA for its radio access. The system requires no actual cell planning.

3G DIGITAL CELLULAR TELEPHONY . . . .

This subsection explains the technologies found in third-generation digital cellular telephony networks and provides some rationalization for moving to such networking.

Portability

Until now, most computer users have had to be satisfied with portable operation (i.e.,
computers that operate at any set of points of attachment, but not during the time that
the computer changes its points of attachment). If the computer is moved from one
place to another, then its network connections have to be shut down and reinitialized
at the new point of attachment to the network. Future mobile users will not be satisfied with this mode of operation, especially if they know that the network could support uninterrupted connectivity between application and resource.

Mobility

Mobility, then, describes protocols that allow truly mobile operation. For example, the
laptop can remain in almost continuous contact with the network resources needed by
its applications. Using these protocols, neither the system nor any of the applications
running on the system needs to be reinitialized or restarted, even when network connectivity is frequently broken and reestablished at new points of attachment.

It is worthwhile to point out that nomadic users of today's Internet are not willing to pay the price of multimodal operation, since nomadic connections maintained
over a telephone link from an airplane cost well over $1 per minute. This is a great
disincentive to keeping idle logins on remote computers.

However, airports and other public areas are already exploring new infrastructures, explained in this subsection, to accommodate the mobile user.

In an office setting, no one would argue about the expense of nomadic connection, since the company experiences productivity gains as a result of having the additional network resources available all the time from anywhere within the office.

EGSM

The evolution of GSM in the years ahead consists of several groundbreaking steps.
The system is known as IMT-2000.

HSCSD

First is the introduction of HSCSD (high-speed circuit-switched data), which enables
data transmission rates of up to 57.6 Kbps.

GPRS

Next, GPRS (general packet radio services) will support data flow rates of up to 115 Kbps. Equally important as speed is the fact that GPRS will allow subscribers to stay connected at all times. GPRS only uses network capacity while transmitting, so subscribers are only charged while they are actually sending or receiving data. This means that users can have an open connection from their laptop to the Internet or their company LAN and do not have to set it up every time they move. GPRS will also allow operators to make more efficient use of radio network resources. GPRS will be the starting point for a completely new range of services and new charging mechanisms.

GPRS provides both point-to-point and point-to-multipoint services. GPRS point-to-point applications include messaging, remote access, Internet access, credit-card validation, roadway tolls, utility meter reading, and many others.

GPRS point-to-multipoint-multicast applications include sending a message to any subscriber located within a geographical area. Interestingly enough, there is no need to maintain a database about the subscribers, since everyone gets messages. Fraud is not an issue. Anyone can be a subscriber of a certain group. This applies to applications such as news, traffic information, weather forecasts, and financial updates.

GPRS point-to-multipoint group applications include sending messages to a given set of subscribers located within a geographical area. There is complete control over which subscribers will get any given message. Only appointed members can be subscribers of certain group, specifically, fleet management (i.e., taxi) and conferencing.

GPRS Features

Here is a list of features that GPRS provides:

- Reuse of the GSM infrastructure.
- Extension of GSM for packet switching end to end.
- Existing circuit-switched services interworks with GPRS.
- HLR-based subscription (one subscription only).
- Fast setup times, from users' perspective.
- Efficient resource utilization (especially radio resources).
- Variable (on demand) user data throughput (up to ~115 Kbps).
- Volume-based and resource-usage-based charging.
- Close interworking with the data communications world, especially IP networks.

- Service
- GPRS multicast radio is one idea that will allow the end user to listen to his or her favorite radio station. This service is already available over the Internet.

GPRS Packet Network

Figure 3-13 contains a GPRS processor diagram of a typical packet network.

GPRS Architecture

Figure 3-14 contains an example of a GPRS architecture.

GPRS Stack

Figure 3-15 shows a GPRS stack.[6]

Table 3.16 shows the GPRS stack layer acronyms.[7]

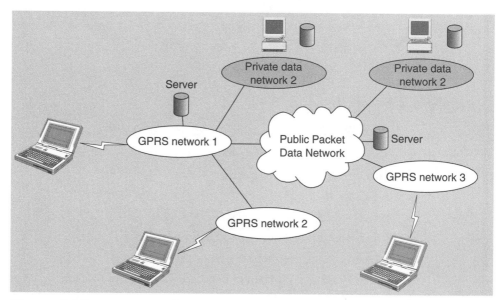

Figure 3-13
Example GPRS packet network.

[6]GSM 4.6 ver. 2.0.0
[7]http://www.lmera.ericsson.se/~epkblom

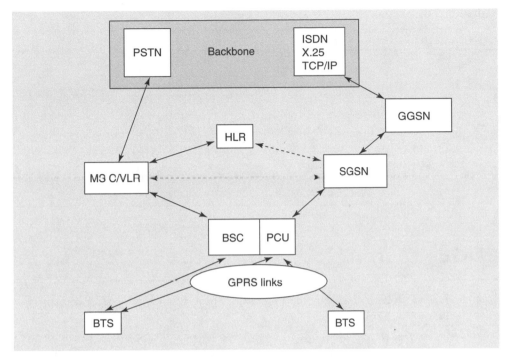

Figure 3-14
Example GPRS architecture.

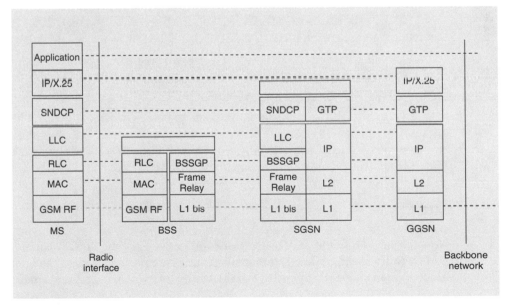

Figure 3-15
GPRS stack.

Table 3.16 *Acronyms*

Abbreviation	Description
PL	Physical link layer.
LLC	Logical link layer between the mobile and SGSN, one LLC entity per mobile.
BSSGP	Base station subsystem GPRS Protocol-conveys routing and QoS-related information between SGSN and BSS.
RLC	Radio link control layer—buffers downlink LL-PDUs, among other things.
MAC	Medium access control layer—multiplexes RLC Data and RLC-MAC control blocks, including priority handling.

EDGE ....

Last, EDGE (enhanced data rates for GSM evolution) will offer transmission rates of up to 384 Kbps.

The EDGE air interface is also the basic component in the 136HS (high-speed) 3G proposal from the North American standardization group R45.3. This enables the same core radio modem to be used in both GSM and in D-AMPS (ANSI-136). Thus, EDGE forms a major step in the convergence of the two leading digital communications standards, GSM and D-AMPS.

EDGE uses the same TDMA, frame structure, logic channel, 200-kHz carrier bandwidth, and spectrum mask as GSM. Existing cell plans can remain intact.

The added capacity is achieved by increasing the data capacity of a single GSM time slot from today's 9.6 Kbps to 48 Kbps per time slot, and even up to nearly 70 Kbps per time slot, under good conditions.

EDGE also allows up to eight time slots to be aggregated, allowing a total bandwidth of more than 384 Kbps. These time slots can be used flexibly to allow several simultaneous services—for example, a voice call in one time slot, Internet browsing in two others, and video conferencing in the fourth.

WCDMA

New frequencies in the 2-GHz spectrum will be used for the third-generation system UMTS (universal mobile telecommunications system), a member of the International Telecommunication Union's IMT-2000 family of systems. The technology chosen for UMTS by the European Telecommunications Standards Institute is wideband CDMA (WCDMA).

Transmission speed in the 3G world will be 2 Mbit/s.

UMTS

CSS will apply a new network architecture that allows combining the three main tracks (GSM, UMTS, and SS over IP) into one common network architecture. The main capabilities of this new architecture are

- Consequent layering—The separation of network functions into distinct layers is a key technique in modern networking. It allows each layer to evolve independently as technology evolves.
- Transport flexibility—This capability allows for different transport technologies (existing and new) to be deployed without affecting the control or service layers.
- Proven and stable base—The new architecture reuses, as much as possible, the installed GSM service base and the established N-ISDN network. This enables a smooth migration.
- Follows general standardization trends—The new architecture adopts the best elements of several ongoing standardization initiatives in ETSI, IETF, and MSF.
- Enables multiservice networks—Several service networks can share the same transport network. This enables the convergence of fixed and mobile networks, as well as the convergence of IT and telecom networks.
- Optimization potential—The new architecture allows optimizing the transmission and the distribution of network resources.

The logical reference model for the new network architecture is shown in Figure 3-16.[8]

G3G

Last, the Operators' Harmonization Group agreed to a third-generation CDMA standard to serve the world market. The agreement addresses the requirements of both the WCDMA and CDMA2000 communities by forming a specification for a direct-

[8]http://www.eed.ericsson.se/CSS/UMTS/NewArch.html

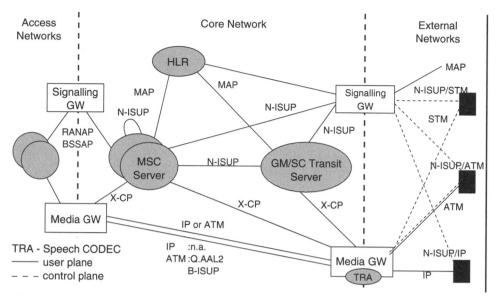

Figure 3-16
Example UMTS architectural framework.

sequence mode for WCDMA, a multicarrier mode for CDMA2000, and a TDD (time division duplex) CDMA mode. The harmonized standard supports the timely development of next-generation radio technology wherever needed.

The agreement is entitled *Harmonized Global 3G (G3G) Technical Framework for ITU IMT-2000 CDMA Proposal* and is in the hands of the ITU TG8/1 and the third-generation Partnership Project (3GPP) hosted by ETSI.

3G ENTERPRISE . . . .

This subsection explains the third-generation wireless technology that is used in the enterprise. Distance is the distinguishing factor between this section and the previous sections on cellular telephony. In addition, it explains some of the services that each provides.

GSM on the Net

Figure 3-17 shows Ericsson's GSM on the Net—a new business communications solution that integrates GSM wireless communications into a LAN-Internet environment.

Ericsson GSM on the Net replaces the complexity of today's business communications environment with one elegantly simple concept: the combined mobility of GSM and the cost efficiency of Internet protocol (IP) networking.

This service allows a business to use a wireless environment in which employees have a wireless terminal with one number that they can use to make and receive calls, access the Internet and company intranets, and use integrated computer telephony applications (e.g., Microsoft Netmeeting) wherever they go at the office, at home, or on a business trip.

GSM on the Net integrates GSM wireless communications into a LAN-Internet environment.

Frequency Reuse

Cell planning is needed due to fixed frequencies. However, it is possible to reuse a GSM frequency every fifth floor.

Operator Issues

The ISPs that desire to get into the wireless extranet business do not own the frequencies, so they are forced to work with local wireless operators. Interoperator or roaming agreements need to be resolved before it will be possible to roam outside the enterprise's intranet. SMS and notification requires custom software, since the standards are just beginning to develop. Flooding the packet network is possible by way of malicious users. Last, the capacity is very low—around 500 subscribers maximum.

Processor Diagram

A GSM on the Net processor diagram is shown in Figure 3-17.

Service Node

Service nodes provide H.323 access, allowing the enterprise user the ability to shift from a circuit-switched PBX environment to an Internet packet-switched environment. In addition, service nodes offer various open APIs for user administration, among other things.

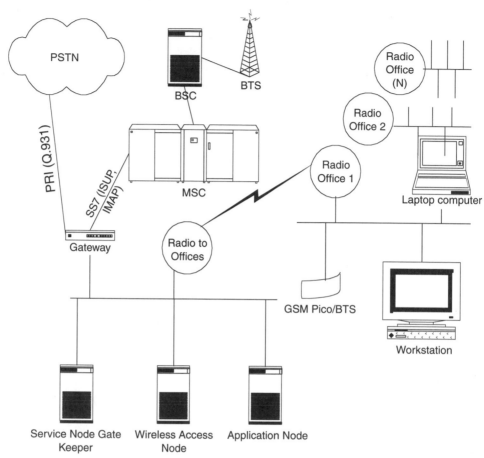

Figure 3-17
GSM on the Net.

Gateway SS7 and ISUP

This gateway is used to convert the RTP stream into the wireless circuit-switched network.

Access Node Handles the GSM Access

The access node handles the GSM access. It includes MSC-VLR and BSC functions interlaced with GSM networks and HLR queries.

Application Node

The applications supported by an application node include voice mail, among other technologies.

Management Node

A Web-based interface is integrated with the service node.

GSM BTS

The base stations are new (e.g., Ericsson BTS 2401). They act as gateways between air interfaces. They tie into the service nodes, not into the micronetwork.

Solsa Chip

Solsa is used to extend remote access to local GSM coverage. Its function is to lock the subscriber on to the local office environment and take the subscriber off of the remote cell.

Logical View

Table 3.17 shows a local view from a developer's perspective:

BLUETOOTH . . . .

Bluetooth is a proposed radio frequency (RF) specification for short-range, point-to-multipoint voice and data transfer. Bluetooth can transmit through solid, nonmetal objects. Its nominal link range is from 10 cm to 10 m, but it can be extended to 100 m

Table 3.17   Logical Layered Architecture for Application Development

Nonsystem	Applications	APIs	
Service Node	GSM on Net		
User Access	GSM Access	Fixed Phone	Fixed terminal access (i.e., PC)

by increasing the transmit power. It is based on a low-cost, short-range radio link, and facilitates ad hoc connections for stationary and mobile communication environments.

Characteristics

Bluetooth characteristics include the following:

- Operates at 2.4 GHz frequency.
- Industrial-scientific-medical (ISM) band.
- Uses frequency hop (FH) spread spectrum, which divides the frequency band into a number of hop channels. During a connection, radio transceivers hop from one channel to another in a pseudo-random fashion.
- Supports up to eight devices in a piconet (i.e., two or more Bluetooth units sharing a channel).
- Built-in security.
- Non-line-of-sight transmission through walls and briefcases.
- Omnidirectional.
- Supports both isochronous and asynchronous services; easy integration of TCP/IP for networking.
- Regulated by governments worldwide.

What Is Bluetooth Used For?

Bluetooth will enable users to connect to a wide range of computing and telecommunications devices without the need to buy, carry, or connect cables. Presently, it delivers opportunities for rapid, ad hoc connections. In the future, it may be used for automatic, unconscious connections between devices. Bluetooth's power-efficient radio technology can be used in many of the same devices that use IR:

- Phones and pagers.
- Modems.
- LAN access devices.
- Headsets.
- Notebook, desktop, and handheld computers.
- Manufacturers' acceptance.

Bluetooth enables portable electronic devices to connect and communicate wirelessly through short-range, ad hoc networks. It is a universal radio interface in the 2.45-GHz frequency band that has gained the support of Ericsson, Nokia, IBM, Toshiba, Intel, and many other manufacturers. In order to function on a worldwide basis, Bluetooth requires a radio frequency that is license free and open to any radio. The 2.45-GHz, ISM band satisfies these requirements, although it must cope with interference from baby monitors, garage door openers, cordless phones, and microwave ovens, which also use this frequency.[9]

IRDA ·

The Infrared Data Association (IrDA) specifies three infrared communication standards: IrDA-Data, IrDA-Control, and a new emerging standard called Air. Since this document focuses on IrDA-Data and its relationship to Bluetooth, for the purpose of this document, IrDA refers to the IrDA-Data standard. In general, IrDA is used to provide wireless connectivity technologies for devices that would normally use cables for connectivity. IrDA is a point-to-point, narrow-angle (30° cone), ad hoc data transmission standard designed to operate over a distance of 0 to 1 meter and at speeds of 9600 bps to 16 Mbps.

Characteristics

IrDA characteristics include the following:

- Proven worldwide universal cordless connection.
- Installed base of over 50 million units.
- Wide range of supported hardware and software platforms.
- Designed for point-to-point cable replacement.
- Backward compatibility between successive standards.

Additional characteristics of IrDA include a narrow-angle (30 degree) cone, point-and-shoot style applications (non-interference with other electronics and low-level security for stationary devices), and high data rates—4 Mbps currently with 16-Mbps technology under development.

[9]http://www.countersys.com/tech/bluetooth.html

What Is IrDA Used For?

IrDA is used by the following devices to transmit data:

- Notebook, desktop, and handheld computers.
- Printers.
- Phones and pagers.
- Modems.
- Cameras.
- LAN access devices.
- Medical and industrial equipment.
- Watches.

Worldwide Acceptance

With a worldwide installed base of over 50 million units and growing at 40% annually, IrDA is widely available on personal computers, peripherals, embedded systems, and devices of all types. In addition, the wide use and acceptance of IrDA standards and robust solutions have accelerated the adoption of IrDA specifications by other standards organizations. The universal adoption and worldwide implementation of IrDA specifications guarantees a universal hardware port, and rapidly emerging software interoperability.

Mobile IP

Mobile IP is IP that allows nodes to continue to receive datagrams no matter where they happen to be attached to the Internet. Additional control messages allow the IP node involved to manage their IP routing tables reliably. Scalability has been a dominant design factor during the development of Mobile IP, because in the future, nodes will be mobile.

802.11

802.11 is the standard for WLANs (wireless local area networks) developed by The Institute of Electrical and Electronics Engineers (IEEE). It can be compared to the 802.3 standard for Ethernet-wired LANs. The goal of this standard is to tailor a model of operation in order to resolve compatibility issues between manufacturers of

WLAN equipment. Thus far, the IEEE 802.11 standards committee is revising a version of MAC-PHY (media access control-physical) level.

The MAC under 802.11 is composed of several functional blocks. These include mechanisms to provide contention and contention-free access control on a variety of physical layers. The functions within the MAC are independent of data rates and physical characteristics.

The fundamental access method of the 802.11 MAC is known as CSMA/CA (carrier sense multiple access with collision avoidance). CSMA/CA works by a "listen before talk" scheme, like amateur packet radio. This means that a station wishing to transmit must first sense the radio channel to determine if another station is transmitting. If the medium is not busy, the transmission may proceed. The CSMA/CA scheme implements a minimum time gap between frames from a given user. Once a frame has been sent from a given transmitting station, that station must wait until the time gap is over before trying to transmit again. Once the time has passed, the station selects a random amount of time (called a backoff interval) to wait before "listening" again to verify a clear channel on which to transmit. If the channel is still busy, another backoff interval is selected that is less than the first. This process is repeated until the waiting time approaches zero and the station is allowed to transmit. This type of multiple access ensures judicious channel sharing while avoiding collisions.

Furthermore, this scheme allows automatic medium sharing between several devices with compatible PHYs. The access method is attractive because it provides spectral efficiency as well as asynchronous data transfer. FDMA and CDMA schemes would not be adequate because they require bandwidth used by the modulation scheme. Strict TDMA would not work well because it requires synchronization. Thus, CSMA/CA—which may be thought of as a version of TDMA—is better suited to wireless LANs.

The PHY under 802.11 includes DFIR (diffused infrared), DSSS (direct sequence spread spectrum), and FHSS (frequency-hopped spread spectrum). Both spread spectrum techniques are used in the 2.4-GHz band because of their wide availability in many countries and lower hardware costs in comparison to the higher microwave frequencies.

The IEEE standard supports DSSS for use with BPSK modulation at a 1-Mbps data rate, or QPSK modulation at a 2-Mbps data rate. The general band plan consists of five overlapping 26-MHz subbands centered at 2.412, 2.427, 2.442, 2.457, and 2.470 GHz. This scheme is used in an attempt to combat both interference and selective fading.

FHSS is supported under 802.11 with GFSK modulation and two hopping patterns with data rates of 1 Mbps and 2 Mbps. Under this scheme, the band is divided into 79 subbands, each with a 1-MHz bandwidth. Each subband is subject to a minimum rate of 2.5 hops/s using any of three available hop patterns (22 hops in a given pattern). The minimum hop rate ensures that each packet sent could be transmitted in a single hop so that destroyed information could be recovered in another hop. This allows an effective frequency diversity that provides excellent transmission characteristics.[10]

Last, for devices operating at speeds higher than 2 Mbps, a project-authorization request (PAR) has been submitted to the IEEE for an extension of the 802.11 standard that will define speeds up to 10 Mbps. Another PAR is being submitted for a 20-Mbps wireless standard in the 5.2-GHz range. The FCC recently approved a new spectrum of unlicensed wireless communications in the 5.2-GHz band for use in the United States. One company, RadioLAN, promises to deliver products soon that will operate in that band.[11]

WECA

WECA (wireless ethernet compatibility alliance) backs the IEEE 802.11 HR standard and is backed by 3COM, Lucent, Nokia, Symbol Technologies, Intersil (formerly Harris Semiconductor) and Aironet Wireless Communications.

OTHER

Other technologies in this space are 3COM's Airconnect product range, providing an access point for 63 clients at 200 feet with an NIC (network interface card) for Win 9X, NT, and WinCE. Acer has brought Warplink to market with a price point aimed at home use, with its ISA card for the PC and PCMIA card for the laptops.

MOBILE TERMINAL SYNCHRONIZATION . . . .

Synchronization technologies provide a solution to managing file distribution, data synchronization, and software distribution for an enterprise's mobile workforce. Various suites provide support for mobile devices and laptops based on Palm OS and Windows CE.

As more and more workers bring handheld computers into the organization, the demand for mobile computing is exploding. Piecing together existing point solutions to support the distribution, collection, and synchronization of data to and from these mobile devices often presents incompatibilities and limitations, extremely high licensing and implementation costs, and exhaustive vendor evaluation and maintenance. Synchronization software aims to eliminate the cumbersome process by

[10]http://www.cwt.vt.edu/faq/80211.htm
[11]http://www.byte.com/art/9803/sec17/art5.htm

consolidating into one product all of the functions needed for developing and implementing a coherent mobile computing strategy. Suites include two standard and essential parts:

- Connecting—Provides "one-click" mobile user updates.
- Administration—Provides a single interface for administration and maintenance of all iMobile suite users and functions.

Between these two supporting parts lies the heart of the suite's functionality: three Internet-oriented products that can be used in any combination. They are

- File Distribution—based on a publish-and-subscribe model, uses Web server technology to provide reliable, secure, and cost-effective transport of information to and from mobile workers.
- Data Synchronization—delivers bidirectional, field-level synchronization between mobile client devices and various enterprise database servers, including Oracle®, Microsoft® SQL Server®, IBM DB2®, and Informix.
- Software Distribution—allows central management and delivery of mobile software applications.

For an example, see the synchronization suite at http://www.synchrologic.com.

Last, IBM's MQ Series Everywhere is designed to address thin client computing (with a kernel less than 50-Kbytes to connect to MQ Series NT server to exchange data), and data synchronization in the area of enterprise applications (i.e., ERRP, billing, orders, job scheduling, credit checks, inventory, accounting, and shipping). The programming interface MQSPI (MQe systems-programming interface) is a low-level interface into MQe and provides direct access to the base objects and their methods (see Figure 3-18). Only the classes that are used need be loaded. Applications written at this level are most compact and most efficient; however, they cannot be ported to MQ Series clients and servers, nor can they be run on other messaging subsystems. The SPI is designed as an object interface, but a procedural version is also provided on some device platforms. On certain device platforms, only a subset of the SPI is available, principally due to resource or operating-system limitations.

INSTANT MESSAGING . . . .

IMPP (instant messaging and presence protocol), which provides a standard method for identifying users involved in instant-messaging sessions, is destined to make it to the wireless terminal in the foreseeable future.

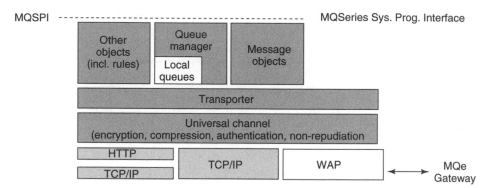

Figure 3-18
MQSeries systems programming interface.

Microsoft opened access to the protocols of MSN Messenger to encourage other instant-messaging applications to communicate with MSN users. This is the next step in MS trying to improve its 1:30 ratio against the 40 million AOL users. IETF's IMPP group is delighted about the move, stating that the publication of different protocols helps in both evaluating the group's requirements document and informing the development group of robust, open protocols for interoperability.

iCALENDAR . . . .

The iCal (iCalendar) specification and related protocols for real-time and e-mail appointment scheduling consitute another IETF protocol that will be used as a wireless service.

WORKFLOW . . . .

The SWAP (simple workflow access protocol) specification for the communication of workflow information over the Internet addresses the interoperability between workflow systems.

SUMMARY . . . .

Table 3.18 summarizes the protocols under review at the IETF.

Table 3.18 *Summary of Protocols under IETF Review*

ICAL	Defines standard format for calendar data.
IMIP	Addresses iCAL data piggybacked on e-mail systems using MIME.
IRIP	Enables calendar searches similar to IMIP but tailored for a real-time environment.
ITIP	Defines an interoperability protocol for scheduling and enables users to send, reply to, and cancel meeting requests.
CAP	Enables mix and match of calendaring and scheduling clients and servers.
SWAP	Supports exchange of workflow information over the Internet and interoperability between workflow systems.
IMPP	Provides standard format for addressing Internet-based user presence awareness and notification.

TRANSCODING

The WAP (wireless application protocol) stack has been developed to provide a user-friendly interface to the Internet from a mobile terminal that has different, and in most cases relatively weak, performance in terms of memory, display size and capabilities, power consumption, and the capacity of the connection used. This means that a WAP application may have to deliver requested data formatted differently, depending on the capabilities of the requesting client. The intention is always to minimize the size of the transferred information over the air interface. WAP is one example of transcoding.

WAPs receive information from

- Browser: version, negotiation information, and so on.
- Application: data types, and so on.

WAP smart proxy transformations include

- Character-set conversion (UNICODE->Shift JIS Characters).
- Content-type conversion.
- Protocol conversion.

Most of the terms used with WAP have their counterparts in the HTML-protocol stack. (See Figure 3-19.) That is natural, since part of a WAP task is to translate resources located on a Web server to formats suitable on a microbrowser running WAP client software. The WAP application relies on a Web server to deliver requested contents to a gateway, which can then transform them into WAP format.

Client Side

It is the WAP gateway function that converts the HTTP side to WAP on a chosen transport layer. Once decided which transport layers to support, the application can deliver any WML code to the client through the gateway. Each type of microbrowser may then interpret the received content and present it to the capabilities of the terminal. Handling the various MIME extensions is key to a successful microbrowser, as far as integration is concerned. Testing is performed with the client simulators included in the development kits. Figure 3-20 shows what transcoding is necessary to provide the mobile terminal with general Internet services.

WAP Service Development Kits

A development kits consists typically of five parts:

- A microbrowser for "test-driving" applications or for surfing the WML Web.
- Device designer for creating new device designs to test out applications.

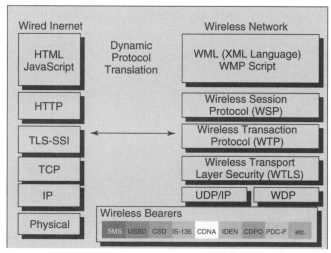

Figure 3-19
Internet and WAP protocols.

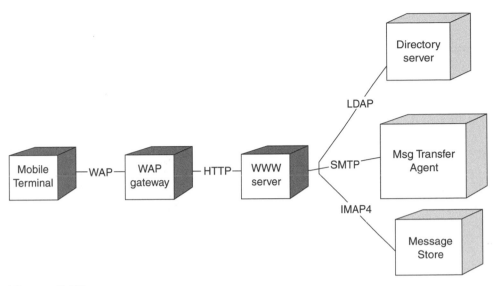

Figure 3-20
Internet services transcoding and processor diagram.

- Application designer for creating Web pages.
- Server tool kit for getting started with creating dynamic WML.
- SIM tool kit for connecting to SIM cards for things like E-commerce.

The package available from Ericsson requires that the following action be performed on the server side:

- Tcl/Tk—used by the WAP client simulator.
- Perl—needed to run Perl scripts in the server tool set
- Erlang—used by the WAP client simulator.
- Configuration of Web server. Add MIME types:
    —application/x-wap.wmlc wmlc.
    —application/x-wap.wmlscripts wmlsc.
    —text/x-wap.wml wml.
    —text/x-wap.wmlscript wmls.

SERVER SIDE . . . .

The WAP application on the server side of the gateway includes all of the WML files and executables. The files and executables cooperate to assemble the information to be formatted into WML documents that can be transferred to the gateway.

FUNCTIONS . . . .

Most of the functionality of a WAP can be performed using CGI. However, below is a list of advantages of joining the features into a single process:

- Since a WAP server runs continuously, it can perform regular jobs, like gathering push information or sending notify messages.
- Requests can be defined, so that the WAP server may perform a number of transactions to complete a request. This way the CGI programs can be kept small and simple.
- A server built of compiled code hides the source from the operator, but can still allow configuration and extensions.
- Compiled servers run faster than Perl scripts.

Input functions include the entering of URLs into the microbrowser. If the associated information is static, like a list of alternatives or a greeting prompt, it can be written directly in a WML page (see Figure 3-21), which will be returned by the Web server if its URL is requested. Dynamic information may be inserted into an information stream using the WML tags in a CGI script. A WML file would usually call scripts with input received from the terminal to produce the complete WML page.

CGI Scripting

When a request is received from a WAP client, some sort of action normally needs to be performed to retrieve information from a source within the messaging system. These actions, which may include interprocess communication, are handled by the CGI scripts called from within WML code. A script may run yet another program, but the final result is, in most cases, that some information is formatted into a WML document.

The normal event flow when a CGI script is run is as follows:

```
<?xml version="1.0"?>
<!DOCTYPE WML PUBLIC "-//WAPFORUM/DTD WML 1.0//EN" http://www.
wapforum.org/DTD/wml.xml>
<WML>
        <CARD NAME="first" NEWCONTEXT="TRUE">
        <DO TYPE="ACCEPT">
                <GO URL="#second"/>
        </DO>
                Enter username:
                <INPUT FORMAT="*m"
                TYPE="TEXT" KEY="username"MAXLENGTH="12"/>
        </CARD>

        <CARD NAME="second">
        <DO TYPE ="ACCEPT">
                <GO URL="login.pl?user=$username
                                &amp;pass=$password"/>
        </DO>
                Enter password:
                <INPUT FORMAT="*M"
                TYPE="PASSWORD" KEY="password"MAXLENGTH="12"/>
        </CARD>
<WML>
```

Figure 3-21
WML page with dynamic login.

- The user triggers an action. For example, clicking OK in one of the WML inputs or entering a WML URL containing dynamic parts.
- The browser passes the name of the script (and any arguments to it) from the terminal to the Web server.
- The Web server starts the script with the passed parameters.
- The script analyzes the parameters received. These parameters may be either information that should be passed to another component, like a message to be transferred, or a request for some information.
- The CGI script sends its formatted output to standard out in the shape of a WML file that the Web server sends back to the client.

Perl scripts are great for manipulating text strings and *awk*. Another advantage of Perl scripts is the high level of abstraction for rapid prototypes. A simple Perl script built on the Ericsson module (wmlib) is shown in Figure 3-22.

```perl
#!/usr/bin/perl-wl..
require 'wmllib/config.pl';
require 'wmllib/demoutils.pl';
require 'wmllib/wmllib.pl';

my $host = 'server'; #Where content is located

%cgivars = $ParseCGIVars();
$user=$cgivars{"userid"};
$pwd=$cgivars{"pass"};

#Init a new WML deck
my($DECK) = &WMLTop;

#Create a card
my(%a) = ("MANE", "cardname", "NEWCONTEXT", "TRUE");

#TASKS
$body.=&Do(&Go("/login.wml"), "PREV");

#Make connection to the server
my $conn = new COMPONENT ($host)
or die ("can't connect to $host:: $!\n);

#login
$response = $conn->login(user,pwd);
$response = $conn->get_info($response)

#Extract info
$body.=$response->theInfo;

#Add card to DECK
$DECK.= &Card($body,%a);

#End this WML deck
$DECK.= &WMLBottom;
print $DECK;
```

Figure 3-22
CGI login script.

For each card, "DO," "GO," or other required WML tags, and retrieval information are written to the cards' bodies and added to the deck. The deck, in its whole, is then written to standard out.

ANALOG WIDE AREA PAGING PERSPECTIVE . . . . .

POCSAG

The term POCSAG (Post Office Code Standardization Advisory Group) refers only to a coding technique, known as the CCIR Radiopaging Code No. 1. It was designed for transmission at either 512 baud (tone pagers) or 1200 baud (alphanumeric pagers up to 2400 baud for other suitable applications) and utilizes a single carrier frequency of 153.275 MHz radiated at sufficient strength to penetrate most buildings.

DIGITAL WIDE AREA PAGING PERSPECTIVE . . . . . .

ERMES

ERMES (European Radio MEssage System) supported by ETSI standards represents a pan-European approach to paging. Unlike the POCSAG code system, the ERMES standard defines the whole system and is intended to meet the European needs for the foreseeable future.

The system operates with 16 channels spaced by 25 kHz within the band 169.425 to 169.80 MHz. Frequency-agile receivers scan all channels. This feature improves the system's roaming characteristics and makes for flexible use of the frequency spectrum. The basic data rate is 6.25 Kbps, but this reduces to 3.125 Kbps due to the use of four-level pulse amplitude modulated frequency modulation (PAM/FM/FSK). A forward-error correctioncode is (30, 18) used to minimize bit errors. This is supplemented by the interleaving of message bits to provide for burst error protection.

Here are facts on ERMES that influence addressing the terminal and data communications:

- ERMES Numbering Plan (ETSI DE/PS 3 01-3).
- ERMES NMsg, AMsg, TMsg character-set conversion is explained in ETS 300 133-2 pg. 116.

Comparing the Protocols

Table 3.19 is a useful comparison of the paging technologies, where data communication speed has the most influence on a wireless service.

TDP Suite

The PCIA (Personal Communications Industry Association) details the specifications for the TDP (telocator data paging) protocol suite. The TDP specification explains how a paging network may be utilized as a one-way or two-way transmission system for transmitting textual and binary data to remote palmtop, laptop, and other portable or desktop computers.

Table 3.20 shows the TDP suite of protocols and services that are used to send information into a paging network.

TNPP

TNPP (telocator network paging protocol) is used for communications between paging terminals or other types of equipment that requires implementing a paging system network. The protocol is ASCII character-oriented, transmitted through a standard RS-232 port. The protocol supports variable-length packets and groupings of different page and data blocks within the same data packet. The protocol uses three types of error recovery methods—two for full-duplex applications and one for broadcast-simplex application.

A common header is used in all of the data formats to indicate the source and destination of each data packet. The header also contains a serial number that is used for identifying the packet with the start-of-text flag (STX). The first 12 bytes of the header are defined in the following sections. After the common header, an optional header extension can be used to extend the source and destination address fields. If a device does not use this feature, the header extension data between the first 12 bytes of the header and the STX flag should be ignored. After the STX flag, the data block is sent. Multiple data blocks can be transmitted within the packet by terminating each block with an end-of-text block flag (ETB) and terminating the last data block with an end-of-text flag (ETX) followed by the block check character bytes (CRC-16). Each data block can have a block modifier optionally added. This modifier is called an ETE request and is used for multiple packet messages and end-to-end control.

Standard RS-232 asynchronous data communication is used in TNPP. The character format used is 8 bit, no parity, one stop bit. The data rate can vary and will be determined by the application and the available data distribution network.

Table 3.19 Paging Protocols Comparison

Protocol	Appl.	Outbound Speed	Outbound Frequency (MHz)	Outbound Channel	Inbound Speed (BPS)	Inbound Freq. (MHz)	Inbound Ch.
POCSAG	OW; Numeric alpha	1200, 2400	Any paging frequency	25 kHz	N/A	N/A	N/A
ERMES	OW; Numeric alpha	6250	'169.425	25 kHz	N/A	N/A	N/A
FLEX	OW; Numeric alpha	3200 6400	Any paging frequency	25 kHz	N/A	N/A	N/A
REFLEX 25	Two-way	3200 6400	'929–'932 '940–'941	25 kHz	800, 1600 6400, 9600	'901–'902	12.5 kHz
IN-FLEXION Voice	Voice paging	Com-pressed Voice	'930–'931	50 kHz	800, 1600	'901–'902	12.5 kHz
IN-FLEXION Data	Two-way data	8000 12K, 16K	'930–'931 '940–'941	50 kHz	800, 1600 6400, 9600	'901–'902	12.5 kHz

Table 3.20 MDP Suite

Protocols	WMF	Wireless message format is an end-to-end application interface, transparent to the paging network, which conveys information from the sender to the wireless recipient.
	TME	Telocator message entry is the entry protocol and data format for sending textual or binary data into a paging company.
Formats	TRT	Telocator radio transport is the protocol used to transfer data messages from a paging message processor to an RF receiving device and a mobile computing device.
	TMC	Telocator mobile computer is the protocol used to transfer data messages from an RF receiving device to a mobile computing device.
Conversion	TFC	Telocator format conversion details the requirements for sending binary data through the TAP protocol.

A packet consists of the following items:

- Start-of-head flag (SOH).
- Header.
- Start-of-text flag (STX).
- Data block(s).
- End flag (ETX).
- Block check code (CRC-16).

TNPP Data Flow

In order to pass data through the network, the address of the final destination is assigned to the data packet by the originator. The data packet is then transmitted on the port that is connected to a path to the destination. Each node in this path must then know the correct path to the destination (routing table), so that the data packet will be routed through the network in the desired manner. A node in the network will then retransmit the data packet without changing the source or the destination address. A new serial number is assigned to the data packet and an error control is implemented each time this new number is transmitted from a node.

The inertia value is decremented whenever the data packet is received by a node in the network and must result in a nonzero value in order to be retransmitted to any other node.

TNPP Block Type

The data portion of a packet may contain one or more data blocks. The format and meaning of these data blocks is determined by the first byte of each data block. Each data block is terminated with an ETB. The last data block in a packet is terminated with an end-of-text flag (ETX). Proposal and acceptance may create new block type definitions by the networking committee. The two control block types, end-to-end request and end-to-end response, are required in all implementations of the protocol. Other block types are application related and are required only to the extent that the application program (paging, data transfer, etc.) must participate in information exchange.

TNPP Control Blocks

There are two types of blocks defined for end-to-end (ETE) control. These blocks are ETE request and ETE response.

The ETE request block is used to request receipt acknowledgement by the destination node and to provide linking information for data blocks that span multiple packets. The ETE request may be applied as a header to any other data block type. This modifier enables end-to-end data block acknowledgement upon appending.

The response block is used to carry receipt acknowledgement or rejection from the destination back to the source and to inform the source if the destination can process multipacket data blocks.

TNPP Paging Blocks

There are two data block types that are currently defined for paging applications. CAP page block is used to send paging information that is ready for encoding. A CAP page block contains all signaling information required to generate the page.

The ID page block is used to send a request for the generation of a page to be sent to a customer. An ID page block contains a customer ID number to be used in determining the signaling information for the pager. This block type requires that a data base record for the customer exists at the destination node.

TNPP Miscellaneous Blocks

There are three data block types currently defined for purposes other than paging or end-to-end communications. These types are COMMAND, DATA, and STATUS.

The COMMAND block is used to send configuration and control commands to a destination. Included in the command block is a three-letter manufacturer code to simplify recognition of manufacturer-specific commands.

The DATA block is used to send generic data to a destination. The data portion of the block is restricted to nonflag characters.

The STATUS block is used for reporting error conditions of external equipment attached to a node in the network. It is not used for reporting network conditions or for data-flow-related functions. Typical uses would be transmitter failure reporting, power loss reporting, external alarm reporting, and so on. The status code value assignments should be coordinated with the networking committee.

Other PCIA Protocols

- TIPP telocator internetworking paging protocol (Version 1.0, June 1994 Chair, Editor) is for two-way paging, and
- TIS telocator interswitch application layer protocol (Version 1.0, June 1994 Chair, Editor) describes the PDU (protocol data unit) for two-way paging.[12]

GLOBAL POSITIONING SYSTEMS . . . .

The U.S. Air Force's Global Positioning System (GPS), which is available for civilian uses, has 24 satellites equally divided among six orbits. Each satellite, 11,000 miles out in space, continuously emits a radio signal that can be received by portable computer devices on land, at sea, or in the air. By picking up the signal from four or more satellites, the computer can determine its location from within 20 to 300 yards of the exact position, depending on how finely the unit is calibrated.

Tech Talk

> **Some foreign countries decided to forego deployment of GPS service in favor of obtaining location information through the wireless terminal networks, due to the U.S. Air Force dependency.**

[12]http://www.pcia.org

Location-Based Services Equation

The service equation goes like this: Location + Data = Information. The process is as follows:

- Locate the device.
- Put the location into context.
- Combine the location with the data.

Invocation

Service invocation methods are shown in Figure 3-23.

Multiple Delivery Responses

The process for multiple delivery response consists of a mobile terminal requesting service from any combination of voice and data service centers, as shown in Figure 3-24.

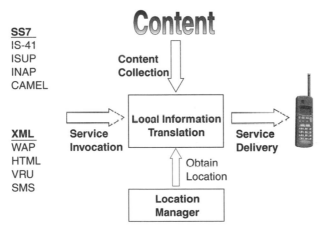

Figure 3-23
Location-based service invocation methods.[13]

---

[13]http://www.signalsoftcorp.com

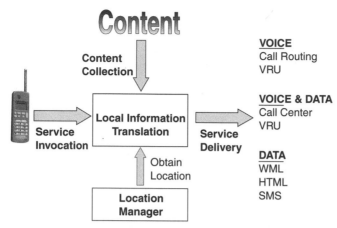

Figure 3-24
Multiple delivery response.

Local Information Translation

Here are a few of the local information translation transformations that are necessary for creating location-based services:

- Cell IDs to latitude, longitude, and zones.
- Routing number assignment, based on service zones.
- Supports single-number services.
- Latitude and longitude to location description.
- Landmarks, addresses, intersections.
- "N" closest searches.
- Supports lists of businesses or services.
- Network transversal algorithms.
- Supports distance and time calculations and driving directions.

Location-Based Services

Wireless location standards development in 1998 paved the way for location services' growth. Table 3.21 shows some of those services. Although the impetus of these standards efforts stemmed from satisfying E911 requirements, the development of the core network capabilities provided a basis for evolution toward commercial location service support.

The TIA has commissioned an enhanced emergency services working group to develop technology that supports E911 requirements.

The TIA TR45.2.2.WIN technology standards group is defining both intelligent network triggers and messages to support these services.

North American T1P1.5 GSM location services working group is defining them for GSM markets worldwide.

MOBILE POSITIONING CENTER · · · · · · · · · · · · · · · ·

The MPC (Mobile Positioning Center), from Ericsson, makes it possible for an application to load local location data about a specified mobile terminal. It is not based on GPS. The wireless network determines the position using three different cells. Consequently, the application can obtain position results with local geographical information.

Server access consists of a user name, a password, and a mobile phone number. Here is an example:

user: ssss

pwd: ssss

MS: 46777100009

All that is needed is an IP address (e.g., 195.58.110.200) and a port number (e.g., 4000). It is also possible to add on unique user and mobile MS in a subscriber database. In addition, it is possible to load local location data. An MPP emulator is available based on Apache Web server. The MPP protocol is loaded as servlets.

Table 3.21   Location-Based Services

Safety	Billing
E911	Location-sensitive billing
Emergency	Wireless office
Early warning evacuation	Residential cordless
Local information	Tracking
Traffic	Fleet
411	Tracking packages
Lifestyle	Tracking children
Roadside	

Example Query

http://195.58.110.200:4000/PositionRequest/Direct?username=ssss&password=ssss&position_itemF777
100009&position_time=(timenow)&geodetic_datum3/4SSEL-1841&coordinate_system=RT90

Figure 3-25
Query MPC.

Example Response

```
<Head RequestID=2.916037719.11 AnswerID=1>
<MSF777100009
RequestedTime_990122084913+0100
Error=0
GeodeticDatum3/4SSEL-1841
HeightDatum=NotAvailable
CoordinateSystem=RT90
PositionFormat=IDMS0
<PositionData
<PositionArea
Time_990122084900+0100
<Area=Arc
<Area=Point
XCoordinated90912
YCoordinate_18131
>
InnerRadiusU0
OuterRadius_00
StartAngle=0
StopAngle60
>
>
<PositionArea
Time_990122084915+0100
LevelOfConfidence_0
<Area=CircleSector
<Area=Point
XCoordinated90912
YCoordinate_18131
>
StartAngle=0
StopAngle60
Radius_43
>
>
>
>
<Tail RequestID=2.916037719.11>
```

Figure 3-26
Response from MPC.

This position information is in Swedish coordinates.

WAP Location-Based Services

The data flow for WAP location-based services is shown in Figure 3-27.

WAP Call Setup

Figure 3-28 shows the WAP call setup.

Chips

One of the paradoxes of mobile data is to have location-independent use while receiving the benefit of location-dependent services.

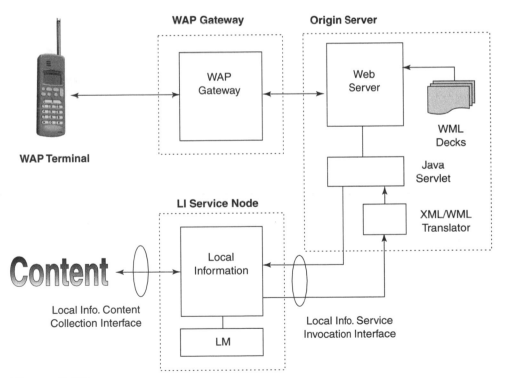

Figure 3-27
WAP Gateway with location-based services.

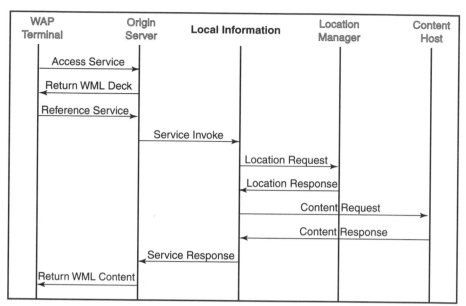

Figure 3-28
WAP call flow.

SiRF Technology, a start-up chip company, recently unveiled new semiconductor technology that will enable cellular phones and handheld computers to have navigation functions and report their location. SiRF has developed a semiconductor architecture that shrinks the size of global positioning system (GPS) technology so that it can fit into small handheld devices. SiRF says it has also increased the accuracy of its GPS devices.

The United States Federal Communications Commission is mandating that by 2001, all cellular phones in the United States must have GPS functionality, so that when calls are made to the emergency services network, the location of the caller can be quickly established. As a result, analysts predict that by 2003, 38 million cellular handsets will be shipped with built-in GPS functions, up from one million phones with GPS in 1999. It is not surprising to learn, therefore, that SiRF's investors include Ericsson and Nokia.

Fitting the GPS functions onto a card only slightly bigger than a credit card, including a GPS chip the size of a single postage stamp, will make it possible for companies to create very small GPS-based products such as wristwatches or lockets, which could be used for locating lost children, criminals, skiers, and hikers. Commercially, it could be used for tracking field workers for job scheduling and progress checking.

The technology also opens up a far more accurate set of location-dependent, value-added services that can be offered by carrier companies. With the combination of the GPS location-sensing capability, business directory, and mapping service, the handset user can inquire about the location of a laundry, courier office, type of restaurant, or gift shop and receive directions to the nearest one. Carriers can then charge a premium to local businesses to have their location data included in the business directory database.

Other users of SiRF technology include Holux Technology, based in Taiwan, which is developing a device the size of a small tape recorder to point out attractions to tourists, and Datus, a subsidiary of Daewoo Telecom, which has a personal navigation assistant for automobiles.

SiRF has also announced partnership with NTT DoCoMo of Japan, the world's largest wireless carrier, which plans to develop a new class of pedestrian navigation service.

SATELLITE-BASED TELEPHONY . . . .

There are three orbits that satellites range (e.g., polar, elliptical, geostationary), but two are optimal for wireless voice and data communications.

Geostationary

Geostationary is the most popular position above the earth, since a satellite can stay in orbit the longest around the equator. However, there are only a fixed number of slots in which they can hover.

GEOs (geostationary satellites) are most commonly used for television transmission. GEOs rely on a passive, "bent-pipe" architecture. Essentially electronic mirrors in the sky, they receive signals from transceivers on Earth, amplify them, and send them back down across their entire footprint. A GEO's footprint can be very large, since a single geostationary satellite can see 42 percent of Earth's surface. This is hardly optimal for data, no matter how it is multiplexed.

Low Earth Orbit

LEO (low earth orbit) satellite constellations orbit the Earth at a height of just 500 to 1000 miles, reducing latency to that equivalent to transcontinental fiber optic cable. Six times more satellites are required to provide the same coverage as GEOs.

Medium Earth Orbit

Like LEOs, medium-earth–orbit satellites are not geostationary. Operating from an elevation between 6250 and 12,500 miles, they take about two hours to pass over any point in their coverage area. Therefore, a constellation of some 20 satellites is sufficient to cover the globe. A few companies intend to turn up services that may yield a bandwidth of 6 Mbps.

Current Systems

Table 3.22 contains the data rates for the deployed satellite-based systems.

Table 3.22   Deployed Satellite-Based Systems

Communication System	RF Channel Rate (BPS)	# of Channels per RF Channel Total User Data Rate Each Data Channel (BPS)	Total User Data Rate Each Data Channel (BPS)	Number of Users per Data Channel	Aircraft User Data Rate per Data Channel	Total User Data Rate per RF Channel (BPS)
	to + from	to + from	to + from		Max., either way	to + from
Inmarsat L	600 + 600	1 + 1	70 + 35	N	70 ÷ N	70 + 35
Inmarsat H/H+	10,500 + 10,500	1 + 1	165 + 500	N	500 ÷ N	165 + 500
Inmarsat I	4800 + 4800	1 + 1	160 + 500	N	500 ÷ N	160 + 500
Iridium	50,000	4 + 4	2400 + 2400	1	2400	9600 + 9600
HFDL	1800	12	10 + 25	N	25 ÷ N	100 + 50
VHF ACARS	2400	shared	100 + 100	N	100 ÷ N	100 + 100
VDL-2	31,500	shared	1200 + 1200	N	1200 ÷ N	1200 + 1200
VDL-3[4]	31,500	4 + 4	1250 + 1250	N	1250 ÷ N	2500 + 2500
VDL-4	TBD	shared	TBD	N	TBD ÷ N	TBD

Planned Systems

Table 3.23 shows the planned satellite systems for wireless voice and data communications. The estimated bandwidth is useful in determining what kinds of services are possible.

Table 3.23 Planned Satellite Systems

System	Lead Investor	Launch Date	Number of Vehicles	Estimated Bandwidth
AstroLink	Lockheed Martin	2001	9 Geostationary satellites (GEOS)	128 Kbps to 10 Mbps
CyberStart	Loral	2001	3 Ka-ban GEOs	6 Mbps downlink, 2.5 Mbps uplink
Halo	Angel Technologies	2000	One aircraft currently being tested; will expand as market requires	Up to 10 Mbps (symmetric)
SkyBridge	Alcatel, Loral	2001	Start with 32 Ku-band low Earth Orbit (LEO) satellites, expand to 80	20 Mbits/src downlink, 2 Mbps uplink
Sky Station	Sky Station	2002	250 sky stations at 12-mile altitude	10 Mbps downlink, 2 Mbps uplink
Spaceway	Hughes Electronics	2002	2 GEOs and 1 Medium Earth Orbit (MEO) satellite, later up to as many as 16 GEOs and 20 MEOs	6 Mbps
Teledesic	Gates, Motorola, McCaw	First launch 2001–2003	288 LEOs	64 Mbps downlink, 2 Mbps uplink. Uses ATM-like mechanisms to transmit inter-satellite data at 155 Mbps
Iridium	Motorola		66 LEOs w/land-based wireless systems	50 Kbps in either direction

Summary of Services

Satellite-based services include a single phone number and a telephone that fits comfortably in the palm of your hand and offers the ability to stay connected anywhere on Earth.

Here is a list of the premier services that are satellite based and offered by service providers:

- World roaming service.
- World paging service.
- World messaging service.
- International satellite service.
- International roaming service.
- International paging service.
- International messaging service.

WIRELESS SURVEILLANCE . . . .

Telecommunications carriers have had to cooperate with law enforcement agencies in conducting electronic surveillance. The CALEA (Communication Assistance for Law Enforcement Act) was enacted by Congress to enable the government to continue to conduct electronic surveillance effectively and efficiently in the wake of rapid advances in telecom technology.

The most notable advances in technology have occurred in digital transmission and processing techniques and in the proliferation of wireless services. These advancements have hampered the law enforcement community's ability to conduct lawfully authorized surveillance. CALEA set detailed capacity requirements for the capability to conduct simultaneous intercepts per region, based on historical incidence.

J-STD-025

J-STD-025 is an interim standard which defines services and features required to support lawfully authorized electronic surveillance. In addition, it specifies interfaces necessary to deliver intercepted communications and call-identifying information to a law enforcement agency. For example, the government may want the ability to tap into all parties on a three-way call, even if the subject under investigation drops off of the call.

Circuit-Switched Tapping

Figure 3-29 shows the current circuit-switched environment for tracing calls:

A5/1

The encryption method known as A5/1 protects the privacy of conversations and data transmissions for millions of GSM subscribers. Without this technology, detecting a phone number and cloning it in another phone to bill calls fraudulently is possible. Underlying the A5/1 encryption method are algorithms thought to have originated from the German or French military, cryptographic experts said.[14] The algorithm uses short keys, so in order to crack the authentication in the encryption scheme, all that is needed is a receiver (i.e., illegally made digital scanner that costs thousands of dollars), a PC with a large amount of disk space, and the code for deciphering the first two minutes of conversation. Once that data is gathered, the eavesdropper can listen to the rest of the conversation, and consequently all GSM-protected conversations.

Tapping into Packet-Switched Voice Networks

Packet-switched voice networks require a mechanism to intercept the packet transmission. Remote monitoring is therefore done on the network's edge (i.e., modem pool). This is due to the very nature of packetized transmission; data transmission can take multiple paths through the network to reach their destinations.

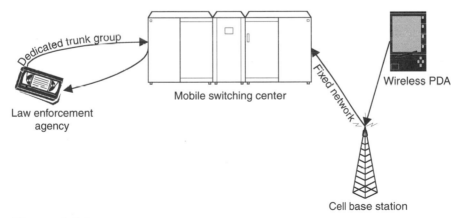

Figure 3-29
Circuit-switched tapping.

[14]Robinson, Sara

Roving Wiretaps

A roving wiretap enables police to monitor all phone calls made by a suspect, rather than just those from a specific telephone. High-speed computers would data-mine calls passing through a certain network, selecting and red-flagging a conversation that contained the voice print–a digitized fingerprint of a person's unique voice characteristics—of a person under investigation. For example, if a suspect made a phone call from his neighbor's house or used a cell phone or a pay phone, his call would be recognized, retrieved, and uploaded to a law enforcement agent by the carrier's "critical electronic equipment." The National Security Agency uses this technology to monitor international telephone calls.

WIRELESS JAMMING . . . .

Handheld consumer devices that jam cellular phones to create essentially a cone of silence are being made illegally. They address the annoyance factor associated with cell phones (i.e., beepers going off in meetings), as well as eavesdropping or tapping.

HIGH-DEFINITION TELEVISION . . . .

For completeness, this section describes HDTV technology and its impact on the wireless terminal.

HDTV (high-definition television, part of Advanced TV, or ATV) is a new television technology that provides picture quality similar to that of 35-mm movies and sound quality similar to that on today's compact disc. The HDTV technology exists, and some television stations have begun transmitting to users on limited channels. HDTV uses digital rather than analog signal transmission.

In the United States, the Federal Communications Commission has assigned broadcast channels for ATV (which includes HDTV) transmissions. ATV also includes the possibility of using the designated channels for multiple signals at current quality levels instead of single signals at HDTV levels. Commercial and public broadcast stations are currently deciding exactly how to implement their use of ATV and HDTV. HDTV is also a standard that will become increasingly available on cable TV.

HDTV uses the MPEG-2 file format and compression standard.

Table 3.24   MUSE Systems Parameters

Parameter	Value
Scanning lines per frame	1125
Active lines per frame	1035
Pixels per line	1920
Field frequency	60 Hz
Interlace	2:1
Aspect ratio	16.9
Luminance bandwidth	20 MHz
Chrominance bandwidth	Wideband Cw 5 MHz
	Narrowband Cn 4MHz

High-definition systems are defined as those capable of providing an image resolution of greater than 1000 lines per picture height (lines/ph), with an aspect ratio of 16:9. To provide such images, a video base bandwidth in the order of 30 MHz is required. Since there is virtually no part of the frequency spectrum available to accommodate such a signal using the modulation techniques of current systems, some form of image compression and processing is absolutely necessary.

The Japanese MUSE/Hi-vision system is already in commercial use. Table 3.24 shows the MUSE system parameters. Most are proprietary but provide a good frame of reference.

Compression

The MPEG standards are an evolving set of standards for video and audio compression developed by the Moving Picture Experts Group (MPEG).

MPEG-1 was designed for coding progressive video at a transmission rate of about 1.5 million bits per second. It was designed specifically for Video-CD and CD-i media. MPEG-1 audio layer-3 (MP3) has also evolved from early MPEG work.

MPEG-2 was designed for coding interlaced images at transmission rates above 4 million bits per second. MPEG-2 is used for digital TV broadcast and DVD. An MPEG-2 player can handle MPEG-1 data as well.

A proposed MPEG-3 standard, intended for high-definition TV (HDTV), was merged with the MPEG-2 standard when it became apparent that the MPEG-2 standard met the HDTV requirements. An MPEG-4 standard is in the final stages of development for release. It is a much more ambitious standard and addresses speech and video synthesis, fractal geometry, computer visualization, and an artificial intelligence (AI) approach to reconstructing images. An MPEG-7 is being discussed.

MPEG-1 and -2 define techniques for compressing digital video by factors varying from 25:1 to 50:1. The compression is achieved using five different compression techniques:

- The use of a frequency-based transform called discrete cosine transform (DCT).
- Quantization, a technique for losing selective information (sometimes known as lossy compression) that can be acceptably lost from visual information.
- Huffman coding, a technique of lossless compression that uses code tables based on statistics about the encoded data.
- Motion-compensated predictive coding, in which the differences in what has changed between an image and its preceding image are calculated and only the differences are encoded.
- Bidirectional prediction, in which some images are predicted from the pictures both immediately preceding and following the image.

Screen Technologies

For the past 10 years, scientists have been able to apply electricity to some plastics, or polymers, to emit visible light.

Just as with the liquid crystal technology that now dominates flat-panel displays, the polymers can be made to glow blue, green, or red, depending upon their particular structure. When combined, they can re-create all the colors in nature.

While liquid crystal displays require a light source and are still relatively bulky and quite rigid, plastics that emit color can be cheaply made into very thin sheets and can be shaped into an endless variety of forms.

Dr. Bill Barnes, senior lecturer in physics at the University of Exeter in England and a researcher in the field, believes that the first applications of light-emitting polymers are most likely to be in devices that display relatively little information, like mobile telephones, which now have simple monochrome displays.

The cell phones of the future, though, will deliver brief messages and also show movies and Web pages. For these applications, users will want a display with color.

"Mobile phones will have color displays and will be much thinner," says David E. Mentley, vice president of Stanford Resources in San Jose, California, a marketing research company that specializes in electronic displays. "The trend is relentlessly toward designs that fit into the pocket without bulge or weight. They will most likely be as disposable as a used credit card, and about the same size."

"People like a display that gives off its own light, rather than a liquid crystal that is using light from the room or backlit," said Mentley.

"Just imagine replacing liquid crystal displays with a thin plastic sheet emitting light in full color spectrum the same as you see on your TV screen—without a bulky cathode-ray tube."[15]

WIRELESS TOYS . . . .

Radio Shack and others are building wireless toys (i.e., remote-controlled automobiles, planes, and boats) that use two frequencies—27 and 49 MHz. The toys are then able to travel more than 150 feet from a multifunction controller.

WIRELESS ELECTRONIC PAPER . . . .

Researchers at IBM Corporation have created a thin, flexible kind of transistor that could one day be used to make, for instance, a computer screen that could be rolled up. Their invention is cheap and can be sprayed onto plastic, making it useful in a variety of areas, they said.

Lucent and E Ink Corporation (which makes "electronic ink" used in billboards and large signs) said that they had teamed up to develop a low-cost "electronic paper." They hope to produce a flexible plastic sheet that would electronically display text and images—a possible replacement for liquid crystal displays, the silver-toned screens used in digital watches, calculators, and cell phones.

Electronic paper uses small beads enmeshed in a flexible binder sheet. They rotate to present one side to the viewer when a pattern of electrical voltage is applied. Xerox Corporation and Minnesota Mining & Manufacturing Company are also working to manufacture electronic paper.

[15]http://www.nytimes.com/library/tech/99/08/circuits/articles/05next.html

HIGH-SPEED FIXED WIRELESS . . . .

High-speed fixed wireless Internet technology fills the gap between the POTS (plain old telephone service) modem and the far faster cable modem. Despite the limitations, fixed wireless offers highly reliable communications with enough bandwidth to deliver television signals and high-speed data as well as telephony. Operating in several frequency bands between 2.4 and 38 GHz, fixed wireless is a viable alternative to conventional (wired) local loops (see Table 3.25).

Wireless systems are desirable because they can be designed quickly and easily. The cost, the slow process of burying copper or fiber lines, and the associated geographic challenges are eliminated.

WinStar Communications offers wireless services at 28-GHz and 30-GHz bands in some 30 markets in the United States and Tokyo. Other services providers include Teligent and Advanced Radio Telecom Corporation. There are a few players in the 38-GHz band. At that frequency, the usable bandwidth is 1400 MHz, which supports a bit rate of 155 Mbps. The reusable millimeter-wave spectrum is ideal for the highly dense, short-haul (2-3-km) urban market. (See HeliOss Communications.) P-Com North America and NEC focused on point-to-point wireless communications used mainly for extending local-area networks to the Internet backbone. These firms' products include wireless links that can deliver up to DS-3 (45 Mbps) and DS-4 (90 Mbps) speeds.

Global Mobile Information System (GloMo)

GloMo aims at standardizing the protocols at access layers of wireless communication, which allows software and hardware developers to mix-and-match digital radio modems. It is sponsored by the information technology office of the U.S. Defense Advanced Research Projects Agency (DARPA).

Internet Radio Operating System

IROS operates in the unlicensed 2.4-GHz ISM band. All nodes have the same transmit and receive capabilities. However, at least one node is wired to the Internet backbone by a high-speed access line (a.k.a., airhead). All of the nodes in the system are aware of all of the other nodes and relay the information forward and backward from node to node. The airhead supports up to 15 clients and maintains a reasonable rate of data flow. The nominal link data rate in either direction is 1 Mbps, although the actual throughput may be somewhat less. In addition, it is possible to use either omnidirectional or directional antennas. The radius is 4.5 km and 15 km.

Table 3.25 Fixed Wireless Communication Frequencies[16]

Frequency, GHz	Usage
2.1500–2.1620	Licensed MDS and MMDS; two bands of 6MHz each
2.4000–2.4835	Unlicensed ISM
2.5960–2.6440	Licensed MMDS; eight bands of 6 MHz each
2.6500–2.6560	Licensed MMDS
2.6620–2.6680	Licensed MMDS
2.6740–2.6800	Licensed MMDS
5.7250–5.8750	Unlicensed ISM-UNII
24.000–24.250	Unlicensed ISM
24.000–25.250	Licensed
27.500–28.350	Licensed LMDS (Block A)
29.100–29.250	Licensed LMDS (Block B)
31.000–31.075	Licensed LMDS (Block A)
31.225–31.300	Licensed LMDS (Block B)
38.600–40.000	Licensed

ISM = industrial, scientific, and medical
LMDS, MMDS = local/multichannel multipoints distribution service
MDS = multichannel distribution service
UNII = unlicensed national information infrastructure

STANDARDS BODIES AND REGULATORS . . . .

Background

Both the ISO and the IEC are world, private, voluntary, nongovernmental, and scientific organizations, affiliated to each other and to the UNO. Together, they represent at least 80% of the world population. The principal members of the ISO and the IEC are the national standards institutes, such as BSI (British Standards Institute), DIN (Deutsches Institute für Normung), ANSI (American National Standards Institute), and JISC (Japanese Industrial Standards Committee). All of the ISO-IEC standards

---

[16]Dutta-Roy.

are published as being international, but it is the responsibility of the national organization to apply these to the local needs, no member state being forced to adopt and enforce a recommendation.[17]

Figure 3-30 shows a high-level overview of the standard-making hierarchy. Use it as a beginning reference point in understanding the wireless standards bodies and acronyms.

Purpose

Specification of standards is important and is designed to

- Ensure the interconnection between different users.
- Allow the portability of equipment between different applications and in different areas.
- Ensure that equipment purchased from one vendor can be interfaced with that from another.

Acronyms

The acronyms associated with this section are shown in Table 3.26.

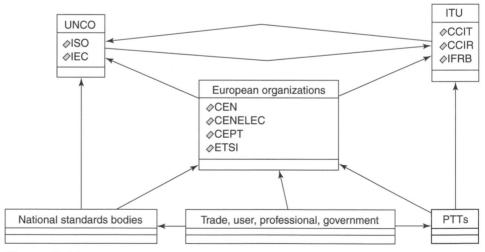

Figure 3-30
Standards-making hierarchy (Europe).

[17]Lewis, Geoff.

Table 3.26 *Standards-Bodies Acronyms*

Acronyms	Description
UNO	United Nations Organization
IEC	International Electrotechnical Commission
ISO	International Standards Organization
ITU	International Telecommunications Union
IFRB	International Frequency Registration Board
CCITT	Consultative Committee for International Telegraph and Telephone
CCIR	Consultative Committee for International Radio
CEN	European Committee for Standardization
CENELEC	European Committee for Electrotechnical Standardization
CEPT	Conference of European Posts and Telecommunications
PTTs	Posts, Telegraph and Telephones (Ministry for)
ETSI	European Telecommunications Standards Institute

TELCORDIA / BELLCORE ....

The RBOCs (regional Bell operating companies) used to depend on what was formally known as Bellcore, but since its sale to Science Applications International Corporation, the company has undergone many changes, including a name change to Telcordia.

Furthermore, the North American Numbering Council (NANC), a Federal Communications Commission (FCC) advisory group, has approved a transition plan that transfers responsibility for administering North America's area codes and other numbering resources from Bellcore to Lockheed Martin IMS. Other major divestitures are sure to follow.

IETF ....

The Internet Engineering Task Force (IETF) is the body that defines standard Internet operating protocols such as TCP/IP. The IETF is supervised by the Internet Society's Internet Architecture Board (IAB). IETF members are drawn from the Internet Society's individual and organization memberships. Standards are expressed in the form of requests for comments (RFCs).[18]

FCC . . . .

The Federal Communications Commission is instrumental for defining the standards for North America. The three most important things the FCC does are as follows:

- Sets prices for interstate radio, phone, data, and video services.
- Determines who can or cannot get into the business of providing telecommunication services or equipment.
- Determines the electrical and physical standards for radio and telecommunications equipment.

The FCC is tempered by the Federal Court, the Justice Department, Congress, and the 50 states' public service commissions.

IMTC

The International Multimedia Telecommunications Consortium, Inc.

The Open Group

The Open Group has created a mobile-computing taxonomy, which assists its members in the understanding of the organizations active in defining standards. Figure 3-31 shows the organizations involved in setting the standards. Table 3.27 provides the glossary for the terms used in the figures.

Figure 3-32 show what the open group perceives as actual activity or even proven success.

---

[18]http://www.whatis.com

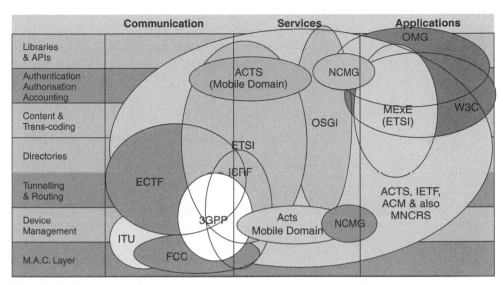

Figure 3-31
Standards Bodies and Regulatory Setting.

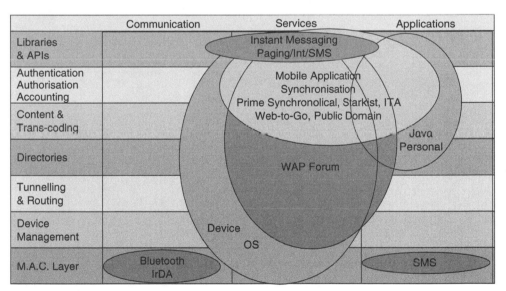

Figure 3-32
Commercial initiatives and consortia.

Table 3.27 Acronyms

Acronym	Description
ACTS	Advanced Communications Technologies and Services
NCMG	Network Computing Management Group
OMG	The Object Management Group
MExE (ETSI)	Mobile Station Application Execution Environment
W3C	World Wide Web Consortium
OSGI	Open Service Gateway Initiative
ETSI	European Telecommunications Standards Institute
ECTF	Enterprise Computer Telephony Forum
ISRF	The Internet Screen Phone Reference Forum
IETF	Internet Engineering Task Force
ACM	Association for Computing Machinery
MNCRS	Mobile NC Reference Specification
FCC	Federal Communications Commission
3GPP	3rd Generation Partnership Project (ARIB, T1, ETSI, TTA, TTC)
UWCC	Universal Wireless Communications Consortium
PCCA	Portable Computer Communications Association

4 Legal Strategies for Software Companies

BACKGROUND . . . .

Before explaining how to develop software for the wireless computing environment, it makes sense to select a strategy for protecting the intellectual property that is about to be created. This section provides such strategies.

Article I, Section 8, of the U.S. Constitution authorizes Congress "[t]o promote the Progress of Science and the useful Arts, by securing for limited Times to Authors and Inventors the exclusive Right to their respective Writings and Discoveries."

STRATEGIES FOR SOFTWARE DEVELOPMENT . . . .

The pendulum in the legal environment of software patents has swung to the right. Companies are more inclined to take legal action to protect their intellectual capital. Therefore, software companies should prepare for legal confrontations.

Litigation is not one of a company's profit centers, as are patents. Therefore, two goals are useful:

- Minimize litigation by knowing the law.
- Maximize output of indisputable patents.

The Strategy

These strategies were developed from an economic analysis of monopolistic and oligopolistic pricing models for software (the reason being that patents provide limited-time monopolies):

- Patent protection is appropriate for highly risky ventures with high costs and great chance of failure.

- Copyright protection is appropriate for projects with modest outlays and predictable chance of success.
- Both patents and copyrights are appropriate when lead time is the most important factor in the project.

Tech Talk

These strategies serve to prohibit direct copying and either will be equivalent in a court of law.

Characteristics of Protective Mechanisms

Table 4.1 shows the general and software-specific protective mechanisms.

Benefits of Software Patents

- Economic incentives.
- Fosters disclosure.
- Recognition.
- Companies can protect themselves.
- Precludes competition.

Less Favorable Issues

- Software patents are difficult to obtain (PTO in state of flux).
- Software patents are difficult to enforce.
- Companies do not know what is already patented.
- Software patents may preempt possible superior technology.
- Big companies can use software patents to crush small companies.

History

- As the industry grew in the 1960s and 1970s, the economic importance of protecting programs grew.
- Congress appointed CONTU, which helped establish the 1980 Computer Software Copyright Act.

Table 4.1   Characteristics of Protective Mechanisms

Consideration	Copyright	Patent	Trade Secrecy
General			
National uniformity	Yes	Yes	No
Protection effective upon	Creation of work	Successful prosecution of application	Entrance into contractual relationship
Cost of obtaining protection	Nil	Moderate	Moderate
Term of protection	Life plus 50 or 75 years	17 years	Possibility of both perpetual protection and termination at any time
Cost of maintaining protection	Nil	Nil	Significant
Cost of enforcing rights against violators	Moderate	Moderate	Higher
Availability of (a) statutory damages; (b) attorney's fees from infringers	(a) Yes (b) Yes	(a) No (b) Yes	(a) No (b) No
Protection lost by	Gross neglect	Unsuccessful litigation	Disclosure
Software, including effects of Commission proposals			
Consistency with other copyright areas	Yes	No	No
Availability of protective mechanism for some programs	Yes	Unclear	Yes
Universal availability of protective mechanism for all programs	Yes	No	No
"Process" protection	No	Yes	Yes
Suited to mass distribution	Yes	Yes	No

- The Supreme Court recognized, in 1981, that a patent could be issued for a process that incorporates a computer program.

Alternative Strategies

- Copyright—term of copyright is life plus 50 years, protection is effective upon creation, cost is next to nil, enforcement cost is moderate, maintenance cost is nil, and protection is lost by gross neglect.
- Trade secret—term of trade secret is any time, entry is by contract, cost to obtain is moderate, enforcement and maintenance costs are high, and secret protection is lost.

RECOMMENDATION . . . .

Here is a list of recommendations for both the businessman and the scientist:

- Promulgate the laws for software throughout the company.
- Identify what characteristics make a software patent good as opposed to bad.
- Defend your software patents after they have been issued.
- Patent software features, since they are most easily noticed by an outside observer.
- Incorporate the aforesaid strategies into intellectual property policy!

Example Patents

- Stac, Inc. Patent #5,146,221—The company continued to update and create new patents from the first compression patent.
- Benson, Pardo, RSA—The firm successfully patented a computer algorithm for encyption. It is not possible to patent a mathmatical equation, since it is considered part of nature. However, they were able to get around this clause.

Non-example Patent

For a non-example, consider Compton's Multimedia Patent #5,241,671—prior art existed, and the claims were too broad in scope.

5 Developing Wireless Services

THE TEAM

This section explains the team needed to support the development of wireless services.

Levels of Complexity

Wireless services are of higher complexity than most other applications. The complexity in relationship to other applications is shown in Figure 5-1.

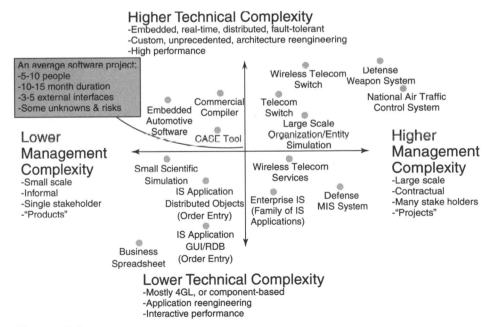

Higher Technical Complexity
-Embedded, real-time, distributed, fault-tolerant
-Custom, unprecedented, architecture reengineering
-High performance

An average software project:
-5-10 people
-10-15 month duration
-3-5 external interfaces
-Some unknowns & risks

Lower Management Complexity
-Small scale
-Informal
-Single stakeholder
-"Products"

Higher Management Complexity
-Large scale
-Contractual
-Many stake holders
-"Projects"

Embedded Automotive Software

Commercial Compiler

CASE Tool

Telecom Switch

Wireless Telecom Switch

Defense Weapon System

National Air Traffic Control System

Large Scale Organization/Entity Simulation

Small Scientific Simulation

IS Application Distributed Objects (Order Entry)

Wireless Telecom Services

Enterprise IS (Family of IS Applications)

Defense MIS System

Business Spreadsheet

IS Application GUI/RDB (Order Entry)

Lower Technical Complexity
-Mostly 4GL, or component-based
-Application reengineering
-Interactive performance

Figure 5-1
Dimension of software complexity.
Source: Royce Walker with the addition of wireless switch and service.

105

Associations in the Team

Shown in Figure 5-2 are the associations in a hyperproductive wireless service development team

Team Members

Here is a summary of the team members:

- Architect.
- Service-creation engineer.
- Wireless standards expert.
- Web-on-line help master.
- Java and C++ integrators and analysts.
- Project manager.
- Release manager.

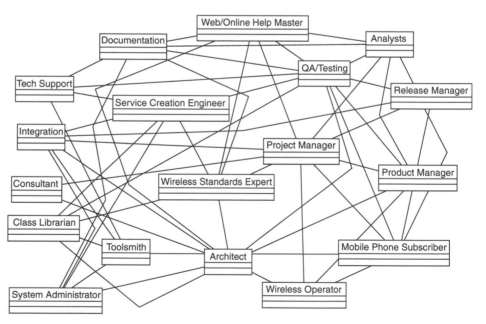

Figure 5-2
Associations in the wireless development team.
Source: Booch Project Management with the addition of wireless and web items.

- System administrator.
- Toolsmith.
- Class librarian.
- Documentation writer.
- QA tester.
- Mobile phone (non)subscriber.
- Consultant.

TEAM COMPETENCE AREAS

The intent of this section is to define areas in which the producer needs to build competence to successfully develop new services.

Rather than list the job descriptions with related tasks to be performed, it is more desirable to have a cross-functional team with backgrounds spanning some or all of the technologies. For this approach to work effectively, the producer will need to hire talent with the capacity to do it all. If a team consists of people from three functions—system, subsystem, and implementation and verification—it is possible to achieve fewer handoffs, quicker feedback, increased quality, and shorter development times.

Occasionally, very low-level, specialized tasks may require a consultant. For example, an anthropologist was used in the creation of new TUIs (telephony user interface) to attain the most ergonomic design. The Microsoft Windows start button evolved from works performed on monkeys. The intent was to design a GUI (graphical user interface) simple enough that even a monkey could use it to operate a computer.

Example Only

This section is provided only as an example. The reason is that each organization has its own unique level of competence.

Competence

Competence can be defined as "the level of skill of a person capable of selecting, implementing, and using various technologies related to wireless services."

Reducing the Scope Principle

When one of the subject areas is too vast for an organization, remedy the problem by considering these options:

- Buy the service off the shelf; /
- Outsource the development of a specific component; or
- Control it by way of the job description (change the scope from "develop" to "integrate").

Missing Section

Last, it is recommended that readers fill in for themselves a subsection entitled "Where to find and build competence." List the internal divisions and external companies that provide support for these specific areas.

FUNDAMENTAL PRODUCT CLASSIFICATIONS . . . . .

Regardless of the company, a computer product has a general classification structure. Planning an organization around such a structure makes the most sense. Table 5.1 shows the four basic classes and the tests that need to be performed.

LAYERED ORGANIZATION . . . .

It has become necessary to organize development around the Internet for many reasons (i.e., public domain software, standard interfaces, code reuse, the competition is doing it, and so on). Furthermore, the Internet protocol developer should not be desig-

Table 5.1   Product Classifications

Product Classifications	Testing
Hardware	Unit
Firmware	Integration
Software	Validation
Documentation	Proofread

nated to a particular product, since application services consist of many Internet component software libraries. For example, a message store service is really a composite of various Internet protocols. LDAP is used to query information about a subscriber, IMAP is used to store or retrieve a message, SNMP is used to alarm us of any malfunctions in a message storage process, and so on.

COMPETENCE AREAS . . . .

This section highlights technological competence areas needed for creating wireless PC-based services using the Internet paradigm. What is more, in job descriptions, the word "integration" is used instead of "develop." This implies that a job is simpler and requires less talent, since all that the job requires is to specify off-the-shelf products, rather than build them from scratch. This is an exemplary alternative available to development organizations lacking either the time, expertise, or resources for another development effort.

Table 5.2 Layered Organization

Org.	Layer	Description	Skill Set	Resource Assignment
A	4	Provisioning off-the-shelf products	No particular skill set required other than a high school or college level aptitude in reading	Designated to product
	3	Application development	Computer programmer or systems analyst	Designated to product
	2	Internet protocol development or circuit-switched telephony development	Computer scientist	Shared resource
	1	Platform, MAC Layer or DSP Layer	Electrical engineer	Designated to product

Application Generators

- Familiarity with application generators is needed—specifically, a service creation tool and associated engine on which to run services.
- Able to handle service creation GUI to develop or modify a service.

Security

- Able to integrate company messaging systems with vendor-selected PKI processing systems.
- Able to work with SMIME and SSL for e-mail encryption.
- Able to mange users' digital identities and certificates and establish systems.

Directories

- Familiarity is needed in directories (e.g., Active Directory, LDAP, X.500) and associated security systems.
- Additionally, some issues with provisioning the de facto schemas (e.g., LIPS) for these kinds of servers.

Messaging Standards and Products

- Familiarity is needed in messaging (e.g., POP3, IMAP4, MAPI, VPIM, IMPP, etc.).
- Able to follow standardization and participate in certain standardization bodies.
- Able to keep track of the top 10 messaging products on the market.
- Familiarity with queuing theory.

Speech Recognition

- Able to acquire and integrate state-of-the-art speech recognition technology to be used in messaging, IVR or personal assistant systems for voice control, voice authentication, and speech-to-text (dictation) technology.
- Knows differences among technologies that exist.
- Knows what the pros and cons are.

- Able to determine what makes a quality service.
- Able to determine what language and dialects are supported.
- Able to determine what the important selection criteria are for a speech-recognition engine.
- Able to determine what impact different voice compressions (e.g., GSM, ADPCM, PCM, CDMA, etc.) used in different networks have on a speech recognizer.
- Has a good understanding of what the competitors are using.
- Has a good understanding of who the suppliers are.
- Knows how to build TUI for voice control.
- Knows issues created by noisy environments (e.g., mobile environments).

Text-To-Speech

- Able to acquire and integrate state-of-the-art text-to-speech technology to be used in messaging, IVR, and information systems.
- Knows the differences in technologies that exist.
- Knows what the pros and cons are.
- Able to determine what makes a quality service.
- Able to determine what language dialects are supported.
- Able to determine what the important selection criteria are for a text-to-speech engine.
- Has a good understanding of what the competitors are using.
- Has a good understanding of the suppliers.

Optical Character Recognition

- Able to integrate mail systems with media conversion component.
- Able to work programmatically with all of the attachment types found in the unified inbox (e.g., voice mail, fax mail, e-mail, RTF, WAV).
- Able to facilitate media conversion on a PC or UNIX work station (e.g., WAV to text, GSM to PCM, TIFF to TEXT).
- Understands statistics.

OPTICAL IMAGE RECOGNITION . . . .

- Able to work with a fax form tool.
- Understands the basics of routing electronic messages to deliver the deciphered message.
- Understands statistics and neural networks.

TELEPHONY AREA . . . .

Call-Handling Models

- Ability to understand call-handling models and how they can be implemented.
- Able to select the appropriate model from a supplier.
- Able to follow the standardization activities in the CT area. (e.g., S.100 from ECTF).

Telephony Signaling

- Able to develop, acquire, and integrate telephony signaling protocols (e.g., SS7, PRI, MAP, IS41, INAP, H.323,ATM, SIP).
- Different standards and statuses.
- Suppliers of signaling protocols.
- Able to determine what technology to use when implementing and testing.

Computer Telephony Hardware

- Able to acquire CT-HW.
- Able to follow the standardization activities in the CT area (e.g., H.110 from ECTF).
- Able to follow the PCI and compact PCI standards.
- Able to read and interpret the document entitled *PC99 System Design Guide: A Reference for Designing PC and Peripherals for the Microsoft Windows Family of Operating Systems.*

- Understands storage subsystems (e.g., RAID).
- Understands regulatory-agency requirements (e.g., NEBS, UL, FCC).

Computer Telephony Software

- Able to acquire CT-SW (e.g., S.100 from ECTF and TAPI).
- Able to track developments in new IETF standards (SIP).
- Able to track developments from ITU (International Telecommunications Union)
- Able to write plug-and-play software.

MOBILE NETWORKS . . . .

- Understands PLMN in order to get the right integration of messaging functionality.
- Understands intelligent-network functionality, including INAP.
- Able to integrate PLMN operation and maintenance platforms.
- Understands mobility information.

INTERNET PROTOCOL . . . .

- Able to build systems based on Internet protocol (i.e., IP switches, IP v.6 and v.4, Ethernet, TCP, Firewalls, WANs).
- Able to track developments from IETF (Internet Engineering Task Force).
- Able to track developments from IMTC (International Multimedia Telecommunications Consortium, Inc.).

TRANSPORT TECHNOLOGIES . . . .

- Able to provision and quantify 10 Base–T, 100 Base–T, 1G Base–T, FDDI, and ATM technologies.

- Understands issues of capacity, throughput, and bandwidth reservation.
- Understands reservation and prioritization for real-time needs.

WEB SERVERS SOFTWARE . . . .

- Able to develop or purchase Web applications (e.g., Web servers, Web development environment).
- Knows how to develop Web applications on popular Web servers offered by industry.
- Able to create NUIs (network user interfaces) for wireless messaging applications.

SYSTEM LEVEL AREA . . . .

- Understands network management and SNMP.
- Understands message and call detail records for billing.
- Understands provisioning service orders.
- Understands traffic engineering.
- Understands operating system maintenance for UNIX and NT.
- Has experience with diagnostic tools.
- Has experience with database maintenance and networking.
- Understands how middleware technologies are used.

WORK METHODS . . . .

- Has an understanding of software design using object-oriented technologies.
- Able to create design guidelines and principles.
- Understands configuration management and change control.
- Project management and software.
- Has supplier management certifications.

- Understands how to document a product.
- Familiar with the processes involved with verification of hardware, firmware, software, and documentation.

CAPABILITY MATURITY MODEL · · · · · · · · · · · · · · · · ·

The vision of most leading software manufacturers is to attain Level 5 on IBM's Capability Maturity Model (CMM), as shown in Table 5.3.

Benefits of Product-Building Process

The product-building processes are intended to provide guidance on how to use product administration tools more effectively. In particular, the processes, along with supporting tools, will help a project achieve the following goals:

- Shorter build intervals due to fewer build failures.
- The ability to reproduce any previous version of the product.
- The ability and flexibility to build whenever needed.
- The ability to provide multiple loads to developers.

Table 5.3   Capability Maturity Model

Level	Description	Focus	Key Process Area
5	Optimizing	Continuous Process Improvement	Defect Prevention, Technology and Process Change Management
4	Managed	Product and Process Quality	Quantitative Process Management
3	Defined	Defined Engineering Process	Quantitative Process Management, Definition, Intergroup Coordination Training Program, Peer Review
2	Repeatable	Project Management and Commitment to Process	Requirements Management, Project Planning, Project Tracking, and Project Assurance
1	Initial Product Creation	Heroes	Not Reproducible

- Isolation of builds—protection of existing development and testing environments form new builds.
- The ability to do multiple, simultaneous builds.
- The ability to access proper versions of the software, including third-party software.
- The ability to deliver high-priority changes quickly.
- A cleaner understanding of the resources required to build and maintain products.

A PROCESS FOR DEVELOPMENT . . . .

Here are the steps in RUP (rational unified process):

1. Business modeling.
2. Requirements.
3. Analysis and design.
4. Implementation.
5. Unit-validation test.
6. Deployment.
7. Configuration management.
8. Project management.
9. Environment.
10. Iterate, don't vacillate.

Assumptions

The processes described in this section apply to medium-sized software projects. Here, "medium" means that the project consists of 5 to 150 people, including developers, system engineers, managers, and testers. Larger and smaller software projects can also benefit from the information provided here. Larger projects may require more rigor, and smaller projects less rigor.

Development Cycle

Figure 5-3 shows the RUP development lifecycle, based on object-oriented programming languages.

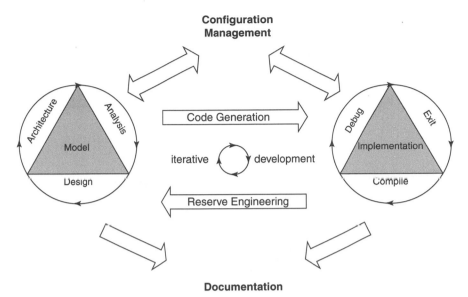

Figure 5-3
Development cycle.

RELEASE MANAGEMENT
AND CHANGE CONTROL . . . .

Release management and change control is the management of changes to any and all intermediate and end products. For some projects, change control refers only to changes in software modules and, perhaps, some of the product-related documents. However, it is important to note that it can also encompass project-related documents, such as the project plan.

Quality Policies

Here are some examples of policies for release management:

- Product release quality statement or phrase [e.g., *We Live to Reject Maintenance Requests* (MR)].
- Maintaining product build node and virtual nodes.
- Avoiding problems at approval time.
- Initialization MRs.
- Releases supported (current and prior).

- Patch release policy.
- Meet or exceed the customer requirements (clarify and verify in release notes).
- MR and file dependency (line level vs. file level).
- Reject these MRs (submitted with no change, tested but not going into OFC).
- Use consistent version numbering and tape labels.

OTHER PROCESSES FOR WIRELESS . . . .

The development process used to create state-of-the-art wireless programs is critical to the success of a software company. Figure 5-4 represents AT&T's SABLIME process. It is included here because it is one of the best for managing software, since the

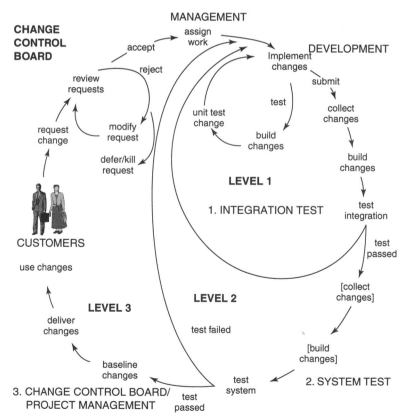

Figure 5-4
Product administration process.

projects support tight associations between changes and MRs, and the project is able to extract product versions given a list of MRs.

Furthermore, AT&T's process uses the most advanced archive software on the planet, the tried and true SCCS (source code control system) and, more importantly, SBCS (source and binary control system). Both programs are used to control versions of nonbinary files in response to MRs, but SBCS goes further. It can control versions on nonbinary files. This means everything can go under version control, including the operating system and digitized voice prompts! SBCS stores only the bits that changed.

Roles in Product Administration

The major roles in product administration are listed in Table 5.4.

Table 5.4 Product Administration Roles

Role	Description
Project manager	The overall project coordinator. Product administration provides the project manager with information (e.g., reports) on the status of the project, and hence can greatly facilitate a project's success.
CCB (change control board)	The central decision-making body for regulating and approving change and its resulting products. The CCB defines the procedures for implementing and approving change, tracks and reports change status, evaluates the impact of changes on various versions of the product, and reviews or audits changes as needed.
	The members of the CCB typically include the project manager, the product-administration manager, various other development managers, and the generic or the release engineer. An empowered delegate who has decision-making authority may replace any or all of these personnel.
Generic engineer	The lead engineer responsible for defining the content of the intermediate and final product versions of the product generic or release. He or she works closely with the project manager, to develop milestones for these versions, and with the CCB, to direct the evolution of the product.

Table 5.4   Product Administration Roles (*continued*)

Role	Description
Product-administration manager	The coordinator and owner of the product-administration process. This individual manages the day-to-day product-administration support activities. The product-administration manager may also head the CCB.
Product administrator	The person or group who maintains the product-administration environment for a project. This environment includes creating, maintaining, and controlling access to builds (product versions). The product administrator is concerned with the integrity of each build and of the product-administration environment. This role is analogous to a system administrator, who maintains the computing environment for a project.
Product-administration users	Anyone who can request and receive a change. This group includes developers, testers, customer-support personnel, customers, and end users. Developers (and sometimes testers) are also responsible for creating change. Ultimately, the purpose of product administration is to facilitate the productivity of all of these individuals.

Product-Building Process

The foundation of the product-building process is the node structure for archiving intellectual capital. Figure 5-5 shows a good example node structure for storing all things pertaining to a wireless project.

Viewpathing

Viewpathing is a mechanism for ordering and searching through one or more nodes in order to create a virtual version (i.e., view) of the product (both source and executables). Products like Clearcase make viewpathing easy. It becomes necessary for large software products and is a by-product of the make command. The main benefit of viewpathing is short build times.

Virtual Node

A virtual node is view of the node, created by viewpathing through one or more nodes (i.e., test node, integration node, packaging node, and production node).

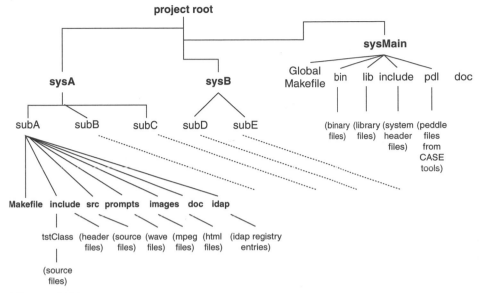

Figure 5-5
Example node structure.

The Product-Building Plan

A product-building plan provides a well-defined way to describe the product-building process, schedules, and deliverables for the project. Table 5.6 shows a scenario of eight loads before the final software release. This scenario is not uncommon for the wireless service program.

Table 5.6 Load Table

Load Name/Feature Content	Integration Test	System Test	Beta Test	General Availability
1	6/7	6/28		
2	6/28	7/12		
3	7/12	7/26		
4	7/26	8/9		
5	8/9	8/30		
6	8/30	9/13	10/1	
7	9/13	9/28	10/18	
8	9/28	10/15	11/1	12/1

Control Points

It is important to have some way to tell whether a project's product-administration process is effective. The best way to gauge the effectiveness is to use check points.

Props

The Ericsson PROPS (no specific meaning) model provides control points throughout out the process, which makes it exemplary. It is shown in Figure 5-6.

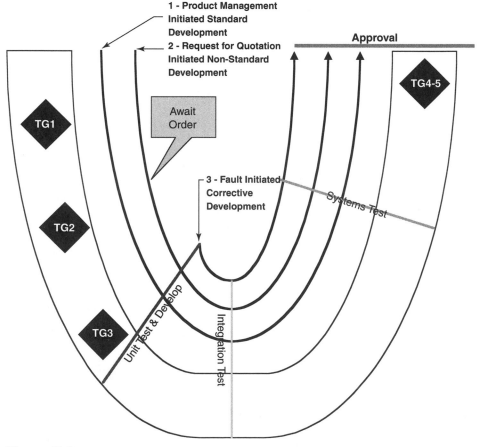

Figure 5-6
Ericsson PROPS development model.

SI Method

Figure 5-7 shows the system integration development process used by IBM. It was provided here to show project status by phase. Phases equate to tasks.

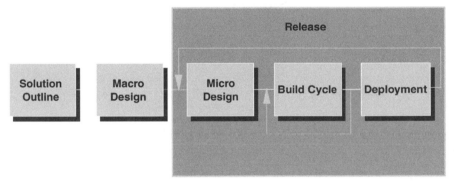

Figure 5-7
Phases in the IBM SI method.

6 Vendor-Neutral Framework for Wireless Services

BACKGROUND . . . .

A framework is an architectural pattern that provides an extensible template for applications within a domain (i.e., wireless system).

MODELING THE ARCHITECTURE OF A SYSTEM . . . .

In this section, models were applied to the wireless space in order to organize the elements used to visualize, specify, construct, and document a wireless system's architecture. The focus was on the implementation, design, and process views, since the use case and the deployment views were considered to be too application specific.

Modeling the UML Way

As a reference, the five UML views are reproduced in Figure 6-1.

THE OPEN GROUP FRAMEWORK . . . .

TOGAF (the open group architectural framework), shown in Figure 6-2, is the most comprehensive model for developing a wireless system, since it factors in APIs. The reason an API is far and away the most important aspect wireless architecture is because API changes to accommodate new protocols or changes to protocols. Version control is key to a successful evolving architecture; without it, the system quality diminishes in proportion to the number of protocols used.

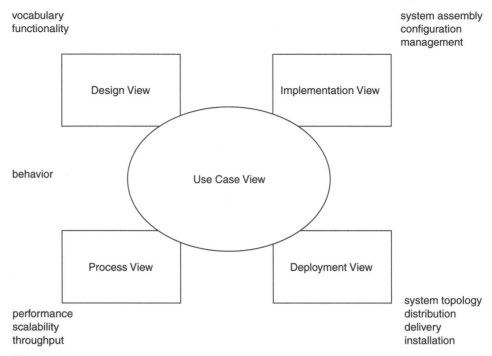

Figure 6-1
Modeling a system's architecture.[1]

Embracing Geography

In addition, TOGAF embraces the concept of local, regional, and global geography, as shown in Figure 6-3. This framework is particularly useful with wireless applications.

TCP/IP Protocol Architecture

The Internet provides a vendor-neutral architecture for development. This came about when the United States Defense Information Systems Agency declared TCP/IP a military standard, forcing computer manufacturers to comply with it in order to sell to the government.

The five-level model illustrated in Table 6.1 is based on a simpler three-layer (application, host-to-host, and network access) model used by the DOD. It was modified for the addition of computer telephony and platform resources.

[1]Booch, p. 424.

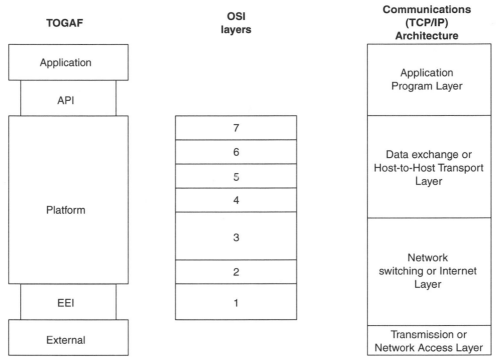

Figure 6-2
The open group architectural framework.

IT-Bus

Figure 6-4 shows a three-dimensional view of the host-to-host transport layer as and information technology bus (a.k.a., IT-Bus). In this figure, there are five services that embrace the bus. They include a text-to-wave file-converting program, an operations

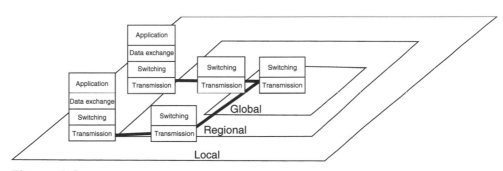

Figure 6-3
Geographic framework.

Table 6.1 Computer Telephony with Internet Messaging Architecture

Applications (X.500/DNS/LDAP)		
Host-to-Host Transport Layer (X.400/IMAP/POP)		
S.100	OS Program Calls (POSIX.1b Real-Time Extension)	RPC/TCP/UDP
H.110		IP
Telephony Resources	Computer and Disk Drives	Network Resources

and maintenance agent that correlates alarms, a screen handler that implements the wireless application protocol, a voice message handler, and an HTML call handler for H.323.

Example of a Host-to-Host Transport

Figure 6-5 provides another example of a wireless host-to-host transport layer while applying the concepts of X.400. The CCITT standard X.400 defines the concept of an MTA (message transfer agent) and a UA (user agent). In this case, the programs surrounding the MTA are called user agents. Each user agent uses a protocol to communicate with his or her respective network. The program is named after the protocol it supports.

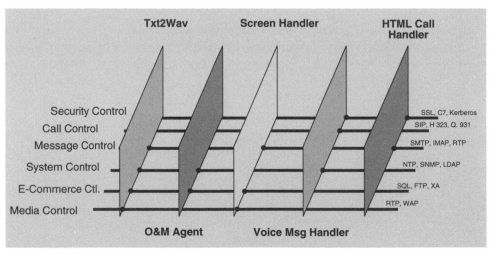

Figure 6-4
Enhanced host-to-host layer for wireless.

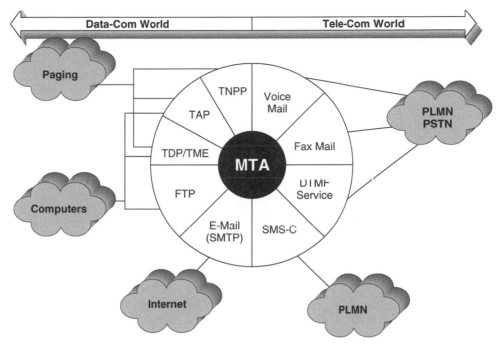

Figure 6-5
X.400 Enhanced for wireless.

UAs Defined

The UAs defined here perform the task of dynamic data conversion to a standard format. In the case of X.400, the standard format is X.409, which is a character-based encoding. The encoding is used even for binary data, but there is a performance penalty that real-time systems cannot afford. Table 6.2 shows a sample of the more frequently used UA conversions.

Scenarios

Table 6.3 shows some paths that a data message might travel. The network type is in parenthesis. The target device determines the network the message will travel over. Each network type has a unique way of identifying the terminal.

Table 6.2 User Agent Descriptions

User Agent	Description
FTP	File Transport Protocol
SMTP	Simple Mail Transport Protocol
SMS-C	Short Message Service Revision C
DTMF	Dual Tone Multifrequency Services
Fax Mail	Fax Mail implies Class 1 or 2 Fax mode.
Voice Mail	Voice Mail implies speech encoding (ADPCM or GSM 6.10)
TNPP	Telocator Network Paging Protocol
TAP	Telocator Alphanumeric Protocol
TME	Telocator Message Entry Protocol

Protocol Conversion

Table 6.4 shows two columns, one with Internet message field identifiers and another with SMS message field identifiers. There is quite a bit of translation required. In the last row, please find both the standard and the version the field names were taken from.

Table 6.3 Data Messaging Scenarios

FROM person	TO person	USING device
Internet	PLMN (D-AMPS)	PDA w/sim card
PLMN (D-AMPS)	Internet	Phone w/alphanumeric display
Internet	PLMN (AMPS)	PC w/analog modem
PLMN (AMPS)	Internet	Voice mail -> E-mail
Internet	ERMES (Paging)	Text -> beeper
ERMES (Paging)	Internet	Two-way beeper
Internet	POCSAG (Paging)	Text -> TNPP
POCSAG (Paging)	Internet	Analog beeper
Internet	PSTN (MF or ISDN)	etc.

Table 6.4   *Example Message Translation*

Internet Text Message Head	SMS Message Head
Apparently to	validity period
bcc*	service-center time stamp
cc*	protocol ID
Comments*	more-message-to-send flag
Content length	priority
Content type	MWI
Date*	alert-SC
Encrypted	options concerning MNRF
. . . , RFC822	. . . , GSM 3.4 ver. 4.7

Copy-Replication Continuum

Three types of channels for communicating with the MTA are recommended for wireless communications due to the instability of the connections, among other things:

- Asynchronous commands and reports.
- Asynchronous bidirectional update for services like logins.
- Synchronous two-phase commit for transactions.

Figure 6-6 shows the spectrum of choices available in the continuum. The only thing that does not apply to the UA is the hot-site/CPU, fail-over.

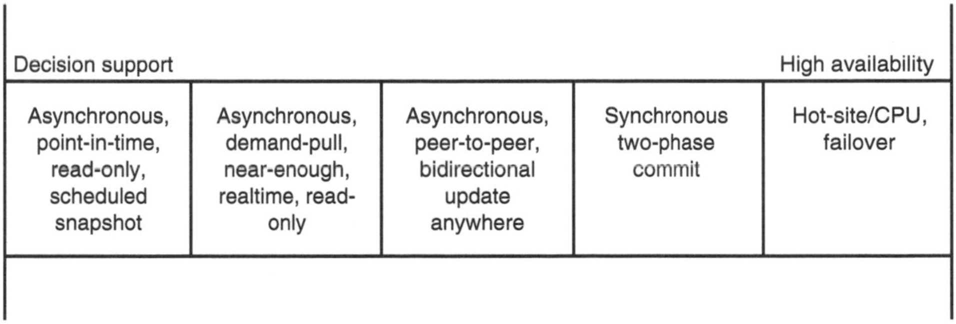

Decision support				High availability
Asynchronous, point-in-time, read-only, scheduled snapshot	Asynchronous, demand-pull, near-enough, realtime, read-only	Asynchronous, peer-to-peer, bidirectional update anywhere	Synchronous two-phase commit	Hot-site/CPU, failover

Figure 6-6
Copy-replication continuum.

Why Use Transactions?

Table 6.5 shows more on the utilization of the telephony resource. State machines are key as well as transactional C for wireless services. The example explains it best. For example, at state 4 in some services, the digit 2 is depressed to record a message, but during the recording, the traveler enters a tunnel and loses the mobile connection. Since the event was contained within a transaction, the message is not lost.

Scalability

A large-scale system may be defined as having these attributes:

- Number of objects $>10^6$
- Number of operations per second $> 10^2$
- Number of transactions per computer per second $> 10^2$
- Number of object creations per server per second $> 10^2$
- Number of clients $> 10^3$

Why Use Queues?

Wireless telephony applications meet all the requirements for when to use queues (see Table 6.6). Queues are short and need fast restart of network connections, parallel operations are high, all information flows in two patterns (call processing and message passing), and dependence on serialization is low.

Why Use the Internet Protocols?

The Internet protocols are open protocols, meaning that the source code is available to everyone by way of university Web sites that have DOD support.

Table 6.5 Example State Machine

STATE	WHEN event	THEN instruction
4	Digit 1	start play msg 1, transition to state 5
	Digit 2	start record msg 2, transition to state 5

Table 6.6 *Queues vs. Connections*

WHEN Wireless Message	USE queues	USE connections
Duration of message exchange	Short (fewer than 10 messages)	Long (10 messages or more)
Criticality of network restart time	High, need fastest restart possible	Low, delayed restart tolerated
Importance of parallel operations	High	Low
Variety of information flow patterns	All information flow patterns	Most closed trees and chains
Dependence upon serialization	Very low	High or medium

Therefore, vendors may create interchangeable programs that allow the consumer to use their product or others in the same system, provided their implementation does not deviate from the standard. Working with standard protocols cuts down the number of interfaces the developer has to contend with, as shown in Figure 6-7

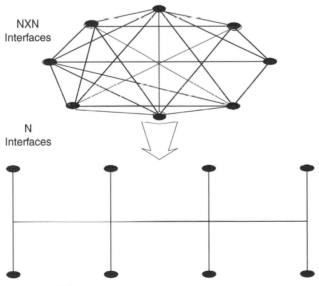

Figure 6-7
Moving toward standard interfaces.

WHAT ABOUT OBJECT MODELS? . . . .

Object models have come and gone, due primarily to complexity. There is a shift from tightly bound and registered COM and DCOM components to loosely coupled, published service events that thin clients subscribe to.

However, components still need to be registered. Active directory helps, since programs will look there for information pertaining to components. This should improve program execution.

Microsoft has decided to give it another try with COM+ (component object model), as shown in Figure 6-8. This is a spin on the Tibco model.[2]

Com

COM is a specification and a set of services that allows you to create modular, object-oriented, customizable, upgradable, and distributed applications using a number of languages. Below is a list of COM facts:

- COM is a specification.
- COM is a set of services (APIs).
- COM allows modular programming.
- COM is object-oriented.
- COM enables easy customization and upgrades to your applications.
- COM enables distributed applications.
- COM components can be written in many languages.
- COM makes a network of computers look like one.

Com+

The COM+ is an enhancement to the COM specification. Here are the improvements:

- Integrates Microsoft transaction server and message queue server as built-in services.
- Provides dynamic load balancing among objects on the network.
- In-memory database supports faster processing and object "persistence."

[2]www.tibco.com

- Queued components let transactions survive system outages and "disconnected users."
- "Publish and subscribe" functions let programmers avoid writing custom software and turn the task into an administrative procedure.

TIBCO Technologies

The foundation of the TIBCO product line is the TIB (TIBCO information bus). TIB/Rendezvous software puts the power of information bus technology in a compact, easy-to-use package for general use. TIB does for software what standardized backplane architectures do for hardware. Developers can easily add or update components in a distributed software system.

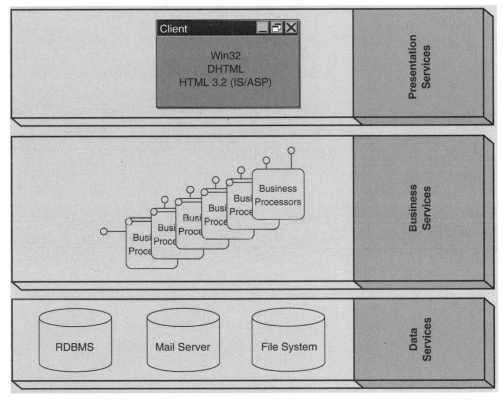

Figure 6-8
COM+ architecture.[3]

[3]http://www.roguewave.com

Messages

TIB/Rendezvous applications communicate by exchanging messages. Messages can contain any kind of data (except memory pointers); they usually contain notifications of business events and any associated data. TIB/Rendezvous software features *self-describing* data—data structures that contain information about their datatypes, sizes, and names. TIB/Rendezvous applications on heterogeneous platforms can communicate easily by exchanging self-describing data.

Publish and Subscribe

TIBCO pioneered publish-subscribe communications technology to expedite the delivery of real-time information in the financial industry. Today, TIB/Rendezvous software lets applications in any environment share up-to-date information reliably and transparently.

Each message traverses the network only once, yet TIB/Rendezvous software carries it to all subscribers on the network. In contrast, point-to-point communications would send the same message individually to each subscriber, wasting network bandwidth and slowing delivery.

The terms "publish" and "send" are synonymous, as are "subscribe" and "listen."

Subject-Based Addressing

TIB/Rendezvous software utilizes TIBCO's powerful patented subject-based addressing technology. A subject name is a character string that describes the content of a message and specifies its destination. Subject-based addressing technology helps messages reach their destinations without involving programmers in the details of network addresses, protocols, packets, ports, and sockets. Application designers devise conventions for intuitive, human-readable subject names.

Traditional network programming uses IP addresses for distribution-binding programs to specific computers. In contrast, TIB/Rendezvous applications share information by subject names, freeing applications to run on any computer, anywhere on the network. Information is sent (published) on a subject name. Interested parties listen for (subscribe to) specific subject names. Any time a message is published on a specific subject name and there are subscribers listening (subscribing) for that subject name, the TIB/Rendezvous software reliably routes the messages to any other applications. Subject-based addressing makes distributed systems more flexible and maintainable. Applications receive messages by listening. Listening associates a subject name with a callback function. When a message arrives, TIB/Rendezvous software dispatches it to the appropriate callback function by matching subject names.

Location transparency is an important consequence of subject-based addressing technology. TIB/Rendezvous senders and listeners can run on any computer on a network. Server applications can migrate or replicate (to share a heavy client load) with no impact on existing clients. Workflow systems that adapt easily to change and growth can be built.

Three Interaction Styles

Three distinct kinds of interaction can occur among applications in distributed environments, and TIB/Rendezvous software supports all three:

1. Publish-subscribe interactions, such as general distribution of information from many sources to many consumers. (See Figure 6-9.)
2. Request-reply interactions, such as queries or transactions. (See Figure 6-10.)
3. Broadcast request-reply interactions, such as queries that may result in several replies from one or more servers. (See Figure 6-11.)

UML COMPONENTS . . . .

This subsection explains how a component is described with UML.

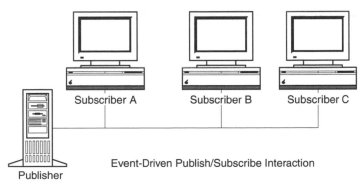

Event-Driven Publish/Subscribe Interaction

Figure 6-9
Event-driven publish-subscribe interaction.

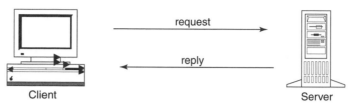

Figure 6-10
Demand-driven request-reply interaction.

Semantic

A component type represents a distributable piece of implementation of a system, including software code (source, binary, or executable), but also including business documents, and so on, in human systems. Components may be used to show dependencies, such as compiler and run-time dependencies, or information dependencies in a human organization. A component instance represents a run-time implementation unit and may be used to show implementation units that have identity at run time, including their location on nodes.

Component

- <<document>>
- <<executable>>
- <<file>>
- <<friend>>
- <<library>>
- <<table>>

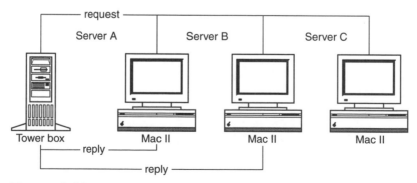

Figure 6-11
Broadcast request-reply interaction.

Auxiliary Elements

Comments and dependencies are auxiliary elements of a component and are listed below for completeness.

Comment

- <<requirement>>

Dependency

- <<becomes>>
- <<call>>
- <<copy>>
- <<deletion>>
- <<derived>>
- <<import>>
- <<instance>>
- <<metaclass>>
- <<powertype>>
- <<send>>

Service

- A service is made up of components heretofore.

CLASS LIBRARIES FOR WIRELESS SERVICES—WHAT IS IT? . . . .

The class library is a collection of descriptors for a set of objects with similar structure, behavior, and relationships specific to wireless and the Internet, among other things. On the physical level, it is made up of source code and UML files.

LIBRARY OBJECTIVES . . . .

Here are some of the objectives of the class library:

- Facilitate reuse (do not build from scratch) of requirements, architectures, components, codes, test artifacts, and so on.
- Increase time to market of software components.
- Off-the-shelf class libraries work almost immediately.
- Improve component quality.
- Provide superior performance.
- Support multiple computing paradigms (NT and UNIX).
- To be easily integrated within an application

KINDS OF C++ CLASSES . . . .

Here are some of kinds of classes in the C++ library:

Internet (Open Protocols)

- ftp++
- http++
- ldap++
- pop++
- smtp++
- snmp++
- iiop++

Vendor (Proprietary Protocols)

- encina++
- mq++

Vendor (Proprietary Extensions)

- threads++
- tools++
- math++
- money++

Enterprise (Open Extensions)

- xa++
- odbc++
- sql92++
- stl++ (N/A)
- dcom++

Domain-Specific (Proprietary Protocols)

- ocr++
- ohr++
- ss7++

KINDS OF JAVA CLASSES . . . .

Here are some of kinds of classes in the Java library:

Graphics

Blend.J, Chart.J, Grid.J, or Jwidgets.

Database

DBTools.J.

Others

Others come with JIDE (Java integrated-development environment).

EXAMPLE VIEW OF OBJECT LIBRARY . . . .

Figure 6-12 is an example Web-site view of a class library that facilitates development and reuse of source code.

Tech Talk

The site contains a UML model for documentation of the library.

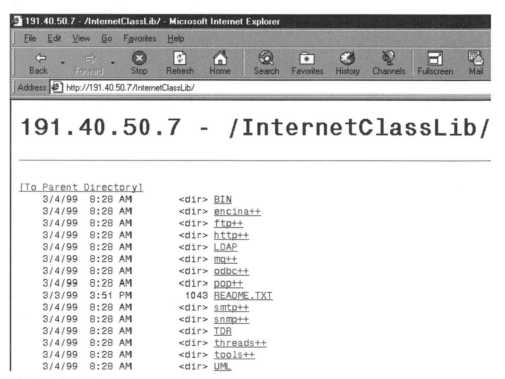

Figure 6-12
Web-site view of source code.

PRODUCT STRUCTURE AND PACKAGING . . . .

The most important high-level decision about the development of a system is the way in which a model is divided into parts.

This requires that the work units be identified and isolated to some extent, so that different work teams do not interfere with each other. In practice, systems can best be understood as collections of loosely coupled subsystems that are connected using well-specified interfaces.

Here are some of the basic principles involved:

- Any complex system must be constructed in parts, so that those teams of developers can work productively in parallel.
- A package must be a name space, because it is a unit of independent work and therefore must isolate itself from naming conflicts.
- Choose package boundaries wisely. If there are too many dependencies among packages, classes can often be moved between packages to reduce the number of dependencies. If moving the classes does not help, sometimes the entire system decomposition into packages must be thought out anew.
- Use the existing Internet architecture packaging principle, which divides client and server by high-level protocols.
- Consider changeable versus reusable. A package that does not lend itself to reuse (i.e., graphic controllers) should lend itself to changeability. Emphasize plug-and-play development instead of focusing on the compile time dependencies.
- Isolate platform dependencies into a single package. Watch for the trade-off between the details of implementation at the possible cost of performance.
- It is useful to show patterns of dependencies using package diagrams. However, a package often has so many services that the dependency diagrams are very dense with linkages.

Tools

The standard, most comprehensive tool set for packaging is UNIX System V packaging commands (pkgadd, pkginfo, etc.). However, this set of tools has its drawbacks. They are hard to use. A separate build cycle just for packaging is recommended, one reason being that the writing of code is needed in most cases. Consequently, making a package add into a system is easy enough, but making a package that is removable is far more difficult.

Therefore, companies like InstallShield Software Corporation developed InstallShield™ to address changing software development needs. InstallShield makes creating reliable installations easier through its all-encompassing installation development environment, new Wizards, and a slew of timesaving features.

7 Vendor-Neutral Framework for Wireless Security

BACKGROUND ·

This section provides a framework for wireless security. It is applicable for third-generation packet mobile networks. See Table 7.1 for a layout of the security framework.

Table 7.1   Security Framework

Data Privacy	Extranet Security — Extranet VPN	E-Firewall with VPN	Secure Security Management Framework	File Encryption — E-Firewall	SMIME
Application/ Data Integrity	Access Control Domain Guard Access	Authorization Authorization Server		Containment Containment with Virtual Vaults	
User Account Integrity	User/Group Adm. Access Manager	Authentication Protect Tools	Single Sign-On DCE/DCOM		
System Integrity	Virus Prevention Antivirus and Guard server		Risk Assessment Tools Satan server		
Network Integrity	Firewalls E-Firewall		Intrusion Detection Node Sentry		
Fraud Prevention	Licensing Flexible Licensing Manager		Hard Locks Aladdin		

DATA PRIVACY . . . .

Extranet VPN

Extranet security manager is a Socksv5-based, client-server software that provides strong encryption for network communications and access control for multiple Web, legacy, and object-based applications. It enables a company to safely build extranets with unmatched levels of protection and versatility of installation and security administration.

E-Firewall with VPN

IPsec-compliant "tunnelling" option for E-Firewall is an IPsec-based encryption for network traffic traveling between firewalls and between remote users and a firewall. It is available on E-Firewall and compatible with other IPsec-compliant security products.

Very Secure Security Management Framework

Exportable strong encryption and policy management technology (strong exportable encryption) is the only strong encryption technology without mandatory key recovery that may be exported from the United States without additional limitation on end-user or intended usage. The advantages of 128-bit and triple-DES encryption are available to users running any computer application, limited only by local laws and regulations. Manufacturers of any network device can adapt their products to changes in national laws quickly and easily.

E-Firewall

Application-level firewall is a third-generation network security software that combines application-level, network access controls, and an ease of configuration and security management that clearly sets the E-Firewall apart from other industry products. It uses a robust set of application proxies to examine the entire data stream of every connection attempted through the firewall. It also filters traffic according to explicit order-independent rules and continuously hardens the host operating system.

Proxy Server

A proxy server is an Internet server that controls client computers' access to the Internet. Using a proxy server like E-Firewall, a company can stop employees from accessing undesirable Web addresses, improve performance by storing Web pages locally, and hide the internal network's identity so that it is difficult for external users to monitor.

Wireless Impact

However, proxy servers are not helpful when the content does not lend itself to be cached, like [Common Gateway Interface] scripts that contain on-the-fly responses. For example, if you go to your unified inbox and listen to messages, you will see that you are receiving a continuous audio, and possibly video, stream. A proxy server makes the audio or video stream less efficient; the movements are jerkier and the sound and lip movements are skewed, because it can only store repeatable information—not unique content.

IPsec/9000

IPsec-compliant virtual private networking (VPN) support for servers (Ipsec/9000). The IPSec/9000 supports standards-based, secure communications both over the Internet and within an enterprise without any modification to applications. With this feature, HP-UX servers can support authentication, data integrity, and data encryption. This security can protect server-to-client, server-to-server, and server-to-gateway network traffic. In addition, the Java GUI provides an easy-to-use interface for configuring application-level, rule-based policies. IPsec/9000 is now available as a standard feature on HP-UX 11.0.

APPLICATION/DATA INTEGRITY . . . .

Domain Guard Access

Web application user access manager is Web security software that "snaps" into Netscape-based server environments and provides "role-based" control over access to Web applications, pages, forms, server-side CGI, and Java programs. It combines

centralized IT control over policy-level security with decentralized security administration by business line managers and enables the sharing of sensitive applications
and data by employees, customers, and business partners who are members of the
same business access domain (See the section titled "The Unified Wireless Inbox,
Access Control Manager.")

Authorization Server

Enterprise user authorization manager is an enterprise security software that provides
"rule-based" control of transactions on both Web and non-Web applications. Features
of the authorization server include:

- Trusted access domain—a simple authorization model based on users, re-
  sources, and access rights.
- Business access controls—rules that implement security for business appli-
  cations, based on the content of the transaction or Web page being accessed.
- Automatic access control for Web content and Web-enabled applications;
  security for static and active Web pages and the transactions behind the
  Web page.
- Flexible security policies that can be changed as business needs change.
- Modular architecture for Web environments.
- Administration that can be partitioned and delegated.
- Support for multiple authentication methods.
- Integration with HP VirtualVault.
- Integration with SNMP.
- Replicated data repository.
- Software developer's kit for custom applications.[1]

Domain Guard Rules

Web application user access and transaction authorization manager is a Web-security
functionality that builds on DomainGuard Access. With DomainGuard Rules, business line managers can create unambiguous rules that either permit or deny Web form
transactions (e.g., entering quantities, dollar amounts, or part numbers), based on user
identity and assigned roles.

---

[1]http://hpcc940.external.hp.com/security/products/authorization_server/papers/whitepaper

Containment with Virtual Vaults

Trusted Web-server platform is a Web-security software that enables businesses to safely provide users Internet and Intranet access to business-critical E-services. It protects confidential information and transactions, the Web site, back-end application resources, and the intranet. Typical applications are E-banking, corporate e-mail, E-collaboration, E-supply chain services, and protection of other security products, like certificate servers.

USER ACCOUNT INTEGRITY . . . .

Access Manager

Enterprise user and group account manager, HP OpenView, is a standards-based solution that provides the IT organization, network administrators, and security managers the tools and processes they need to take control of their networking environment. Access Manager is a powerful, flexible, and comprehensive solution for managing enterprisewide employee access to operating systems, databases, and applications.

Protect Tools

A smart-card and single sign-on authentication accessory for a PC is an HP Vectra PC smart-card accessory, which enables IS managers to quickly and easily implement a corporate smart-card program. It includes a smart-card reader, smart-cards, Windows NT compatible login software, and single sign-on software.

PKC Accelerator Card

User authentication performance accelerator for servers is an encryption processor card for servers. It accelerates the processing of both the secure electronic transaction (SET) and secure sockets layer (SSL) authentication protocols.

SYSTEM INTEGRITY . . . .

Virus Prevention

The idea here is to include virus prevention software systemwide.

Risk Assessment Tools

Risk assessment tools include software for determining risk by way of decision tree analysis and operations research.

NETWORK INTEGRITY . . . .

Network Node Manager and Node Sentry

IBM's Tivoli, used for enterprise network intrusion detection and response, is another standards-based solution that provides the IT organization, network administrators, and security managers the tools and processes they need to take control of their networking environment. Node Manager and Node Sentry is an intrusion detection system that includes distributed Node Sentry software that plugs into TCP/IP networks, integrating with routers, relational databases, trouble-ticket systems, and e-mail and pager applications. Working with the centralized network node manager, the system continuously examines network traffic to identify patterns of misuse. When a violation is found, Node Sentry raises alarms and removes offending traffic from the network.

PUBLIC KEY INFRASTRUCTURE . . . .

The Microsoft Windows 2000 operating system introduces a comprehensive public key infrastructure (PKI) to the Windows platform. This infrastructure utilizes and extends the Windows-based public key (PK) cryptographic services introduced over the past few years, providing an integrated set of services and administrative tools for creating, deploying, and managing PK-based applications, and allows application developers to take advantage of the shared-secret security mechanisms or the PK-based security mechanism, as appropriate. At the same time, enterprises gain the advantage of being able to manage the environment and applications based on consistent tools and policy mechanisms.

The remainder of this chapter provides an overview of the PKI in Windows 2000.

Public Key Cryptography

Cryptography is the science of protecting data. Cryptographic algorithms mathematically combine input *plain text* data and an *encryption key* to generate encrypted data (*ciphertext*). With a good cryptographic algorithm, it is computationally infeasible to reverse the encryption process and derive the plain text data starting with only the ciphertext; some additional data, a *decryption key*, is needed to perform the transformation. In traditional *secret (*or *symmetric) key cryptography*, the encryption and decryption keys are identical and thus share sensitive data. Parties wishing to communicate with secret-key cryptography must securely exchange their encryption-decryption keys before they can exchange encrypted data. In contrast, the fundamental property of *PK cryptography* is that the encryption and decryption keys are different. Encryption with a public key encryption key is a *one-way* function; plain text turns into ciphertext easily, but the encryption key is irrelevant to the decryption process. A different decryption key (related but not identical to the encryption key) is needed to turn the ciphertext back into plain text. Thus, for PK cryptography, every user has a pair of keys consisting of a *public* key and a *private* key. By making the public key available, it is possible for you to enable others to send you encrypted data that can only be decrypted using your private key. Similarly, you can transform data using your private key in such a way that others can verify that it originated with you. This latter capability is the basis for digital signatures, as discussed next.

Public Key–Enabled Functionality

The separation between public and private keys in PK cryptography has allowed the creation of a number of new technologies. The most important of these are digital signatures, distributed authentication, secret key agreement by public key, and bulk data encryption without prior shared secrets. There are a number of well-known PK cryptographic algorithms. Some, such as RSA (Rivest-Shamir-Adleman) and ECC (elliptic curve cryptography), are general-purpose algorithms; they support all of the foregoing operations. Others support only a subset of these capabilities. Some examples include the Digital Signature Algorithm (DSA, part of the U.S. government's Digital Signature Standard, FIPS 186), which is useful only for digital signatures, and Diffie-Hellman (D-H), which is used for secret key agreement. The following paragraphs briefly describe the principal uses of PK cryptography. These operations are described in terms of two users, Scott and Alice. It is assumed that Scott and Alice can exchange information but do not have any prearranged shared secrets between them.

Digital Signatures

Perhaps the most exciting aspect of public key cryptography is that of creating and validating *digital signatures*. This is based on a mathematical transformation that combines the private key with the data to be *signed* in such a way that

- Only someone possessing the private key could have created the digital signature.
- Anyone with access to the corresponding public key can verify the digital signature.
- Any modification of the signed data (even changing only a single bit in a large file) invalidates the digital signature.

Digital signatures are themselves just data, so they can be transported along with the signed data that they *protect*. For example, Scott can create a signed e-mail message to Alice and send the signature along with the message text, providing Alice the information required to verify the message origin. In addition, digital signatures provide a way to verify that data has not been tampered with (either accidentally or intentionally) while in transit from the source to the destination. Because of this, they can be exploited to provide a very high-assurance data integrity mechanism.

Authentication

One can exploit PK cryptography to provide robust distributed *authentication* services. *Entity authentication* guarantees that the sender of data is the person that the receiver thinks it is. One possible method involves the data receiver, Alice, sending a challenge to the data sender, Bob, encrypted with Bob's public key. Scott then decodes this challenge and sends it back to Alice, proving that he has access to the private key associated with the public key Alice used to issue the challenge. An alternative is for Alice to send a plain text challenge to Bob. Scott then combines the challenge with other information, which is digitally signed. Alice then uses Bob's public key to verify the signature and prove that Scott has the associated private key. The challenge makes this message unique and prevents replay attacks by a hostile third party. In either case, this is known as a *proof of-possession* protocol, because the sender is proving that he has access to a particular private key.

Secret Key Agreement by Public Key

PK cryptography also permits two parties to agree on a shared secret using public, nonsecure communication networks. Basically, Scott and Alice each generate a random number that will form half of the shared secret key. Scott then sends his half of the secret to Alice encrypted, using her public key, while Alice sends her half to Bob, encrypted with his public key. Each side can then decrypt the message received from the other party, extract the half of the shared secret generated by the other party, and combine the two halves to create the shared secret. Once the protocol is completed, the shared secret can be used for securing other communications.

Bulk Data Encryption Without Prior Shared Secrets

The fourth major technology enabled by PK cryptography is the ability to encrypt bulk data without the establishment of prior shared secrets. Existing PK algorithms are computationally intensive relative to secret key algorithms. This makes them ill-suited for encrypting large amounts of data. To get the advantages of PK cryptography along with efficient bulk encryption, PK and secret key technologies are typically combined. This is accomplished by first selecting a secret key encryption algorithm and generating a *random session key* to use for data encryption. If Scott is sending the message, he first encrypts his session key using Alice's public key. The resulting ciphertext key is then sent to Alice along with the encrypted data. Alice can recover the session key using her private key and then use the session key to decrypt the data.

Protecting and Trusting Cryptographic Keys

In secret key cryptography, Alice and Scott trust their shared secret key because they either mutually agreed on it or exchanged it in a secure manner, and each has agreed to keep it stored securely to prevent access by a malicious third party. In contrast, using PK cryptography, Alice need only protect her private key and Scott his private key. The only information they need to share is each other's public key. They need to be able to identify each other's public key with high assurance, but they need not keep it secret. This ability to trust the association of a public key with a known entity is critical to the use of PK cryptography.

Alice might trust Bob's public key because Scott handed it to Alice directly in a secure manner, but this presupposes that Alice and Scott have had some form of prior secure communication. More likely, Alice has obtained Bob's public key through a nonsecure mechanism (for example, from a public directory), so some other mechanism is needed to give Alice confidence that the public key she holds, claiming to be from Scott, is really Bob's public key. One such mechanism is based on certificates issued by a certificate authority (CA).

Certificates

Certificates provide a mechanism for gaining confidence in the relationship between a public key and the entity owning the corresponding private key. A certificate is a particular type of digitally signed statement; the subject of the certificate is a particular subject public key and the certificate is signed by its issuer (holding another pair of private and public keys). Typically, certificates also contain other information related to the subject public key, such as identity information about the entity that has access to the corresponding private key. Thus, when issuing a certificate, the issuer is attesting to the validity of the binding between the subject public key and the subject identity information.

The most common form of certificates in use today is based on the ITU-T X.509 standard. This is a fundamental technology used in the Windows 2000 PKI. It is not, however, the only form of certificates. Pretty good privacy (PGP) secure E-mail, for example, relies on a form of certificates unique to PGP.

Certificate Authorities

A certificate authority (CA) is simply an entity or service that issues certificates. A CA acts as a guarantor of the binding between the subject public key and the subject identity information contained within the certificates it issues. Different CAs may choose to verify the binding by different means, so it is important to understand the authority's policies and procedures before choosing to trust that authority to vouch for public keys.

Trust and Validation

The fundamental question facing Alice when she receives a signed message is whether she should trust that the signature is valid and was made by whoever claimed to make it. Alice can confirm that the signature is mathematically valid; that is, she can verify the integrity of the signature using a known public key. However, Alice must still determine whether the public key used to verify the signature does in fact belong to the entity claiming to have made the signature in the first place. If Alice does not implicitly trust the public key to be Bob's, she needs to acquire strong evidence that the key belongs to Bob.

If Alice can locate a certificate for Bob's public key issued by a CA that Alice implicitly trusts, then Alice can trust that Bob's public key really belongs to Bob. That is, Alice will likely trust that she really has Bob's public key if she finds a certificate that

- Has a cryptographically valid signature from its issuer.
- Attests to a binding between the name Scott and Bob's public key.
- Was issued by an issuer that Alice has chosen to trust.

Assuming that Alice finds such a certificate for Bob's public key, then she can verify its authenticity using the public key of the issuing CA, Ira. However, Alice is now faced with the same dilemma. How does she know that public key actually belongs to Ira? Alice now needs to find a certificate attesting to the identity of Ira and the binding between Ira and Ira's public key.

Ultimately, Alice will end up constructing a chain of certificates leading from Scott and Bob's public key through a series of CAs and terminating in a certificate issued to someone that Alice implicitly trusts. Such a certificate is called a "trusted root certificate," because it forms the root (top node) of a hierarchy of public keys and identity bindings that Alice will accept as authentic (see the section "Certificate Hierarchies"). When Alice chooses to explicitly trust a particular trusted root certificate, she is implicitly trusting all of the certificates issued by that trusted root, as well as all certificates issued by any subordinate CA certified by the trusted root.

The set of trusted root certificates that Alice explicitly trusts is the only information that Alice must acquire in a secure manner. That set of certificates bootstraps Alice's trust system and her belief in the public key infrastructure.

SIM SECURITY . . . .

Cellphones use SIM (subscriber identity module) chips to provide authorization for each call made and provide storage for both programs and data. The programs determine how the phone will function, and the storage is for messages and a telephone directory. The SIMs can be small (i.e., postage-stamp size) or full-size (credit-card size). They are interrogated and reprogrammed through wireless communications.

Planned

The plan is to make the handset interface with SmartCards, so that the user can telephone shop or bank.

8 Wireless Fault Tolerant System Example

HARDWARE BACKGROUND . . . .

Figure 8-1 shows a fault tolerant system example based on the ECTF (Enterprise Computer Telephony Framework) and the NEBS (Network Equipment Building System) standard from Telcordia Technologies, Inc. A fault tolerant system should have these characteristics:

- All of the computer chassis are based on PCI (peripheral component interconnect) or CompactPCI, making parts interchangeable (i.e., memory, VGA cards, I/O cards, H.110 cards).

- N + 1 means that it is possible to have many stacks of PCI-based computer chassis loaded with any mixture of H.110 devices (i.e., DSP resources) and routers with one hot spare in each stack. The limiting factor is the bus speed to the minicomputers.

- The topology is ring or dual bus. The routers make them interchangeable.

- There is a redundant CPU inside a minicomputer. In addition, this minicomputer does not have to be colocated with the TFEs.

- A distributed file system is needed in Subnet/Cell 3, like the Andrew File System from IBM, which is capable of providing a file server network interface that runs free of volume access inconsistency. This means that the outside world would not know if the system contained one PC or 512; it would all look the same.

Tech Talk

The Cornell Theory Center and IBM Corporate Internet Projects Group have validated AFS 3.4 beta at the 1995 U.S. Open and the 1996 Olympic Games.

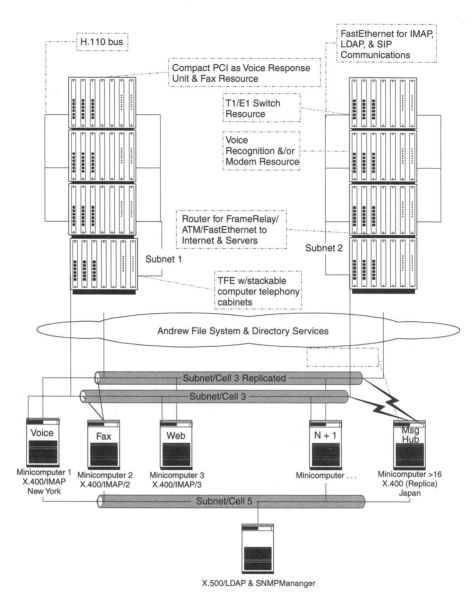

Figure 8-1
Example computer telephony processor diagram.

THREADED MULTILINE APPLICATIONS . . . .

Most telephony applications are designed to handle several phone lines. Multiline telephony applications need to be designed to handle the multiple input channels in such a way that one channel does not slow down or harm the other. In Figure 8-1 on the previous page, the T1 or E1 shelves interface the wireless telephone network. T1 has a capacity of 24 simultaneous telephone conversations; E1 has a 32-channel capacity.

Therefore, the easiest and most stable multiline telephony design is to have one process per phone line, or T1 channel. This ensures that one phone line cannot crash and pull down the other lines. This design also parallelizes well. One simple technique is to create a process that works for one telephone line and then create a symbolic link, named "line two," to the line-one executable. This makes the system easy to administer, since each process has its own identity.

Alternatively, the multiline application has one process running at least one thread per phone line. Because each line has its own thread, the lines are independent, and (generally) one line will not cause another to slow down. Multithreaded lines also allow for improved performance on multiprocessor CPUs. However, if one of the lines in a multithreaded application causes a GP fault, all of the threads will die.

SYNCHRONIZATION OBJECTS SUMMARY . . . .

Table 8.1 is a useful reference for programmers writing real-time wireless services, since performance (i.e., see columnar relative speed) is key to a good service.

Table 8.1   *Sychronization Objects under Windows NT*

Name	Relative speed	Cross process	Resource counting	Supported platforms
Critical Section	Fast	No	No (Exclusive Access)	95/NT/CE
Mutex	Slow	Yes	NO (Exclusive Access)	95/NT/CE
Semaphore	Slow	Yes	Yes	95/NT
Event	Slow	Yes	Yes	95/NT/CE
Metered Section	Fast	Yes	Yes	95/NT/CE

COMPACT PCI ·

The PCI architecture has become the most common method used to extend PCs for add-on adapters. Windows, Windows NT, Linux, and Solaris use the basic PCI infrastructure to gain information about devices attached to the PCI bus. The ability of PCI to supply such information makes it an integral part of the plug-and-play architecture.

Please see http://www.pcdesguide.org for more information.

Diagram

Figure 8-2 is an inside view of a Compact PCI shelf.

H.110 Bus

The H.110 bus rides on top of the Compact PCI cards in the shelf, as shown in Figure 8.3

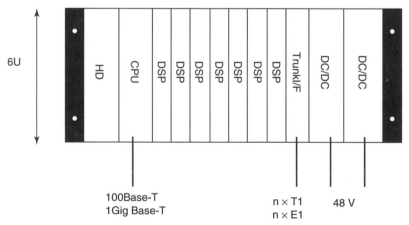

Figure 8-2
Compact PCI shelf.

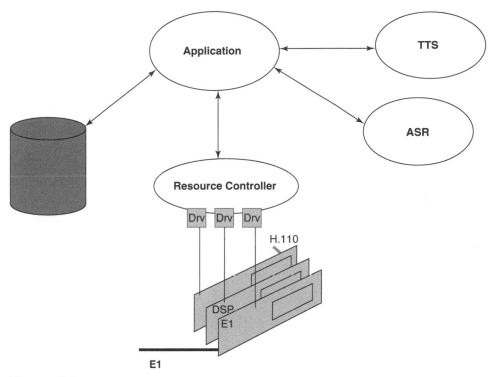

Figure 8-3
View of H.110 Bus.

I₂O BEATS I-O BOTTLENECKS . . . .

PCs face ever-daunting demands on their resources. Besides traditional roles of file, mail, and print services, such machines must handle new tasks, such as wireless call processing, database queries, online transaction processing, and streaming video for multimedia applications. Now, servers must manage numerous high-speed network connections and churn out graphics and Java applets for content-rich Web applications.

Therefore, a new I-O architecture was recently introduced, called Intelligent I-O, or I₂O. I₂O-compliant servers can administer more tasks, despite a limited amount of hardware, because the architecture off-loads portions of the work onto intelligent I-O subsystems. Dedicated I/O processors (IOPs) on these subsystems take care of the gritty details of interrupt handling, buffering, and data transfers. This improves the server's I-O throughput and frees the server's main processor so that it can handle more critical tasks (i.e., incoming calls). Look for it in all new computers.

What to Look for in I₂O Servers

Look for the following I₂O server features:

- Flash memory for the boot ROM: I₂O requires a revised boot sequence to detect I₂O-compliant devices and install the drivers. If the server's current firmware does not support I₂O, its flash memory provides the ability for inexpensive downloads.
- ISA buses need not apply: I₂O leverages off the capabilities of the PCI bus for device installation performance. There is no support for the older bus architectures.

Types Of I₂O Designs

Table 8.2 shows the pros and cons associated with the different type of I₂O designs.

Table 8.2   Types of I₂O Designs

Single IOP on main logic board	IOPs on peripheral cards
Pros	Low cost
Pros	Concurrent processing possible Improved availablity because I-O interrupts handled by I-O processor (IOP) Good scalability—more peripherals add more IOPs
Cons	Little to no concurrent processing
Cons	Raises price of peripheral boards Limited scalability Overkill in a small server

More information may be obtained from the I₂O special interest group (SIG) Web site, http://www.i2osig.org/.

9 Computer Language Performance for Wireless Services

BACKGROUND . . . .

For the following reasons, the very core of any new software service is the programming language and the compiler used to create it.

- Software quality is impaired if the language does not guard against human error.
- Hardware goes underutilized if the compiler is unable to address all of the various hardware components.
- Time to market the application is affected when the language is difficult to learn and to use.
- Fundamental libraries are nonexistent and, therefore, need to be written from scratch.
- Portation and maintenance efforts take longer than the time it takes to create an application in the first place.

Within this context, the performance of computer languages was judged for wireless services. Therefore, this section examines and evaluates several computer languages' suitability for developing applications. The evaluation was achieved with special test classes. The tests ranged from the very simple "for" loop (language dependent), with increment instruction, to the more complex "client-server" application (language independent, since the bottleneck is in the network). Each test had a timer, which made it possible to calculate the execution time and the instruction-per-second metric. Given the object-oriented design of this test suite, more tests can be added easily. The application was written in both C++ and Java. It was not written in C, but an examination in C was performed for completeness.

Finally, this application was ported from NT to Solaris 2.5.1 and Solaris 2.6 for several reasons:

- To investigate the complexities of working in a multiplatform environment.
- To benchmark the various platforms in order to understand their behavior.
- To learn about the 64-bit instructions set of Solaris 2.6.
- To see which integrated development environment (IDE) is the best.
- To explore the optimization features of the compilers.

In summary, much was learned and documented here within these pages for the purpose of eliminating software development risk for the developer. Furthermore, the approach is reusable for understanding future releases of operating system software and compilers.

INTRODUCTION . . . .

Products Tested And Evaluated

Here is a summary of the materials used in this examination:

- Sun's C++/C SPARCworks 4.1.
- Sun's C++/C SPARCworks 4.2 thirty-day evaluation.
- Microsoft's Developers Studio C++ 5.0.
- Microsoft's Developers Studio J++ 1.0.
- Supercede 1.02 Integrated Development Environment for Java.
- GNU C++ 2.7.2.
- NT 5.0 beta and NT4.
- Solaris 2.5.1 and 2.6.
- Rational Rose 4.0.14 and Analyzer.

Report Layout

Since it may not be clear from the Table of Contents, the structure of this section is as follows:

- Language.
- Development Environment.
- Problems Identified.

- Possible Resolutions.
- Notable Mentions.
- Results.
- Conclusion, which contains comparison of results for all of the languages.

THE TEST APPLICATION ....

Why These Tests?

It is better to benchmark using the hardware and tools onsite, since those published in industry magazines do not factor in the following:

- Local machine or operating systems configurations.
- Unique compiler settings specific to a shop.
- Different versions of compilers, operating systems, patches, firmware, and so on.

APPLICATION TEST OUTPUT ....

This section explains the program output columnar. The application has no inputs. Currently, only one test has a dependency, which means for the client-server test to operate, the server must be started before beginning the test. For example,

Test	Iterations	Time(ms)	Num/Second

Test

The tests were selected using information found on Java's bulletin board. They mapped to the very foundation of each of the languages.

Iterations

The loop is based on the largest possible integer divided by 10. The division is to prevent overflow. The loop increments by multiples of 10. However, the test breaks the loop when the previous loop time is greater than the current loop time. This prevents runaways (i.e., memory test absorption).

Times

The timer uses the ANSI clock function, which returns the number of clock ticks of elapsed processor time. The returned value is the product of the amount of time that has elapsed since the start of a process and the value of the CLOCKS_PER_SEC constant. If the amount of elapsed time is unavailable, the function returns –1, cast as a clock_t.

Numbers Per Second

The numbers per second columnar was calculated with the expression: (Iterations*CLOCKS_PER_SEC/last), where "last" is the duration of the test. It represents the amount of iterations—specific function, or instruction, that can be performed in one second. For example, the calibration test tells us the maximum number of increments that can be performed in one second. This is a standard loop that would operate the same in C or C++.

THE "C++" LANGUAGE EXAMINATION . . . .

This section explains what it took to make the test application work (if possible in the time provided) in both environments and shows the results for NT and Solaris.

NT/4 Development Environment Problems

- The service packs did not come with the Visual Studio compilers (C/C++/Java/HTML). They were obtained separately.
- The Visual Studio service packs are dependent on the NT service packs, which means that three more CD-ROM of patches and documentation are needed.
- Anticipate service packs every three to six months (high churn).
- Rational Rose tool is not set up for Microsoft Visual C++ 5.0—service pack is required.

Possible Resolutions

- Download the service packs.

- Subscribe to the Microsoft Developers Network at a cost of greater than $2000, since they deliver the CD-ROMs as they become available.
- Plan for high maintenance expenses due to software churn.

Notable Mentions

- Visual C++/5.0 appears to be current with the ANSI C++ specification. I was unable to find a feature that was not supported.
- Visual C++/5.0 documentation contains sample code that works very well. This allows the developers to focus their attention on their applications rather than on the sample fixture.

Results

On an HP Vectra 266-MHz Pentium with 128 Mbytes of RAM, the following results were made:

Tech Talk

NT/4 optimized: Executables were made with Visual C++. They are forthcoming.

Test	Iterations	Time (ms)	Num/Second
Calibration	100000000	751	133,155,792
Pure	100000000	3766	26553372
Virtual	100000000	3766	26553372
None	100000000	3565	28050490
Memory	1000000	6179	161838
Ctor	1000000	3986	250878
DefCtor	1000000	3956	252780
ArrayCtor	100000000	7461	13403029
InitializeString	1000000	8873	112701
CopyString	100000000	18426	5427113

SOLARIS/2 DEVELOPMENT ENVIRONMENT . . . . . .

SPARCworks C++/4.1 Problems

- The SPARCworks C++/4.1 compiler did not contain ANSI C++ keyword "namespace," which means that the code from the NT environment did not compile.
- Even after the removal of this keyword, the code did not compile because of special Microsoft compiler settings.
- Microsoft employed special conventions that are not part of the ANSI convention. For example, the compiler will convert an "include" file that does not end with ".h" into a MFC (Microsoft foundation classes) extension. When compiled under SPARCworks, the compiler cannot locate the file of the same name. One good thing about this convention is that we can quickly identify MFC code.
- The SPARCworks C++/4.2 demo compiler did not recognize files without ".h", which is a newer convention.
- SUN support of C++/C is lagging behind Java.
- Solaris 2.6 is a 64-bit operating system, which means that the developer will need to go through another portation of its applications! The benchmark program was moved from Solaris 2.5.1 to 2.6. A large effort was required to port this very simple program. The problems were in both compilation and run time. The constants have changed in the standard libraries (i.e., time.h).

Possible Resolutions

- Purchase the 4.2 upgrade for SPARCworks, since it is documented to contain more of the ANSI C++ conventions.
- Download the 4.2 evaluation of SPARCworks.
- Purchase a multioperating system class library (e.g., Rogue Wave).
- Create your own foundation classes.
- Use a GNU 2.7.2 compiler and libraries, since they worked with some bastardization.

Results

Sun Ultra 2 with 250MHz processors and 64 Mbytes of RAM yielded the following results:

Tech Talk

Solaris 2.6 optimized: Executable made on Solaris 2.5.1 w/GNU C++.

Test	Iterations	Time(ms)	Num/Second
Calibration	100000000	820	121951219
Pure	100000000	13040	7668711
Virtual	100000000	12100	8264462
None	100000000	5150	19417475
Memory	10000000	16160	618811
Ctor	10000000	16550	604229
DefCtor	10000000	16140	619578
ArrayCtor	100000000	7950	12578616
InitializeString	1000000	6360	157232
CopyString	100000000	10110	9891196

THE "JAVA/J++" LANGUAGE EXAMINATION . . . . . .

Java may operate in two modes (interpreted or compiled). Interpreted is slower than compiled, and therefore, the results are not shown here. Everything shown in this section is based on the Java compiled executable.

NT/4 DEVELOPMENT ENVIRONMENT JAVA . . . . . .

Problems

- Visual J++/1.1 was not up to the newer networking standard, and therefore, the application did not compile until the TCP/IP test was removed. In addition, service packages were needed.
- Visual J++/1.1 was not capable of producing an executable.
- SuperCede/1.2 was not up to the newer networking standard and therefore the application did not compile or run. It is not known if the jc.exe program can be swapped out for another vendors' compiler, but it is unlikely.

Possible Resolutions

- Use SuperCede/2.0 to create executables that incorporate the latest Java standard, available since the end of Nov. 1997.
- It is not known if the jc.exe program can be swapped out for another vendors' compiler, but it is unlikely.
- Remove network classes, which was done.
- Use the beta version of Sun's 1.1.4 for NT.

Notable Mentions

- The program was written and operational within half a day.
- Sun's 1.1.4 for NT has been downloaded, but not tested, due to the complexity of the Java run time environment.

Results

NT 5.0 beta: Executable made with Supercede 1.2

Test	Iterations	Time(ms)	Num/Second
Calibration	100000000	4887	20,462,451
PureVirtual	100000000	11216	8915834
Virtual	100000000	10975	9111617
NoneVirtual	100000000	9784	10220768
Memory	100000	3976	25150
Ctor	10000000	18005	555401
DefCtor	1000000	2223	449842
ArrayCtor	10000000	18887	529464
InitializeString	10000	591	16920
CopyString	1000000	4035	247831

SOLARIS/2 DEVELOPMENT ENVIRONMENT JAVA . .

Problems

- IDE (integrated development environment) for Java in the Solaris/2 environment is needed.
- Makefiles need to be created manually.
- Solaris 2.6 is required for green threads and the just-in-time compiler from Sun.

Possible Resolutions

- It was possible to create an IDE using XEMACs and the Sun Java compiler. All that was needed was the makefile and XEMACs know-how. XEMACs is Java aware and is quite good, if you like emacs.
- Purchase an IDE that embraces Java and C++, like that of Visual Studio for all platforms.
- JavaPlan (Sun's IDE) was evaluated some time ago, and it was unstable and difficult to use. Asymmetric has since created a product for Sun.

Notable Mentions

- The Java command executes Java bytecodes created by the Java compiler, javac. The JIT (just in time) compiler compiles these bytecodes into machine instructions by default in the Solaris Java VM when using Java. It is a nice feature, and makes Java 50 times faster without the extra step of creating an executable, as we did with SuperCede 1.2.

Results

Solaris 2.6: Executable made with Java Virtual Machine 1.1.3.

Test	Iterations	Time(ms)	Num/Second
Calibration	100000000	4870	20533880
PureVirtual	100000000	19866	5033725
Virtual	10000000	2094	4775549
NoneVirtual	100000000	18235	5483959
Memory	1000000	11733	85229
Ctor	1000000	3595	278164
DefCtor	1000000	3461	288933
ArrayCtor	1000000	3899	256476
InitializeString	1000000	8443	118441
CopyString	1000000	17709	56468

THE "C" LANGUAGE EXAMINATION . . . .

One test was conducted and the performance of the C language was researched. This section explains what was learned.

NT/4 Development Environment "C"—Problems

- The SUN SPARCworks & Solaris C code did not compile when moved to Microsoft's Visual C/C++. The "include" files were named differently or were not found at all. Even if an equivalent file was located, the compiler settings were invalid.
- The SunOS/Solaris Berkley sockets library for interprocess communications are incompatible with Winsock 2.0.

Possible Resolutions

- Go outside the framework of Visual Studio and export the project to a makefile. Work the makefile and write C code to cover the deficiencies or just copy it from Solaris.
- Purchase a development environment in which you can write once and run everywhere, or use another language like Java. What was not determined was how well each compiler adhered to the ANSI C compiler.

- Make wrappers around the Berkley socket libraries or purchase a multi-platform C library off the shelf. However, I do not recommend C at all for networking. Justification for that is provided in the next section.

Results

No results could be found without platform-specific portation work, which could prove useful when time permits.

SOLARIS DEVELOPMENT ENVIRONMENT "C" . . . . .

A working Solaris C program called "bmark.c", was ported to NT. This program is a benchmark (test) for both TCP/IP sockets and UNIX domain (named pipes) sockets, the core interprocess communication (IPC) technologies used in the current MXE platform.

Problems and resolutions do not apply, since the program was created in this environment.

Results

Here are the results of running on a 170-MHz computer with 32 Mbytes of RAM:

1. TCP/IP

   Sender Started Default rebuff = 0 TxBuff = 0
   Tx and Rx Buffer Set to 7168
   TCP Server Finished Sending 102403 K Bytes
   Received 102403 K Bytes in 9 Seconds
   Data Rate = 11378.1 KBytes/Sec

2. UNIX

   Sender Started Default rebuff = 0 TxBuff = 0
   Tx and Rx Buffer Set to 7168
   UNIX Server Finished Sending 102403 K Bytes
   Received 102403 K Bytes in 8 Seconds
   Data Rate = 12800.4 KBytes/Sec

Comparison of Results: C

Without the portation, a comparison is not possible at this time.

Research on the C language

Programming directly with C, Solaris threads, and Berkley sockets will yield a correct program. However, in summary, developing concurrent applications at this level of detail has several drawbacks:

- Lack of portability.
- Lack of reusability.
- Lack of robustness.

Countless studies have been made in comparing alternative programming languages; one such article is provided in the document titled, *Object Interconnections: Comparing Alternative Programming Techniques for Multi-threaded Servers*. Douglas C. Schmidt (Department of Computer Science at Washington University), and Steve Vinoski (Hewlett-Packard Company) arrived at the aforementioned drawbacks.

As explained within the article, they used the C language in a stock-quote server application, but quickly learned that the C language was cumbersome, especially when it came to threading technology. One way they overcame these deficiencies in the C language was with C++ wrappers, which simplified the complexity of programming concurrent network servers.

CONCLUSION . . . .

The final comparisons are shown in this section, so that readers may draw their own conclusions. A personal commentary appears at the end of the section.

Comparison of Results: C++

Following is the comparison of the number of tests per second that were calculated on an HP Vectra 266 MHz (NT 5.0 beta), as compared to the Ultra AX 250 MHz (Solaris 2.6):

Tech Talk

The Microsoft compiler was used for the HP, and the GNU compiler was used for creating the Ultra AX binaries.

C++ on Two Platforms	From HP Vectra 266 M	To Ultra AX 250 MHz	Improvement?
Calibration	133,155,792	121,951,219,	−9.19%
Pure	26,553,372	7,668,711	−246.26%
Virtual	26,553,372	8,264,462	−221.30%
None	28,050,490	19,417,475	−44.46%
Memory	161,838	618,811	382.36%
Ctor	250,878	604,229	240.85%
DefCtor	252,780	619,578	245.11%
ArrayCtor	13,403,029	12,578,616	−6.55%
Initialize String	112,701	157,232	28.32
Copy String	5,427,113	9,981,196	45.13%

Tech Talk

A ±5 percent confidence interval should be used.

Comparison of Results: Java on Cisc Vs. Risc

Here is the comparison of a Java application on two platforms (HP Vectra 266 MHz and the Ultra AX 250 Mhz):

JAVA on Two Platforms Test	From HP Vectra 266 MHz	To Ultra AX 250 MHz	Improvement?
Calibration	20,462,451	20,533,880	0.35%
Pure	8,915,834	5,033,725	−24.60%
Virtual	9,111,617	4,775,549	−53.56%
None	10,220,768	5,483,959	−60.19%
Memory	25,150	85,229	29.51%
Ctor	555,401	278,164	−50.08%
DefCtor	449,842	288,933	−64.23%
ArrayCtor	529,464	256,476	−57.01%
Initialize String	16,920	118,441	700.01%
Copy String	247,831	56,468	−438.89%

Comparison of Results: C++ to Java Same Platform

Here is the comparison of a C++ application to a Java application on the same platform (i.e., Ultra AX):

C++ vs. Java Test	C++ on Ultra AX 250 MHz	Java on Ultra AX 250MHz	Improvement?
Calibration	121,951,219	20,533,880	−593.90%
Pure	7,668,711	5,033,725	−152.35%
Virtual	8,264,462	4,775,549	−173.06%
None	19,417,475	5,483,959	−354.08%
Memory	618,811	85,229	−726.06%
Ctor	604,229	278,164	−217.22%
DefCtor	619,578	288,933	−214.44%
ArrayCtor	12,578,616	256,476	−4904.40%
Initialize String	157,232	118,441	−132.75%
Copy String	9,891,196	56,468	−17516.46%

Comparison of Results: C++ to Java Different Platforms

Here is the comparison of a C++ application to a Java application on the same platform (i.e., Ultra AX):

C++ vs. Java Test	C++ on HP Vecta 266 Mhz	Java on Ultra AX 250 Mhz	Improvement?
Calibration	133,155,792	20,533,880	−648.47%
Pure	26,553,372	5,033,725	−527.51%
Vital	26,553,725	4775,549	−556.03%
None	28,050,490	5,483,959	−511.50%
Memory	161,838	85,229	−189.89%
C tor	250,878	278,164	9.81%
DefC tor	252,780	288,933	12.51%
Array Ctor	13,403,029	256,476	−5225.84%
Initialize String	112,701	118,441	4.85%
Copy String	5,427,113	56,468	−9610.95%

Tech Talk

A ±5 percent confidence interval should be used.

Tech Talk

The results indicate that the HP Vectra is better at integer arithmetic and looping (i.e., the calibration test). But, memory allocation and real-location are better on the Ultra. This may be because the HP Vectra 266 MHz-Pentium is using a low-quality SIMS, whereas the Ultra has DIMs of higher quality. To verify this result, it might pay to replace the memory in the HP Vectra with some higher quality SIMS to see if this were true. It also may be due to the parameter settings used to initialize Java Virtual Machine. The heap size was set to 12000000 and the maximum Java heap size was set to 12000000. As for the other results (Pure, Virtual, None), it would be safe to say that the compiler implementation is responsible for the variations in these tests.

COMMENTARY ·

Java

Overall, Java lives up to its reputation, because it is possible to write a program once and run it everywhere, provided that you use the same version of the Java Virtual Machine and the same development kit on each node. Note the following facts about Java:

- Java's performance is improving.
- The Java engine runs real-time applications.
- Performance is becoming less important with advances in distributing computing (i.e., Compact PCI).
- Increased focus is on time to market.
- Breadth of market (i.e., heterogeneous internet) takes precedence.

Java is extremely attractive for prototyping and for making products. Furthermore, Java exceeded the performance of C++ on dynamic function calls (constructors). These calls are extremely important when creating flexible and reusable software products that adapt to changing requirements. This translates into quicker time to market in a heterogeneous data network!

C++

The portation of even a simple C, or C++, program took an enormous amount of time compared to the Java code. Even to port the code from Solaris 2.5.1 to Solaris 2.6 was troublesome, because Solaris 2.6 is now using both 64-bit addressing and instructions. Java makes it possible to focus on the business model, not the platform-specific nuances.

What is now obvious from the C/C++ compiler analysis is that

- SUN Microsystems' maintenance of the C++ compiler is lagging.
- One optimization flag improves performance by as much as 380% on NT.
- Java is easier than C++ to use in a heterogeneous environment.
- C++ is quite a bit faster than Java in most areas.

In summary, with the materials at hand, telecommunication and messaging applications are better off being built with C++ on the CICS machines (HP Vectra), in which the application memory is statically allocated prior to the execution of the main routines. The trade-off with the C++ approach is time to market—Java might be just enough to meet the requirements!

ACCOMPLISHMENTS . . . .

This study accomplished the following:

Tech Talk

This intellectual capital is reusable when comparing new platforms, operating systems, or compilers.

- It is now possible to build advanced (C++/Java) applications in both the NT and Solaris environments.
- The performance was verified of the Ultra AX and the HP Vectra.
- The optimizing of applications under both NT and Solaris is now understood.
- A test application has been created that will allow the developer the ability to validate third-party vendor components to ensure that they meet the developers' requirements.
- Several IDE (integrated development environments) have been tested, which will aide any study aimed at selecting the best one for a multi-operating system environment.
- The Rational Rose installation has been validated. As a result, it was determined that the ROSE analyzer needed a service pack in order for it to work with MSVC 5.0.
- SPARCworks was validated for its compliance with C++.
- MS Visual J++ was validated for its compliance with Java.
- Three service packs were identified for Visual Studio, which prompted us to become members of the Microsoft Developers Network.

TO DO LIST . . . .

Here is what can still be done to improve the performance results of these tests:

C++

- Create a GNU compiler under Solaris 2.6, when it becomes available.
- Get the SPARCworks 4.2 compiler for 2.6 and work around the inadequacies of the product for the purpose of creating an application.
- Benchmark with NT 5.0, when available.
- Benchmark using the real-time features of NT and Solaris.
- Add Rogue Wave classes and test the individual components (i.e., LDAP, POP, etc.)
- Test the symmetric multiprocessing capabilities of both NT and Solaris.
- Analyze the object-time implementation.
- Download SuperCede 2.0, when it becomes available for NT.

- Use Java run-time environment 1.1.4.
- Benchmark without the garbage collection routines turned off in Java.
- Benchmark DEC Alpha (Done…optimized code core dumps).

APPENDIX: TESTS CODE DESCRIBED . . . .

UML Notation

Figure 9-1 was automatically generated from UML source code using ROSE tool.

Component View

Figure 9-2 was automatically generated from C++ source code using ROSE tool.

Source Code Described

Table 9.1 shows the test source codes used in the analysis.

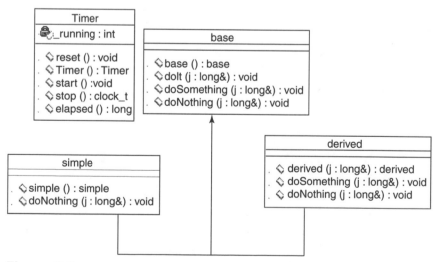

Figure 9-1
Timer and test base class diagram.

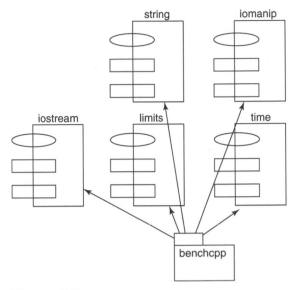

Figure 9-2
Bench C++ include files.

Table 9.1 Test Source Code

Test	Test name	Description

1	Calibration	This test measures the time it takes to execute this simple operation "k+=I" within a "for" loop. The reason it is called calibration is because it is the best case for all of the tests, since a loop is used throughout with the addition of more complex operators.
		
		 ```clock_t calibrate(long count)```
		
		 ```{```
		
		 ```...```
		
		 ``` timer.start();```
		 ``` for (long i=0; i<count; i++)```
		 ``` k+=i;```
		 ``` return timer.stop();```
		
		 ```}```

2	Pure Virtual	This test measures the time it takes to reference a pure virtual function (function with no objects, like "C"). This type of function is used to define a set of operations for the most general version of

(continued)

Table 9.1   Test Source Code (*continued*)

Test	Test name	Description
		a concept (a base class). When necessary, the interpretation of these operations can be refined for a particular special case (derived class).

```
class base

{

public:

      virtual void doNothing(long & j)=0;

...

};

clock_t purevirt(long count)

{

      base *pBase=new derived(k);

...

      timer.start();

      for (long i=0; i<count; i++)

            pBase->doNothing(k); //Does nothing but
            create a

      last=timer.stop();

      delete pBase;

      return last;

}

class derived : public base

{

public:

        virtual void doNothing(long& j);

...

};

void derived::doNothing(long& j)

{

      j+=2;

}
```

Table 9.1 Test Source Code (*continued*)

Test	Test name	Description
3	Virtual	This test measures the time it takes to make a virtual function call, with no derivations.

```
class base
{
public:
        ...
        virtual void doSomething(long& j);
};
clock_t virt(long count)
{
    base *pBase=new derived(k);
...
        for (long i=0; i<count; i++)
                pBase->doSomething(k);
...
}
void derived::doSomething(long& j)
{
        j+=2;
}
```

| 4 | Nonvirtual | This test measures the time it takes to make a function call (nonvirtual) that was part of the class called "base." |

```
class base //declaration
{
public:
        base();
        void doIt(long& j); //notice no virtual
...
};
clock_t nonvirt(long count)
```

(continued)

Table 9.1 Test Source Code (*continued*)

Test	Test name	Description
| | | ```
{
    ...
        base *pBase=new derived(k);
    ...
        timer.start();
        for (long i=0; i<count; i++)
                pBase->doIt(k);
        last=timer.stop();
    ....
        return last;
}
void base::doIt(long& j)
{
    j+=1;
}
``` |
| 5 | Memory | This test measures the time it takes to construct the code which specifically handles the allocation of arrays. <br><br> ```
clock_t memory(long count); //declaration
clock_t memory(long count)
{
    ...
Timer.start();
    for (long i=0; i<count; i++)
    {
            char *pArray=new char[1024];
            pArray[512]=(char)9;
            delete pArray;
    }
    last=timer.stop();
    ...
}
``` |

Table 9.1   Test Source Code (*continued*)

Test	Test name	Description
6	Ctor	This test times how long it takes to construct a derived object.

```
clock_t construct(long count); //declaration

class derived : public base

{

public:

        derived(long& j);

        virtual void doSomething(long& j);

        virtual void doNothing(long& j);

};

derived::derived(long& j)

{

        j+=2;

}

clock_t construct(long count)

{

...

        long k;

...

        timer.start();

        for (long i=0; i<count; i++)

        {

                derived *pArray=new derived(k);

                delete pArray;

        }

        last=timer.stop();

...

}
```

| 7 | DefCtor | The time it takes to deallocate the memory for the destruction of an array was measured using this code. |

```
clock_t defconstruct(long count); //declaration
```

(continued)

Table 9.1   Test Source Code (*continued*)

Test	Test name	Description
| | | ```
class simple : public base
{
public:
      simple();
      virtual void doNothing(long& j);
};
simple::simple()
{
}
void simple::doNothing(long& j)
{
      j+=2;
}
clock_t defconstruct(long count)
{
...
      timer.start();
      for (long i=0; i<count; i++)
      {
            simple *pArray=new simple();
            delete pArray;
      }
      last=timer.stop();
...}
``` |
| 8 | ArrayCtor | The time it takes to allocate the memory for the creation of an array is measured using this code. The Microsoft string extension libraries were used. |
| | | ```
clock_t arrayconstruct(long count); //declaration
class simple : public base
{
public:
      simple();
``` |

Table 9.1 Test Source Code (*continued*)

Test	Test name	Description

```
                        virtual void doNothing(long& j);
    };
    simple::simple()
    {
    }
    void simple::doNothing(long& j)
    {
        j+=2;
    }
    clock_t arrayconstruct(long count)
    {
    ...
      const int arraysize=1000;
      long loopcount=count/arraysize;
      timer.start();
      for (long i=0; i<loopcount; i++)
        {
        simple *pArray=new simple[arraysize];
            delete pArray;
        }
        last=timer.stop();
    ...
    }
```

| 9 | InitializeString | The time it take to allocate the memory for the creation of a string is measured using this code. The Microsoft string extension libraries were used. |

```
Clock_t initializestring(long count); //declaration
clock_t initializestring(long count)
{
...
```

(continued)

Table 9.1   Test Source Code (*continued*)

Test	Test name	Description
| | | ```
timer.start();
for (long I=0; i<count; i++)
{
        string *pString=new
        string("0123456789ABCDEF");
        delete pString;
}
last=timer.stop();
...
}
``` |
| 10 | CopyString | clock_t copystring(long count); |
| | | ```
clock_t copystring(long count)
{
...
  string a("0123456789ABCDEF");
  string b;
...
        timer.start();
        for (long I=0; i<count; i++)
        {
                b=a;
        }
        last=timer.stop();
...
}
``` |
| 11 | Timer | The timer class in C++ is subject to change. It is dependent on the platform. Be careful when using it. |
| | | ```
const char *IllegalStateException="IllegalState
Exception";
class Timer
{
public:
``` |
```

Table 9.1 Test Source Code (*continued*)

Test	Test name	Description

```
                                    Timer()
                                    {
                                        reset();
                                    }
                                    void start()
                                    {
                                        if (_running)
                                            throw IllegalStateException;
                                        _running=1;
                                        _started=clock();
                                    }
                                    clock_t stop()
                                    {
                                        if (!_running)
                                            throw IllegalStateException;
                                        _elapsed+=(clock()-_started);
                                        _running=0;
                                        return _elapsed;
                                    }
                                    long elapsed()
                                    {
                                        if (_running)
                                        {
                                            clock_t now=clock();
                                            _elapsed+=now-_started;
```

(_elapsed/CLOCKS_PER_SEC) << endl;

If elapsed time greater than 2147 seconds of //CPU, the clock command wraps around on SUN boxes

```
                                            _started=now;
                                        }
```

(continued)

Table 9.1   Test Source Code (*continued*)

Test	Test name	Description
|      |           | ```
                return _elapsed;
        }
        void reset()
        {
                _running=0;
                _elapsed=0L;
        }
private:
        clock_t _started;
        clock_t _elapsed;
        int _running;
};
``` |
12	tcpSocket	To be provided using the WINSOCK class unless the Rogue Wave library is purchased.
13	tcpPipe	To be provided using the named pipes.
14	MqAsync	See the *Queuing Theory For Wireless Communications* section.
15	LdapD	To be provided.
16	MapiD	To be provided.
17	SqlD	To be provided.

APPENDIX: NT/4 COMPARISON: OPTIMIZED VS. UNOPTIMIZED . . . .

To formulate the percentage improvement, the column titled, "Num/Second" was taken from each section of the NT/4 C++ results. This table shows the difference of running with optimized code as compared to optimized code.
```

Test	Unoptimized	Optimized	Improvement?
Calibration	34,916,201	133,155,792	381.36%
Pure	11,544,677	26,553,372	230.01%
Virtual	11,845,534	26,553,372	224.16%
None	13,511,687	28,050,490	207.60%
Memory	160,025	161,838	1.13%
Ctor	262,054	250,878	−4.26%
DefCtor	263,435	252,780	−4.04%
ArrayCtor	6,595,435	13,403,029	203.22%
Initialize String	98,570	112,701	14.34%
Copy String	999,600	5,427,113	542.93%

Nt/4 Unoptimized Vs. Optimized C++

For completeness, here are the results for the unoptimized code.

Tech Talk

The optimized results are shown in the previous section.

Test	Iterations	Time(ms)	Num/Second
Calibration	100000000	2864	34916201
Pure	100000000	8662	11544677
Virtual	100000000	8442	11845534
None	100000000	7401	13511687
Memory	1000000	6249	160025
Ctor	1000000	3816	262054
DefCtor	1000000	3796	263435
ArrayCtor	100000000	15162	6595435
InitializeString	1000000	10145	98570
CopyString	10000000	10004	999600

10 The Unified Wireless Inbox

WIRELESS CLIENT TERMINAL . . . .

Figure 10-1 shows a typical mobile phone. The interface is text based. Even with such a small display, a vast amount of information may be presented. The presentation of the data is dependent on both the air interface and the network serving these clients. This type of client is managed differently than the standard computer or PC. The security is usually built into the service that the user subscribes to. For example, a user can make a call only after entering a PIN number to avoid fraud in older network types. These services require that the subscribers' SIM cards be equipped with SIM application tool kit (SAT) applications. The SAT application management (SAM) module of the AviSIM OTA service center solution from AU-System provides operators with a powerful, efficient, and secure tool for managing and distributing SIM applications over the air, both before and after SIMs are delivered to subscribers.[1]

OUTLOOK . . . .

Figure 10-2 is an example of a unified inbox in which voice mail, fax mail, wav. files, and e-mail are contained in one mailbox on an IMAP server. This is not Web based, but will show up on PDAs that run the Windows CE operating system.

UNIFIED INBOX . . . .

Web messaging server software lets users integrate voice mail, e-mail, and fax messaging on the desktop, but does not require new client software for each user. The Web-server software can be accessed through a standard Web browser. It can be used in

[1]www.ausys.com

193

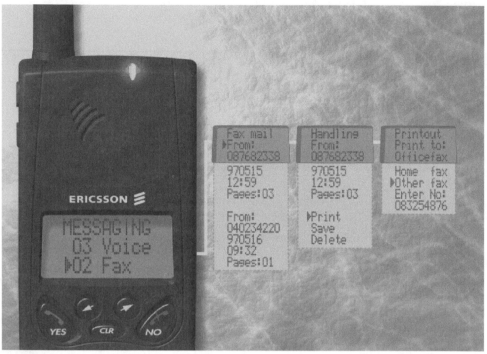

Figure 10-1
Wireless client terminal.

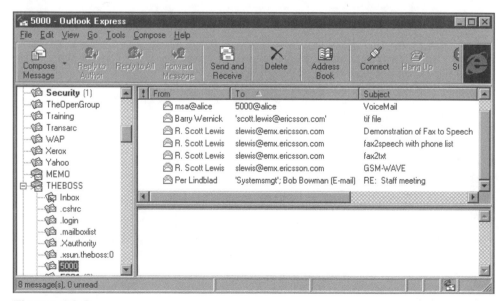

Figure 10-2
Unified Outlook Express inbox.

Windows, Macintosh, and Sun UNIX networking environments and can be deployed on voice-messaging servers that can connect to a wide range of PBXs or central offices.

Users can go to a personalized Web site and quickly scan a list for important voice messages, rather than sequentially listening to individual voice-mail messages. Users can double-click on messages and hear them on their PCs or have them sent to a telephone. Users can also store messages on disks and listen later.

It can support up to nine different languages such as French, German, and Spanish across all servers.

NETSCAPE . . . .

Figure 10-3 shows a voice message in the Netscape (Iplanet) Messenger Express unified inbox.

CLIENT PROGRAMS SUMMARY . . . .

Both Messenger Express and Outlook Express have either IMAP4 or POP3 interfaces for downloading or viewing messages on a standard Internet server. Unfortunately, these interfaces are not available over the wireless networks. To facilitate these interfaces, a WAP (wireless application protocol) gateway is used.

WEB-BASED INBOX SECURITY . . . .

Web-based inbox security begins with a login and a password. This can be accomplished two ways—by the individual program (i.e., Outlook), or by Web-based security products that protect an entire domain. One such product is Hewlett-Packard's DomainGuard.

ACCESS CONTROL MANAGER . . . .

The Netscape Express Message Web page shown in Figure 10-3 is protected by HP's DomainGuard. Figure 10-4 shows the DomainGuard administrator screen used to protect the root directory and subdirectories of the Web page, including Netscape Express Message.

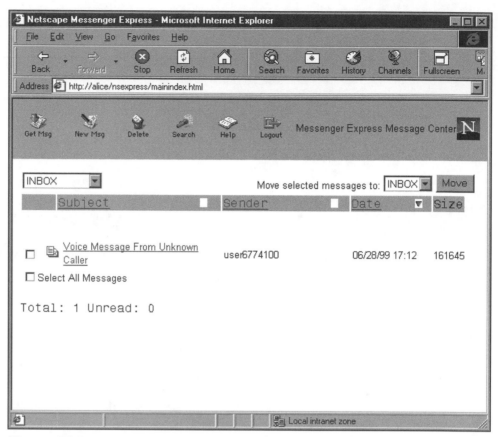

Figure 10-3
Messenger Express unified inbox.

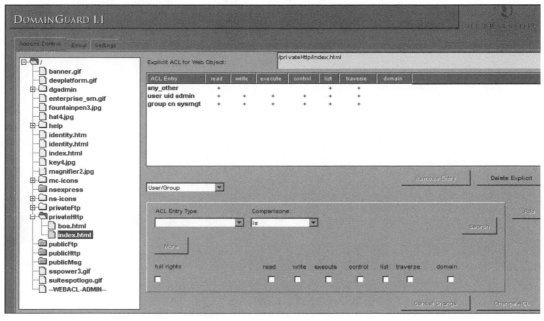

Figure 10-4
HP's DomainGuard administrator screen.

11 Wireless Call Processing (S.100) Service

BACKGROUND . . . .

This section describes a call processing service structured around an IT-bus architecture and the Enterprise Computer Telephony Forum Application Interoperability Framework ECTF A.001 Revision 1.0. The framework includes the S.100 API, which allows computer telephony applications to cooperate and interoperate, hence diminishing the cost and complexity to integrate CT applications and providing unique services.

Introduction

The call processing service is the termination point for the telephony networks towards the messaging system. The call processing service explained in this section includes telephony HW and SW, as well as the service application. As such, it controls the calling and called parties telephony dialog, also known as the telephone user interface (TUI). The users navigate through the dialogs by speaking command words or by pressing DTMF keys on their telephone.

The main functions of the call processing service are to

- Interact with the caller for message deposit.
- Interact with the mailbox account owner for message retrieval.
- Interact with the mailbox account owner for user profile administration (limited implementation).
- Perform an outdial alert and delivery to the mailbox account owner (not implemented, even though the outdial capabilities have been verified).

Products

The call processing service is based on and created with the OmniVox application generator tool, which is a commercial product sourced from APEX Voice Communications, Inc.

The major functions of the OmniVox tools are

- OmniVox administrative utility, which includes the application builder.
- OmniView applications generator, used to define and build the call flow diagram.
- OmniView project, which uses the project concept to organize the OmniVox application and its associated call flows, voice recordings, and output fields.
- Speech editor, which is used to record and edit voice prompts.
- C/C++ interface, which allows for interfacing to other components and services such as the directory server and the message store.

Applications can be created and tested in a few hours, and seemingly complex outcomes are performed easily, without the need to write computer programs. OmniVox status utilities include an online display screen showing the progression of each call and a system error log. System utilities include both line and application assignment (with dialed number identification service) and start-stop utilities for lines and applications. OmniVox provides a call count reporting facility from call detail records (CDR). An OmniView project can be managed completely from within the OmniView environment. (See Figure 11-1.) Voice messages can be recorded, modified, and reviewed from within OmniView as well, since the speech editor is an integrated component, rather than a stand-alone tool. The OmniVox tool is based on Dialogic® hardware and software for computer telephony (CT), which comes with the product. Voice Control Systems, Inc. (VCS) provides the automatic speech recognition (ASR) technology. The ASR function is integrated into OmniVox, which makes it easy to load different vocabularies and play appropriate prompts. The VCS firmware runs on Dialogic's Antares boards. The current licensing, controlled by a "dongle" on the Antares board, allows four channels of discrete speech recognition with cut-through technology and two channels of continuous speech recognition with cut-through. Please see Ref. [1] for available vocabularies and a description of the ASR technology. The OmniVox tool is licensed on a per-telephone-channel basis. The license is controlled by a software key and a "dongle" connected to the parallel port. Please see Ref. [2], OmniVox® System for Windows NT User's Manual, for a full description of the OmniVox tool.

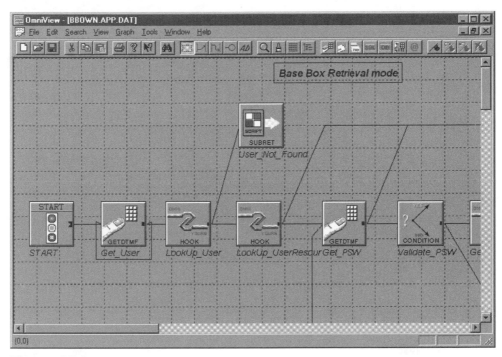

Figure 11-1
Service create viewing tool example.

IT-BUS INTERFACES . . . .

Table 11.1 shows how the call processing service is connected to the IT buses.

FUNCTIONS . . . .

Meter

The call processing service is built using the graphical application generator Omni-Vox, which allows for a rapid development of different service applications. Four basic applications include support DTMF- and ASR-controlled deposit and retrievals (i.e., DTMF deposit), DTMF retrieval, ASR deposit and ASR retrieval. The retrieval applications include the user profile administration. The application project flowcharts give an underview of each of these four applications. OmniView is used to browse the flowcharts, (See Figure 11-1).

Table 11.1 IT-Bus for Call Processing

IT Bus	Protocol	Service
Call Control	Dialogic® R4.2 API[1]	CT SW and HW Resources
System Control	LDAP	User and Directory Service
	TRP	Meter Data Repository
Message Control	IMAP4	Message Store
	NOP	Notification Server
OAM and P	Report Event(NT)	Management Agent
	SNMP	

Administrative Functions NT Event Reports

The call processing service, which includes the OmniVox and Dialogic software, reports internal anomalies to the NT event log.

SNMP

The call processing service has defined an SNMP MIB, VoiceDll.mib. Examples of information available through the MIB are a gauge for the number of concurrent calls and a counter for total number of calls since the SNMP agent was started.

Meter Data Reporting

Meter data are collected for each call. The unique handle for reporting on resource usage is the user ID. The following meter data are generated for each incoming call:

- User ID (handle).
- Time stamp.
- Channel ID.
- Call duration.
- Call status.
- Message size, in number of bytes.

[1]This is a proprietary interface and therefore has been encapsulated in the call processing service. S.100 shall replace it when Dialogic has made it available.

The record format is plain text with each field delimited by a ^ and terminated with a new line. The following is an example of meter data reporting:

```
19980504_00:00:08^TINA^COMP^5035^16^HangUpMsgSendOk^d28^r28^50
35^104040^<new_line>
```

```
The format for meter data reporting is
Date_time^host^service^user_id^call_duration_in_sec^call_
status^channel_id_deposit^
channel_id_retrieval^user_id^voice_message_size_in_bytes^
new_line
```

Tech Talk

XML tags and delimiters are more appropriate format (i.e., <Field_ Name="field_data">).

CONFIGURATIONS . . . .

OmniVox Tool

OmniVox is delivered on a CD and is installed using InstallSHIELD™. To install OmniVox, please follow Ref. [3], OmniVox® System for Windows NT Installation Manual. The manual contains information on how to install the Dialogic HW and SW, as well as the license dongles.

Directory Server

After installation, the call processing service must be registered in the directory server. The registration has to be entered manually. Below is an example of a call processing service entry in an LDAP directory server:

```
dn: mcn=Comp@tina.dilbertville, msn=Dilbertville,
o=MessagingSystem, c=US
objectclass: messagingservice
mcn: Comp@tina.dilbertville
mcc: CallProcSrvc
rev-level: A
host: tina
port: Unknown
service: Telephony User Interface
```

```
patch-level: 0
service-path: c:\USR\APEX\AppBin\comp.exe
control-bus-name: ANY.TO.VPC
snmp-dll-path: C:\USR\APEX\App_gen\Bin\snmp\Voicedll.dll
description: Dilbertville DTMF controlled Telephony User
Interface.
```

Internal Service Architecture

Figure 11-2 shows the internal architecture of a call processing service.

Tech Talk

Apex OmniVox without CT Media (S.100).

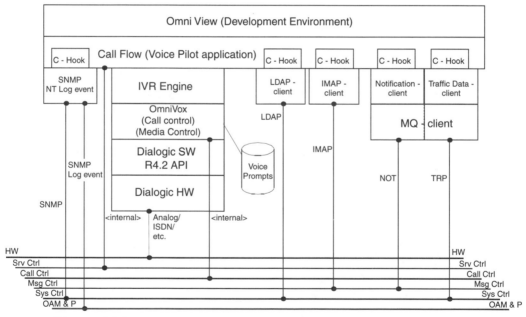

Figure 11-2
Call processing service IT-bus diagram.

INTERPRETATION ························

Processes and Threads

OmniVox uses one process for each telephone line or channel. This process contains channel-specific data as well as static-linked C hooks. The code behind each "Icon" is executed in a DLL, which is shared between the processes. This configuration promotes a stable system (if a process dies, only one line is affected) and still allows for each process to be reasonably small, regarding memory usage.

Each process contains two threads. The main thread that runs the OmniVox engine spawns from a thread that initializes the channel to SNMP and waits for an SNMP set.

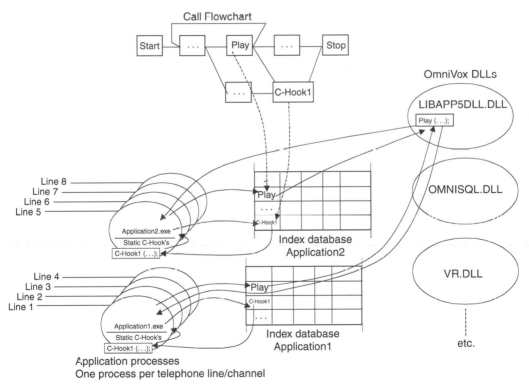

Figure 11-3
OmniVox call flow.

Call State Table

OmniVox maintains the call flow states in an index database that is accessed when moving from one state to another during the call. This implies that the call flow, viewed and edited in the OmniView tool, can be changed during a call if desired. As long as the "current" state exists in the updated flow chart, the new call flow will take effect as soon as it is stored without compilation or any other "hocus-pocus."

REFERENCES . . . .

- [1]   Antares VCS ASR Software Reference for Windows NT.
- [2]   OmniVox® System for Windows NT User's Manual.
- [3]   OmniVox® System for Windows NT Installation Manual.

12 Wireless Directory Services

BACKGROUND ·

The recommended course of action for wireless services is to depend on a directory for everything. Therefore, this section gives a brief introduction to the LDAP protocol as used within a directory server. The intention is not to fully describe LDAP as such, but rather to build a basic understanding. For the interested reader, this document refers to other documents in which an LDAP is fully described.

Consequently, DNS and NTP are explained, since LDAPs are dependent upon them. Proxies are another LDAP dependency, but they were explained in the security section.

What Is a Directory Service?

A directory is an information source that is used to store information about objects of interest. For example, a telephone directory stores information about telephone subscribers. In a file system, the directory stores information about files. In a distributed computing system, or in a public computer network like the Internet, there are many objects, such as printers, fax servers, applications, databases, and other users. Users want to find and use these objects. Administrators want to manage how these objects are used.

In this document, the terms "directory" and "directory service" refer to the directories found in public and private networks. A directory service differs from a directory in that a directory service is both the directory information source and the service making the information available and usable to the users.

A directory is like a database, but tends to contain more descriptive, attribute-based information. The information in a directory is generally read much more often than it is written. As a consequence, directories do not usually implement the complicated transaction or rollback schemes that regular databases use for doing high-volume complex updates. Directory updates are typically simple all-or-nothing changes, if they are allowed at all. Directories are tuned to give quick response to high-volume lookup or search operations. They may have the ability to replicate information widely in order to increase availability and reliability, while reducing response time.

Why Have a Directory Service?

A directory service is one of the most important services of an extended computer system. Users and administrators frequently do not know the exact name of the objects that they are interested in. They may know one or more attributes of the object and can query the directory to get a list of objects that match the known attributes; for example, "find all duplex printers in Building 26." A directory service allows a user to find any object given one of its attributes.

A directory service can

- Enforce security defined by administrators to keep information safe from intruders.
- Distribute a directory across many computers in a network.
- Replicate a directory to make it available to more users and resistant to failure.
- Partition a directory into multiple stores to allow the storage of a large number of objects.

A directory service is both a management tool and an end-user tool. As the number of objects in a network grows, a directory service becomes essential. The directory service is the hub around which a large distributed system turns.

How Directory Services Work

A directory consists of entries containing descriptive information. For example, a directory might contain entries describing people or network resources, such as printers or fax machines.

The descriptive information is stored in the attributes of the entry. Each attribute describes a specific type of information. For example, attributes describing a person might include the person's name (common name, or "cn"), telephone number, and e-mail address.

The entry for Barbara Jensen might have the following attributes:

```
cn: Barbara Jensen
mail: Barbara.Jensen@us.ibm.com
telephoneNumber: 555-1212
roomNumber: 3995
```

An attribute can have more than one value. For example, a person might have two common names (a formal name and a nickname) or two telephone numbers:

```
cn: Barbara Jensen
cn: Barbara Jensen
mail: jen@ace.com
telephoneNumber: 555-1213
telephoneNumber: 555-2059
roomNumber: 3991
```

Attributes can also contain binary data. For example, attributes of a person might include a JPEG photo of the person or the voice of the person recorded in an audio file format.

Acronyms and Basic Concepts

ASN.1   Abstract Syntax Notation 1

BER   Binary Encoding Rules

PDU   Protocol Data Unit

SASL   Simple Authentication and Security Layer

HOW LDAP SERVERS ORGANIZE DIRECTORIES . . .

Because LDAP is intended to be a global directory service, data is organized hierarchically, starting at a root and branching down into individual entries. Entries are typically arranged geographically and by organization.

At the top level of the hierarchy, entries represent countries or international organizations. Examples of entries are US or Canada (countries) or Ace Industry (an organization). Under each country entry in the hierarchy might be entries for states, provinces, or national organizations. The hierarchy might end with entries for people or resources.

Figure 12-1 illustrates a hierarchy of entries in an LDAP directory service.

Each entry is uniquely identified by a distinguished name. A distinguished name consists of the name of an entry (for example, Barbara Jensen) and a path of names tracing the entry back to the root of the tree.

For example, this might be the distinguished name for the Barbara Jensen entry:

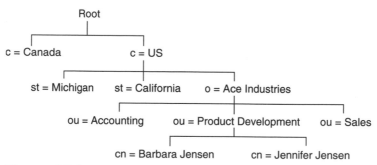

Figure 12-1
Entries hierarchy in LDAP directory.

cn=Barbara Jensen, ou=Product Development, o=Ace Industry, c=US

Here, "cn" represents the common name of the entry, "ou" represents the organizational unit (such as a department or a division) in which the entry belongs, "o" represents the organization in which the entry belongs, and "c" represents the country in which the entry belongs. For more information on the syntax of distinguished names, see Ref. [3].

Figure 12-2 shows how distinguished names are used to identify entries uniquely in the directory hierarchy.

At any level of the directory hierarchy, a service of a distinguished name is itself a distinguished name. For example, at the country level in the directory hierarchy, the service "c=US" is a distinguished name that uniquely identifies the entry for the United States at that level.

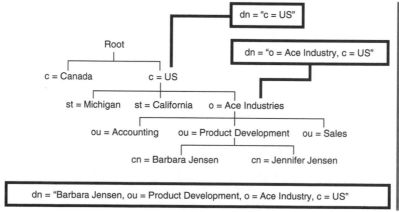

Figure 12-2
Distinguished names.

The data stored in a directory can be distributed among several LDAP servers. For example, an LDAP server at Ace Industry might contain entries representing the Ace Industry organizational units and employees, whereas an LDAP server at the University of Michigan might contain entries containing the organizational units, faculty, and students at that campus.

Some LDAP servers are set up to refer requests to other LDAP servers. In this way, LDAP servers can appear to be a single source of directory information. Even if an LDAP server does not contain the information you request, the server can refer you to another server that does contain the desired information.

THE LDAP PROTOCOL . . . .

The general model adopted by the LDAP protocol is one of clients performing protocol operations against servers. In this model, a client transmitting a protocol request describes the operation to be performed to a server, which is then responsible for performing the necessary operations on the directory. Upon completion of the necessary operations, the server returns a response containing any results or errors to the requesting client.

LDAP, Lightweight Directory Access Protocol

LDAP, lightweight directory access protocol, is a directory service protocol that runs over TCP/IP. It is a connection-oriented transport in which communication proceeds through three well-defined phases: connection establishment, data transfer, and connection release.

LDAP is defined in RFC 1777 "The Lightweight Directory Access Protocol." (See Ref. [1].)

LDAP was originally developed as a front end to X.500, the OSI directory service. X.500 defines the directory access protocol (DAP) for clients to use when contacting directory servers. DAP is a heavyweight protocol that runs over a full OSI stack and requires a significant amount of computing resources to run. LDAP runs directly over TCP and provides most of the functionality of DAP at a much lower cost.

The LDAP directory service model is based on *entries*. An entry is a collection of *attributes* that has a name, called a *distinguished name* (DN). The representation of distinguished names is defined in RFC1779. (See Ref. [2].) The DN is used to refer to the entry unambiguously. Each of the entry's attributes has a *type* and one or more *values*. The types are typically mnemonic strings, like "cn" for common name, or "mail" for e-mail address. The values depend on the type of attribute.

In LDAP, directory entries are arranged in a hierarchical, tree-like structure that reflects political, geographic, or organizational boundaries. An entry in the tree is referenced by its distinguished name, constructed by taking the name of the entry itself (called the relative distinguished name, or RDN) and concatenating the names of its ancestor entries.

In addition, LDAP allows you to control which attributes are required and allowed in an entry through the use of a special attribute, called "objectclass." The values of the objectclass attribute determine the *schema rules* that the entry must obey.

LDAP defines operations for interrogating and updating the directory. Operations are provided for adding or deleting an entry from the directory, changing an existing entry, and changing the name of an entry. Most of the time, though, LDAP is used to search for information in the directory. The LDAP search operation allows some portion of the directory to be searched for entries that match some criteria specified by a search filter. Information can be requested from each entry that matches the criteria.

Finally, LDAP provides a method for a client to authenticate or prove its identity to a directory server, paving the way for rich access control to protect the information that the server contains.

LDAP Operational Model

LDAP directory service is based on a *client-server* model. One or more LDAP servers contain the data making up the LDAP directory tree. An LDAP client connects to an LDAP server and asks it a question. The server responds with the answer, or with a pointer to where the client can go to obtain more information (typically, another LDAP server). The latter is called "referral." No matter which LDAP server a client connects to, it sees the same view of the directory; a name presented to one LDAP server references the same entry it would at another LDAP server. This is an important feature of a global directory service like LDAP.

Note that, although servers are required to return responses whenever such responses are defined in the protocol, there is no requirement for synchronous behavior on the part of either client or server implementations. Client and servers may exchange requests and responses in any order for multiple operations, as long as clients eventually receive a response for every request that requires one.

Consistent with the model of servers performing protocol operations on behalf of clients, it is also to be noted that protocol servers are expected to handle referrals without resorting to the return of such referrals to the client. This protocol makes no provisions for the return of referrals to clients, as the model is one of servers ensuring the performance of all necessary operations in the directory, with only final results or errors being returned by servers to clients.

A referral entry acts as a mount point, gluing two directory servers together. A referral entry has an objectclass of "referral" and is named by a ref attribute containing a URL pointing to the directory server holding the data below the mount point. A referral entry can be defined as follows:

```
dn: ref="ldap://new.host/o=New Company,c=US", o=Your company,
c=US
objcctclass: referral
```

For each directory server, part of a directory server cluster must have referral entries defined.

MAPPING ONTO TRANSPORT SERVICES . . . .

The LDAP protocol is designed to run over connection-oriented, reliable transports, with all eight bits in an octet being significant in the data stream. A specification for one underlying service is defined here, though others are also possible.

Transmission Control Protocol (TCP)

The LDAP message PDUs are mapped directly onto the TCP byte stream. Server implementations running over the TCP should provide a protocol listener on port 389.

LDAP ELEMENTS . . . .

For the purposes of protocol exchanges, all protocol operations are encapsulated in a common envelope, the LDAP message, which is defined as follows using ASN.1 (see Ref. [5]):

```
LDAPMessage ::=
     SEQUENCE {
          messageID      MessageID,
          protocolOp     CHOICE {
          bindRequest        BindRequest,
          bindResponse       BindResponse,
```

```
            unbindRequest        UnbindRequest,
            searchRequest        SearchRequest,
            searchResponse       SearchResponse,
            modifyRequest        ModifyRequest,
            modifyResponse       ModifyResponse,
            addRequest           AddRequest,
            addResponse          AddResponse,
            delRequest           DelRequest,
            delResponse          DelResponse,
            modifyRDNRequest     ModifyRDNRequest,
            modifyRDNResponse    ModifyRDNResponse,
            compareDNRequest     CompareRequest,
            compareDNResponse    CompareResponse,
            abandonRequest       AbandonRequest
    }
}
MessageID ::= INTEGER (0 .. maxInt)
```

The function of the LDAP message is to provide an envelope containing common fields required in all protocol exchanges. At this time, the only common field is a message ID, which is required to have a value different from the values of any other requests outstanding in the LDAP session of which the message is part.

The message ID value must be echoed in all LDAP message envelopes, encapsulating responses corresponding to the request contained in the LDAP message in which the message ID value was originally used.

BindRequest

This command is used by a client to log in and authenticate with the directory server.

BindResponse

This command is used by the directory server to acknowledge a log in and authentification request (BindRequest).

UnbindRequest

This command is used by a client to log out from the directory server.

SearchRequest

This command is used by a client to search the directory.

Parameters of the SearchRequest are:

- baseObject: An LDAP DN that is the base object entry relative to which the search is to be performed.
- scope: An indicator of the scope of the search to be performed. The semantics of the possible values of this field are identical to the semantics of the scope field in the directory search operation.
- derefAliases: An indicator as to how alias objects should be handled in searching. The semantics of the possible values of this field are, in order of increasing value,
  - neverDerefAliases: Do not dereference aliases in searching or in locating the base object of the search.
  - derefInSearching: This command dereferences aliases in subordinates of the base object in searching, but not in locating the base object of the search.
  - derefFindingBaseObject: This command dereferences aliases in locating the base object of the search, but not when searching subordinates of the base object.
  - derefAlways: This command dereference aliases both in searching and in locating the base object of the search.
  - sizelimit: A size limit that restricts the maximum number of entries to be returned as a result of the search. A value of zero in this field indicates that no size limit restrictions are in effect for the search.
  - timelimit: A time limit that restricts the maximum time (in seconds) allowed for a search. A value of zero in this field indicates that no time limit restrictions are in effect for the search.
  - attrsOnly: An indicator as to whether search results should contain both attribute types and values, or just attribute types. Setting this field to TRUE causes only attribute types (no values) to be returned. Setting this field to FALSE causes both attribute types and values to be returned.
  - filter: A filter that defines the conditions that must be fulfilled in order for the search to match a given entry.
  - attributes: A list of the attributes from each entry found as a result of the search to be returned. An empty list signifies that all attributes from each entry found in the search are to be returned.

SearchResponse

This command is used by the directory server as a response to a search request.

To simply the wireless services framework, it is recommend not to use these methods:

- ModifyRequest.
- ModifyResponse.
- AddRequest.
- AddResponse.
- DelRequest.
- DelResponse.
- ModifyRDNRequest.
- ModifyRDNResponse.
- CompareRequest.
- CompareResponse.
- AbandonRequest.

Tech Talk

The directory database is loaded by an initialization file at start-up rather than by the aforementioned commands.

Protocol Element Encodings

The protocol elements of LDAP are encoded for exchange using the basic encoding rules (BER) [4] of ASN.1 [5]. However, due to the high overhead involved in using certain elements of the BER, the following additional restrictions are placed on BER-encoding of LDAP protocol elements:

- Only the definite form of length encoding will be used.
- Bit strings and octet strings and all character string types will be encoded in the primitive form only.

Users

Normally, services of the target system will use the LDAP protocol.

APPLICATION PROGRAM INTERFACE . . . .

There are several software developers' kits (SDKs) for LDAPs. There is also an informal RFC (RFC1823) describing an LDAP-API.

For the prototype, the Netscape LDAP SDK has been used. It is available from Netscape free of charge.

READING AN ENTRY . . . .

To read an entry, set the starting point of the search to the entry, set the scope of the search to `LDAP_SCOPE_BASE`, and specify (`objectclass=*`) for the search filter. Figure 12-3 shows a typical LDAP search session.

Search PDU

For this example, the SearchRequest PDU would be set to (see Figure 12-4):

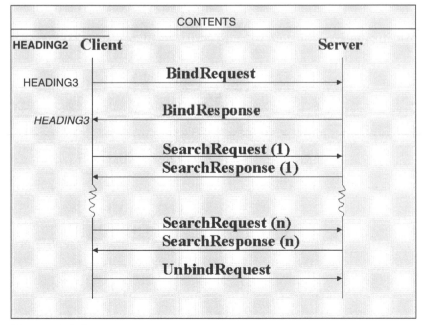

Figure 12-3
LDAP search session.

```
baseObject: "o=Ace industry, c=US".
scope: LDAP_SCOPE_BASE.
derefAliases: neverDerefAliases
sizelimit: 1
timelimit: 0
attrsOnly: FALSE
filter: (objectclass=*)
attributes: NULL
```

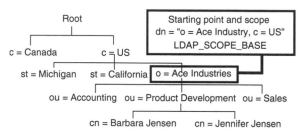

Figure 12-4
Search PDU.

Listing Subentries

To list subentries, set the starting point of the search to the entry and set the scope of the search to LDAP_SCOPE_ONELEVEL.

For this example, the SearchRequest PDU would be set to (see Figure 12-5):

```
baseObject: "o=Ace industry, c=US".
scope: LDAP_SCOPE_ONELEVEL.
derefAliases: neverDerefAliases
sizelimit: 0
timelimit: 0
attrsOnly: FALSE
filter: (objectclass=*)
attributes: NULL
```

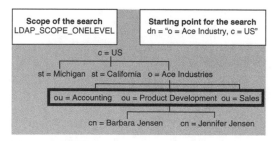

Figure 12-5
Set scope level one.

Future Considerations

LDAP version 2 has been used in the prototype. LDAP version 3 is now on the proposed standards track within IETF. Products supporting LDAPv3 are also starting to hit the market. It is very likely that LDAPv3 will be used shortly.

Key aspects of this version of LDAPv3 are

- All protocol elements of LDAPv2 (RFC 1777) are supported. The protocol is carried directly over TCP or another transport, bypassing much of the session and presentation overhead of X.500 DAP.
- Most protocol data elements can be encoded as ordinary strings (e.g., distinguished names).
- Referrals to other servers may be returned.
- SASL mechanisms may be used with LDAP to provide association security services.
- Attribute values and distinguished names have been internationalized through the use of the ISO 10646 character set.
- The protocol can be extended to support new operations, and controls may be used to extend existing operations.
- The schema is published in the directory for use by clients.

DNS AND BIND . . . .

This section explains several strategies for setting up DNS for wireless services like e-mail, ftp, and the WWW in an ISP (Internet service provider) environment.

DNS is the distributed namespace used on the Internet to resolve computer and service names to TCP-IP addresses. It handles mapping between host names, which humans find convenient, and Internet addresses, which computers deal with.

DNS is the standard mechanism on the Internet for advertising and accessing all kinds of information about hosts, not just addresses.

DNS distributes the management of host information among many sites and organizations. It is not necessary to submit your data to some central site or periodically retrieve copies of the "master" database.[1]

---

[1]Albitz, pg. 1.

The domain name space distributed database is indexed by domain names. Each domain name is essentially just a path in a large inverted tree, called the domain name space. The tree's hierarchical structure is similar to the structure of the UNIX file system. The tree has a single root at the top. In the UNIX filesystem, this is called the root directory and is represented by a slash ("/"). DNS simply calls it "the root." Like a filesystem, DNS's tree can branch any number of ways at each intersection point, called a node. The depth of the tree is limited to 127 levels.

Domain Names

Each node in the tree has a text label (without dots) that can be up to 63 characters long. A null (zero-length) label is reserved for the root. The full domain name of any node in the tree is the sequence of labels on the path from that node to the root. Domain names are always read from the node toward the root ("up" the tree) with dots separating the names in the path.

Windows NT and 2000 Active Directory

The active directory is tightly integrated with the domain name system (DNS). Most enterprises with intranets use DNS as the name resolution service. The active directory uses DNS as the *location service*. Windows 2000 domain names are DNS domain names. For example, "Microsoft.com" is a valid DNS domain name and could also be the name of a Windows 2000 domain. Tight DNS integration means that the active directory was designed to fit naturally into Internet and Intranet environments. Clients find directory servers like any other Internet user. An enterprise can connect active directory servers directly to the Internet to facilitate secure communications and electronic commerce with customers and partners.

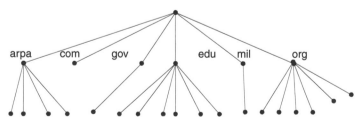

Figure 12-6
Domain tree.

Wireless Domains

At this time, a wireless domain (i.e., .wom or .tel) does not exist, but there is a need for such a space. Imagine a group of machines that facilitate wireless telephony billing services—for example, a soda machine that accepts a wireless phone call as a method of payment. The wireless operator acting as the clearing house or credit-card company for making sure the soda distributor is paid. A special designation like ".tel" would make these machines easily identifiable on the Internet.

Other Domains

The IAHC has defined an additional set of seven gTLDs. Any additional gTLDs will be defined under the aegis and policy coordination of the gTLD-MoU. The newly defined gTLDs are shown in Table 12.1.

REFERENCES . . . .

- RFC1777 Lightweight Directory Access Protocol.
- RFC1779 A String Representation of Distinguished Names.
- RFC1823 The LDAP Application Program Interface.

Table 12.1 The International Ad Hoc Committee[2]

Postfix	Description
.firm	for businesses or firms
.store	for businesses offering goods to purchase
.web	for entities emphasizing activities related to the WWW
.arts	for entities emphasizing cultural and entertainment activities
.rec	for entities emphasizing recreation or entertainment activities
.info	for entities providing information services
.non	for those wishing individual or personal nomenclature

[2]http://www.iahc.org

- Specification of Basic Encoding Rules for Abstract Syntax Notation One (ASN.1). ITU-T Recommendation X.209, 1988.
- Specification of Abstract Syntax Notation One (ASN.1). ITU-T Recommendation X.208, 1988.

1. Albitz, Paul & Criket, Liu. <u>DNS and Bind</u>, 3rd ed. (Beijing, Cambridge, Koln, Paris, Sebastopol, Taipei, Tokyo O'Reilly & Associates, Inc., 1998).
2. http://www.isc.org/bind.html.
3. RFC2251 Lightweight Directory Access Protocol (v3).

<u>TimeServ</u>'s home page (includes list of changes from previous versions and any changes in progress such as new and updated phone numbers; if not found try searching for a Time-TimeServ link under <u>http://www. niceties.com</u>)

http://www.iahc.org.

NTP CLOCK SYNCHRONIZATION SERVICES . . . . . .

This section explains how to keep a system clock in synchronization within a specified domain. The configuration of this service depends upon the domain type (DNS, DHCP, DCE, etc.). In addition, it contains a composite of articles that deal with everything from the various configuration options available, as well as known problems and how to rectify them.

Network administrators may establish one or more time-source servers as domain time standards and modify client login scripts to synchronize workstation time to that of the time-source servers. Network environments that require high accuracy will need to use the Windows NT 4.0 Resource Kit and Windows NT 4.0 Server Resource Kit, since they include many useful utilities for Windows NT domain administrators. The administrator may install the *TimeServ* utility (included in the Windows NT 4.0 Server Resource Kit). This utility synchronizes a Windows NT computer to a remote time standard through either modem dial-up or a network connection.

The **timeserv.exe** program keeps the local system clock synchronized with a time server that is independent of a logged-on user. It is an actual Windows NT service that comes from the Windows NT 4.0 Server Resource Kit.

Acronymns

DCE—Distributed computing environment from the open systems forum.
DHCP—Dynamic host configuration protocol.

DNS—Domain naming service.

NTP—Network time protocol.

TIMESERV—Time server program from NT 4.0 Server Resource Kit.

HOW TO SYNCHRONIZE WITH DOMAIN TIME SOURCE SERVERS . . . .

This subsection describes how to set up a Windows NT server to act as a domain time source server and enable client computers to synchronize with it.

Network administrators may establish one or more time-source servers as domain time standards and modify client login scripts to synchronize workstation time to the time-source servers. Network environments that require high accuracy may install the *TimeServ* utility (included in the Windows NT 3.5 Resource Kit). This utility synchronizes a Windows NT computer to a remote time standard through modem dial-up. For more information about *TimeServ*, refer to the Windows NT 3.5 Resource Kit Help file (RKTOOLS.HLP).

Source Server Setup

WARNING: Using Registry Editor incorrectly can cause serious systemwide problems, corrective only by reinstalling Windows NT. Microsoft cannot guarantee that any problems resulting from the use of Registry Editor can be solved. Use this tool at your own risk.

Start the Registry Editor (REGEDT32.EXE) and locate the following Registry subkey:

HKEY_LOCAL_MACHINE\SYSTEM\CurrentControlSet\Services
\LanManServer\Parameters

From the Edit menu, select Add Value.

1. Add the following:

   Value Name: TimeSource

   Data Type: REG_DWORD

   String: 1

2. Choose OK and quit the Registry Editor.

3. Shut down and restart Windows NT.

Enabling Client Computers to Synchronize with Source Server

For client computers, type the following in the MS-DOS command prompt, or add the following to the log-in script:

```
NET TIME /DOMAIN:<domain name> /SET
```

For Windows or MS-DOS–based client computers, such as Windows, Windows for Workgroups, LAN Manager for MS-DOS, or Microsoft Network Client for MS-DOS, type the following in the MS-DOS command prompt, or add the following to the log-in script:

```
NET TIME /WORKGROUP:<domain name> /SET
```

Tech Talk

You can also synchronize all timesource computers with a master timesource computer using the command NET TIME \\<computername> /SET. The master timesource computer can also be synchronized to an external time standard using the *TimeServ* utility.

TIMESERV.EXE utility causes 100% CPU utilization

A Windows NT 4.0 computer that is running the Windows NT 4.0 Resource Kit utility *TimeServ*.exe may slow down in its performance or even stop responding. If you check Performance Monitor or Task Manager, you may notice the *TimeServ* utility displays the CPU utilization at 100%. This happens when no data is sent in the return TCP packet from the servers contacting the source Internet time server.

Resolution

To resolve this issue, edit the *Timeserv.ini* file:

Click the Start button, point to Settings, click Control Panel and double-click the Services icon. Click Time Service, then click Stop. Using a text editor (such as Notepad.exe or Edit.com), open the *Timeserv.ini* file in your %SystemRoot% folder. Below the section heading [*TimeServ*], add the following line:

USNOServer=192.5.41.41

Save the file and close the text editor. From a command prompt, type "time-serv-update" (without the quotes). Click the Start button, point to Settings, click Control Panel, and double-click the Services icon. Click Time Service, then click Restart.

More Information

More information may be required when the Windows NT server computer running Time Service receives no data in the TCP packet from the Internet server when Internet type is selected in the Timeserv.ini file.

When Internet type is selected, your Windows NT server computer will attempt to connect to one of the two United States Naval Observatory (USNO) Internet time servers. These time servers provide an accurate time that Windows NT uses to synchronize its time. The time servers are

```
tick.usno.navy.mil    192.5.41.40
tock.usno.navy.mil    192.5.41.41
```

Occasionally, the server at IP address 192.5.41.40 might not accept time requests sent to the TCP port daytime(13) and will send a TCP RST in return. This will prompt your Windows NT server to try the alternate server, 192.5.41.41, and continue with time synchronization. Alternately, the first server may accept a TCP connection request but will not send any data in the reply message packet. This causes CPU utilization to go to 100% on the Windows NT Server.

Tech Talk

The above USNO servers also provide network time protocol (NTP) service. NTP uses UDP port 123. To use NTP service, enable NTP in the Timeserv.ini file before updating Time Service by adding the following line: NTPServer=192.5.41.41.

TIME SERVICES . . . .

This section describes the *TimeServ* program included in the Windows NT 4.0 Resource Kit. This service has two main goals. The first goal is to be able to set the system time of Windows NT accurately from a variety of sources. The second goal is to help synchronize the time easily between multiple machines on a local area network. (Links embedded in this document require access to the Internet.)

NTP Sources

To set the time accurately, *TimeServ* can access the following sources:

- National Institute of Standards and Technology ACTS.
- US Naval Observatory.
- National Research Council Canada INMS.
- BBC Radio Time Standard Dial-in Time Service.
- Computime from Telstra.
- TUG/PTB/Precision Timing/IEN/Netherlands (and others).
- New Zealand's MSL.

By Internet TCP/IP, the following sources may be used for the synchronization:

- US Naval Observatory—http://www.eecis.udel.edu/~mills/database/rfc/rfcl1769.txt
- National Institute of Standards and Technology—http://www.bldrdoc.gov/timefreq/service/nts.htm.
- Heath "Most Accurate Clock" GC-1000 or GC-1001WWV(H)–http://www.bldrdoc.gov/timefreq/service/swb.htm.
- Spectracom NETCLOCK/2(R) (WWVB)—http://www.bldrdoc.gov/timefreq/service/lfb.htm.
- TimeLink—http://www.truetime.com/ttlow.htm (WWV(H)) or PC-SG2 or serial format
- Arbiter Systems serial broadcast format.
- Hewlett-Packard's GPS receivers.
- Trimble GPS receiver.
- Rockwell GPS receiver.
- Motorola GPS receiver.
- Bancomm bc620AT, bc627AT (GPS-based), bc630AT, or PC03XT.

To synchronize the time easily, *TimeServ* can access the time from other Windows NT machines or many other machines running networking software from Microsoft. A machine can synchronize from a "primary" source (one server or a list of specific servers) or a "secondary" source. A secondary source is defined as a machine within a domain or workgroup that sets the "timesource" bit, and there is a feature in *TimeServ* which allows the easy setting of this bit on a Windows NT machine.

Installation Instructions

1. COPY TIMESERV.EXE and TIMESERV.DLL to %SystemRoot%\system32
2. COPY TIMESERV.INI to %SystemRoot%.
3. EDIT TIMESERV.INI as necessary (see below for details).
4. Log on with administrator privileges, if not already done.
5. Run TIMESERV-AUTOMATIC or TIMES-MANUAL, depending on how you want the service to start.

Tech Talk

TimeServ **requires Windows NT 3.5 or later to operate. An error message will appear if trying to run under Windows NT 3.1.**

Starting *TimeServ*

After performing the preceding steps (with -automatic), a reboot would start *TimeServ*. *TimeServ* runs as a service, so you do not need to be logged on. If you specified -manual, you must start *TimeServ* by using the Control Panel, then Services, selecting Time Service, and then pressing the Start button. You can also use this interface to change the start-up type or stop the service. If you decide to edit TIMESERV.INI later, you must stop the service and run TIMESERV-UPDATE from a command line, since the actual parameters are stored in the registry.

Checking Status

When *TimeServ* is running, it places any errors, warnings, or other information into the application log in the Event Viewer. Therefore, start Event Viewer and select application log to review the operational status. If there are no events in the log, *TimeServ* should be running fine. If desired, an option is available to write an event in the log for successful sets (Log = yes in timeserv.ini). Although the event description should be self-explanatory, more information appears later in this section.

In addition, perform a sanity check on both the operation and system time. When setting the time by modem, watch for the modem to operate. Check the time after about a minute, looking for any change. It should be accurate, and this would be easy to detect if the time was not accurate before. Also, check the date. If either the time or the date is off by an hour or more, set the time-zone setting in the control panel.

ACCURACY INFORMATION . . . .

A default entry in timeserv.ini is TASync = no. This is one of the main reasons *TimeServ* is not supported for Windows NT 3.1. It specifies that the TimeAdjustment flag in the system be fixed and skew compensation allowed. By default, Windows NT regularly syncs the time to the CMOS RTC (on 3.51 or later, it only does this when time is off by at least one minute). By specifying this option on the first time set after each boot, the clock will run using only the 8254-based timer, which has greater precision and can result in greater stability. In this mode, skew compensation is possible (for error in the rate of the system timer). Of course, if CMOS sync is not disabled, the long-term clock will take on the characteristics of the CMOS RTC with poor precision. Assuming that CMOS sync is disabled and using the popular i486 or uniprocessor Pentium CPU type, setting your time daily should result in a clock with maximum ±0.45 second error (twice daily ±0.22s, four times daily ±010s, etc.). These figures are for *TimeServ* obtaining the time from a nonnetwork source. Detailed skew compensation is not normally attempted when using a network source because of inconsistent delays over the network. In such cases, when the time drifts more with *TimeServ* than without, try setting TASync = yes.

Tech Talk

For skew compensation to work properly, never set the time manually while *TimeServ* is running. Either stop the Time Service first (and restart it after, if desired), or set TASync = yes.

Supplemental Instructions for Using *Time- Serv* with Board Level (ISA) Devices

In order for Windows NT to access I-O ports, a device driver is necessary (which is not normally included). For the purposes of *TimeServ*, it is easiest to use a sample device driver from the DDK, called *PortIO* or *GenPort*. Like an .exe or .dll file, there is a different file (genport.sys) for each processor architecture. The driver takes two parameters: the base port and the number of addresses. For example, the default might be port 300h for 10h addresses for the bc62xAT and bc630AT, port 320h for 20h addresses for the PC-SG2, port 2A0 for 10h addresses for the PC-LTC/IOR, port 300 for 20h addresses for the PC03XT, or port 200 for 8h address for Kallisto– http://ion.le.ac.uk/kallisto.

To obtain the driver and data files, type "genport -d" from a command prompt after obtaining genport.exe from a place such as http://home1.gte.net/dougho/ GENPORT.EXE (if not found, try searching for a Time–*TimeServ* link under http:// www.niceties.com, or perhaps ftp://ftp.microsoft.com/bussys/winnt/winnt-unsup-ed/ reskit/timeserv).

To install the driver, log on with administrator privileges and copy genport.sys (for the appropriate processor architecture) to your %SystemRoot%\system32\drivers directory. Next, you must create certain registry entries. Be careful to follow the instructions exactly, because the registry is vital to the operation of Windows NT and the Registry Editor is powerful. Select File-Run-REGEDT32 (or Start-Run if using the new shell). You should see four windows open within REGEDT32. Select the window titled HKEY_LOCAL_MACHINE on Local Machine.

Next you will double-click on a number of "keys" to expand down a tree: First double-click on SYSTEM, then CurrentControlSet, and then Services.

Now use the Edit menu and select Add Key. In the dialog box, type GenPort and then press the Enter key (or OK). Next, scroll down using the down-arrow key until GenPort is highlighted. Now, use the Registry menu, select Restore.

Enter the filename G30010.REG for the default bc62xAT or bc630AT (port 300, length 10), or the filename G32020.REG for the default PC-SG2 (port 320, length 20), or the filename G2A010.REG for the default PC-LTC/IOR (port 2A0, length 10), or the filename G30020.REG for the default PC03XT (port 300, length 20).

After pressing the Enter key (or OK), a warning message appears. If you are sure that you had highlighted (selected) *GenPort*, press Yes. To specify a different base port, it is fairly easy to follow the above steps, then double-click on *GenPort*, double-click on Parameters, then double-click on the line to the right which says *IoPortAddress*. You can then enter a new value (in hex) and press the Enter key (or OK).

Finally, use the Registry menu and select Exit.

Now shut down and reboot the machine, and the device driver should automatically start (watch for any error).

Tech Talk

If you attempt to run *TimeServ* with type =bc62xAT or =bc630AT or =PCSG2 or =PCTLC or =PC03XT (or PPSPort=Kallisto) without the above steps, you should get an error message stating that *TimeServ* was unable to open the I-O driver. Another way to verify that the driver installed and started correctly is to use Control Panel-Devices, and scroll down to the entry for GenPort (which should say Started Automatic). You can use the Start-up button to disable the driver if necessary at some future point.

13 Wireless Message Storage Service Based On E-Mail

ORIGIN . . . .

This section discusses using Internet standard e-mail services for storing all message types (i.e., voice, fax, and e-mail). In addition, it describes the associated protocols (i.e., IMAP4rev1 and SMTP) for use in wireless networks. A limited discussion about multipurpose Internet mail extension (MIME) is also included. The wireless aspects of service are addressed last.

Internet Messaging Background

As the Internet has emerged as a global network, the push toward e-mail service standardization has gained momentum. Most efforts have been aimed at closing the gap between Internet e-mail and proprietary e-mail systems, like those used by America Online and CompuServe, as well as proprietary systems. The gap has been narrowing from both sides. Proprietary systems now offer gateways that translate between their own formats and the Internet, and will be available in the future in versions that connect directly to the Internet. Conversely, developers of Internet mail systems have attempted to catch up with proprietary systems.

MIME

Until a few years ago, there was no simple way to send multimedia messages over the Internet. An image had to be translated into a transmittable form and cut and pasted into a document. The recipient would then cut it out of the document and put it in its own file, which was then decoded. Although some systems allowed images to be inserted easily, only recipients on the same system could read them.

All that began to change in 1992, when an Internet standards group led by Nathaniel Borenstein of Bell Laboratories generated the first prototype of a message known as MIME (multipurpose Internet mail extensions). MIME is a specification—like a container—for telling how to transport multimedia objects through the Internet.

The user clicks on the files to be attached, and the mail system does all the encoding, decoding, preparing, and then untangling when the message arrives. In 1994, MIME was deployed as the Internet standard for multimedia messages.

Now that the message format has been standardized, accessing mail protocols (POP and IMAP) are on their way to becoming standards.

POP3

POP3 serves as the Internet equivalent of your home mailbox.

Essentially, the mail program delivers your mail into your mailbox, and your mail product has to get the mail out. As with a real mailbox, however, capacity is limited; if your virtual mailbox overflows, messages are lost forever. Another drawback is that you typically cannot go back into your mailbox to retrieve a message you have already read on a different computer.

POP Status

The text-only e-mail format of the Internet was no match for some of the sophisticated functions that the proprietary systems offered.

IMAP4

This is where the newer schemes such as IMAP4 (Internet message access protocol version 4) come in. The system works like an enormous file cabinet full of drawers and folders with sorting and searching functions. The mail stays on the server, so if you are traveling, you could download part of your mail to your laptop, work on the mail off-line, resynchronize with your mailbox, and send some back. It is not necessary to carry all of your mail—wasting all that disk space—all of the time.

IMAP4 Status

IMAP4 is not yet fully deployed because it requires service providers to adopt new administrative procedures that have yet to be worked out.

Tech Talk

This was confirmed in our prototype effort.

But even with enhancements like IMAP4 on the way, the MIME standard is, in Internet terms, archaic. Over the past four years, the needs and expectations of users have changed dramatically.

MIME does not currently have the following qualities:

- Message encryption and authentication services, which are now standard in proprietary mail systems and are crucial to the future of the Web and digital commerce.
- A standard format for combining text and images, the way Web pages are presented, not just cover letters and attachments.
- Return receipts or delivery notification; when you send a piece of mail, you do not know if it has been received.
- Message authentication, preventing fraud.

Tech Talk

SMIME is on its way to becoming a standard.

Overall Status

The goal now for the Internet community is to create a set of standards that incorporate all of these services. Internet groups are working on protocols for providing message authentication and delivery notification, and for combining MIME with HTML.

Goal

A company's clients will be able to use electronic mail, not just to send personal messages, but also to engage in digital transactions and to manage entire systems of mobile workers and computers. The eventual aim is to develop a system as easy to use and as reliable as a wireless telephone—where the user can reach anyone regardless of their ISP.

Acronyms

ACAP   Application configuration access protocol.
base64   Binary data-encoding scheme.

c-client	IMAP Client library nickname.
e-mail	Electronic mail.
ESMTP	Extended simple mail transfer protocol.
IETF	Internet engineering task force.
IMAP4	Internet message access protocol (version 4).
MIME	Multipurpose Internet message exchange.
MTA	Message transfer agent.
POP3	Post office [Mail] protocol (version 3)
RFC	Request for comment.

IMAP4 . . . .

The IMAP protocol includes operations for creating, deleting, and renaming mailboxes. It supports checking for new messages, permanently removing messages, and setting and clearing attributes flags. Client authentication to the server is included as well.

Internet standards for electronic mail transfer, such as RFC822 and RFC1911 (MIME), are also supported. Searching and selective fetching of message attributes, texts, and portions is thus enabled.

Definition and Usage

Messages in IMAP4rev1 are accessed by the use of numbers. These numbers are either message sequence numbers or unique identifiers. IMAP4rev1 supports a single server. A mechanism for accessing configuration information to support multiple IMAP4rev1 servers is discussed in an Internet draft [ACAP].

The IMPA protocol does not specify a means of posting mail; this function is handled by a mail transfer protocol, such as [SMTP]. An effort is made to design IMAP4rev1 to be upwardly compatible with the RFC1176 [IMAP2] and unpublished [IMAP2bis] protocols.

Acronyms

Table 13.1 contains the concepts and acronyms for this section.

Table 13.1 *Acronyms*

Authentication	Establish the IMAP4 server as worthy of trust.
Log-in	Connect and authenticate to the IMAP4 server.
Expunge	Permanently remove "deleted" messages from a mailbox.
Log-out	Disconnect from the IMAP4 server. The protocol allows silent activity on the IMAP4 server after disconnection (*e.g.,* "expunge").
Select	Choose among several mailboxes.
Examine	Select a read-only mailbox.

IMAP4 Models

There are three fundamental models of client-server e-mail: off-line, on-line, and disconnected use.

Each of these models has its own strengths and weaknesses:[1]

IMAP PROTOCOL . . . .

The IMAP protocol allows a client to access and manipulate electronic mail messages on a server. IMAP4rev1 permits manipulation of remote message folders, called "mailboxes," in a way that is functionally equivalent to that of local mailboxes. See Figure 13-1. IMAP4rev1 also provides the capability for an off-line client to synchronize with the server.

Table 13.2 *E-mail Client/Server Models*

Feature	Off-line	On-line	Disconnected
Can use multiple clients	No	Yes	Yes
Minimum use of server connect time	Yes	No	Yes
Minimum use of server resources	Yes	No	No
Minimum use of client disk resources	No	Yes	No
Multiple remote mailboxes	No	Yes	Yes
Fast start-up	No	Yes	No
Mail processing when not on-line	Yes	No	Yes

[1]RFC1733, pg 2

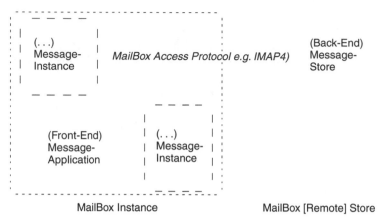

Figure 13-1
Mail box access protocol.

Protocol Overview

Figure 13-2 is a diagram presenting valid transitions during mailbox access using the IMAP4 protocol.

The following transitions are marked on the diagram in Figure 13-2:

- Connecting without preauthentication.
- Preauthentication connection.
- Rejected connection.
- Successful LOGIN or AUTHENTICATE command.
- Successful SELECT or EXAMINE command.
- CLOSE command, or failed SELECT or EXAMINE commands.
- LOGOUT command, server shutdown, or connection closed.

Table 13.3 shows a limited set of commands that are available at each state (as an example).

Link Level

The IMAP4rev1 protocol assumes a reliable data stream, such as that provided by TCP. When TCP is used, an IMAP4rev1 server listens on port 143.

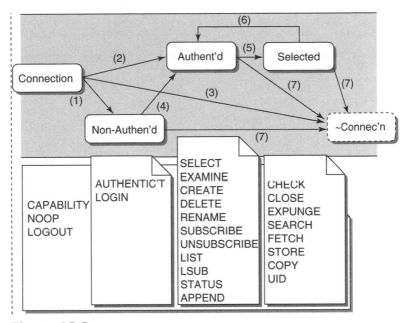

Figure 13-2
Mailbox access in IMAP4.

Commands and Responses

An IMAP4rev1 connection consists of the establishment of a client-server network connection, an initial greeting from the server, and client-server interactions. These client-server interactions consist of a client command, server data, and a server completion result response (demonstrated below).

Table 13.3　Commands at Each State

Connected	Not Authenticated	Authenticated	Selected
CAPABILITY	AUTHENTICATE	SELECT	CHECK
NOOP	LOGIN	EXAMINE	CLOSE
LOGOUT		CREATE	EXPUNGE
		DELETE	SEARCH
		RENAME	FETCH
		STATUS	STORE
		APPEND	COPY

Typically, the IMAP client and server are on dispersed systems. Thus, the protocol includes an "inactivity timer," which monitors a valid connection between an IMAP client and server. The server terminates a connection if it is not active for some time (e.g., 40 seconds).

Message Flags

Message flags are limited attributes attached to a message while it is inside a scope of a mailbox. Other message attributes, which are irrespective to a mailbox scope, are not considered at this time (e.g., SIZE, DATE). Applications context may include additional flags or attributes as necessary (e.g., "AUDIO").

> **Tech Talk**
>
> **In the wireless IT architecture, a message is considered "SEEN" once it has been played back (not when it was retrieved from the Message Store)! Please see Table 13.4 for a list of all the Flags.**

Version

Currently, IMAP is at version 4, revision 1. Thus, the short term "IMAP4rev1" is used. It is specified in RFC2060 (December 1996), which obsoletes RFC1730 (IMAP2). RFCs are published on the Internet "Standard Track," with limited duration for collecting comments.

Mailbox and Message Access

Table 13.5 introduces mailbox states in a limited messaging application.

Table 13.4 *Flags*

Flags	Notes
SEEN	This message has been reviewed before
ANSWERED	A reply has been sent
FLAGGED	Urgent message, limited priority
DELETED	Waiting for expunge (or flush)
DRAFT	Incomplete
RECENT	Arrived in this mailbox, since last accessed

Table 13.5 Mailbox States

Context or /State	Notes
Connected	A mailbox server is identified (i.e., Message Store)
Authenticated	Mailbox selection allowed (user logged in)
Selected	A mailbox is identified, found, and accessed
Disconnected	No mailbox access

It is possible to recognize two trades in mailbox access at this time. In IMAP, a message is delivered between a mailbox client and server upon explicit dialog. In POP3, a message is "pushed" toward the mailbox client upon server access. Additional trades deal with storage policy and copying of a message between the mailbox client and its server.

In the IMAP4 protocol, a message is copied toward the client, while an original copy is retained by the server. Thus, explicit deletion of "old" messages is necessary. No update or "restore" is necessary for messages with no modifications reviewed by the mailbox client.

Mailbox Library

Figure 13-3 shows the 'C' client library linked in with a client program. This provides access to the messaging service.

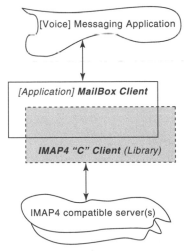

Figure 13-3
Mailbox library and linking.

Table 13.6 IMAP Functions

Function	Notes
Server	Connect, authenticate, disconnect, ping
Selection	Select mailbox, message
Management	Create, delete, get and set attributes (flags)
Deposit	Append, send, copy message(s)
Retrieval	Fetch message(s)
[Mailbox Events]	Contents' arrival and departure, attributes changed

Messaging Functions

Preliminary mailbox access for messaging applications supports the functions shown in Table 13.6.

Tech Talk

Messaging classes (Java or C++) were not commercially available at the time this book was written.

Example Client Access

Below is an example of a functioning IMAP client program called "mtest." The user is authenticated before being allowed to retrieve an audio message.

```
D:\Slewis\CTI\imap-4.1.BETA\mtest>mtest
MTest  -  C client test program
Personal name: slewis
Debug protocol (y/n)?n
Mailbox ('?' for help): {191.40.50.131}mbox
[ratbert IMAP4rev1 v10.214 server ready]      (<- Version )
{191.40.50.131/imap} username: slewis         (<- Authenticate )
Password: xxxxx
[[UIDNEXT 119] Predicted next UID]            (<- Selected )
[[UNSEEN 1] 1 is first unseen message in
/export/home/slewis/mbox]
[[READ-WRITE] SELECT completed]
Thu, 21 May 1998 11:44:24 -0400 (Eastern Daylight Time)
  imap mailbox: {191.40.50.131:143/imap/user=slewis}mbox, 1
messages, 0 recent
MTest>b 1                                      (<- Retrieve )
```

```
    1 AUDIO/BASIC (44140 bytes)              (<- Body Part )
    MTest>c                                  (<- Status )
    [Check completed]
    Thu, 21 May 1998 11:45:25 -0400 (Eastern Daylight Time)
     imap mailbox: {191.40.50.131:143/imap/user=slewis}mbox, 1
    messages, 0 recent
```

MULTIPURPOSE INTERNET MAIL EXTENSION (MIME) . . . .

RFC 822 defines a message representation protocol which specifies considerable detail about message headers, but which leaves the message content, or message body, as flat ASCII text. RFC1521 (MIME) redefines the format of message bodies to allow multipart textual and nontextual message bodies to be represented and exchanged without loss of information. This is based on earlier work documented in RFC 934, STD 11, and RFC 1049, but extends and revises that work. Because RFC 822 says so little about message bodies, MIME is largely orthogonal to (rather than a revision of) RFC822.

Content Types

MIME is built around the notion of "content-type." If a header of an electronic mail message contains the `Content-Type:` header, then its value indicates the type of data contained in the body of the message.

Multipart

The multipart type is used to convey a content value that contains several subordinate parts. It basically conveys zero or more body parts (each separated by a delimiter). Each of the body parts is structured in a similar fashion to an electronic mail message. Unlike a message, however, no header fields need be present (see RFC822).

Content Transfer Encoding

The `Content-Transfer-Encoding:` field is designed to specify an invertible mapping between the "native" representation of a type of data and a representation that can be readily exchanged using 7-bit mail transport protocols, such as those defined by RFC 821 (SMTP).

For example, the encoding mechanisms defined here explicitly encode all data in ASCII. Thus, for example, suppose an entity has header fields such as

```
Content-Type: text/plain; charset=ISO-8859-1
Content-transfer-encoding: base64.
```

This must be interpreted to mean that the body is a base64 ASCII encoding of data that was originally in ISO-8859-1 and will be in that character set again after decoding. A "base64" encoding scheme is used when the content value is a string of octets. Although the encoded value is one-third larger than the original value, it is immune to "diddling" by all known character set translations (e.g., LINE-FEED).

REFERENCES . . . .

- RFC2060   Internet message access protocol.
- RFC2045   Multipurpose Internet mail.
- RFC1911   MIME voice profile.
- RFC822,821   Message format, SMTP support.
- RFC1521,1522,1864 MIME support.
- RFC1939   Remote mail access (POP).

Good sources of information are the respective Internet bodies http://www. washington.edu/imap, for IMAP issues, and http://www.ema.org, for e-mail issues (*e.g.,* MIME).

MAILBOX CLIENT ACCESS (SUBSERVICE OF IMAP) . . . .

This section introduces design issues with the previously discussed mailbox concepts for wireless devices and the required access to E-mail messages. It is assumed that *Messages* are typically stored and managed through a *Mailbox* scheme.

Purpose

The purpose of this section is to expose the underlying structures in an application mailbox, thus soliciting design review and progress status for the "CallProcSrvc" prototype effort in particular.

Application Context

Remote mailbox access for a [local] messaging application or resources (e.g., media resource unit) provides a wide range of message store providers. A "client/server" model is typically being applied to e-mail delivery; thus, messages are "stored" on a server and "forwarded" to a client (as example).

Voice mail delivery with reasonable delays (< 2 sec) may require prefetching and overlapping message transfer schemes between the client and server(s). Thus, a prefetched message to the client may not be reviewed if a subscriber had "hung-up" the phone line (as example).

Tech Talk

It is thus necessary to augment a typical e-mail "client/server" setup with an application specific context!

Sample Application

The following diagram demonstrates a "limited" messaging application context. A "limited" playback and recording session is included.

```
ServiceLogic        Prompt, message play or record
LocalStore          e.g., local "file" entry.
MailBoxClient       Transfer messages to and from message
                    store.
```

Table 13.7   *Mailbox Signals*

Signal	Note/Function
P1	ServiceLogic requests subscriber's mailbox [content] retrieval
P2	[Partial] Subscriber's mailbox content is retrieved into LocalStore
P3	A "Message Ready" indication is now sent to ServiceLogic
P4	ServiceLogic invokes a message player (. . . reads from LocalStore)
R1	ServiceLogic invokes a message recorder (. . . writes to LocalStore)
R2	ServiceLogic requests subscriber's mailbox deposit [Transaction]
R3	Subscriber's mailbox content is being updated in [Remote] mailbox store
R4	ServiceLogic [Transaction] is acknowledged by the MailboxClient

Tech Talk

Message attributes management and content encoding are omitted from this limited context, as are timers and exceptions. Otherwise, it is most likely to be supported by the mailbox client.

Mailbox and Message Contexts Transitions

The following transitions schemes are somewhat compatible with the IMAP4 (RFC2060) protocol. The IMAP4 protocol supports Internet mailbox access. A "C" client library skeleton is provided by the University of Washington (UW) for interactions with e-mail servers, which support this protocol and compatible mailbox storage. Various mailbox storage schemes are supported through "drivers". The IMAP4 protocol and its "C" client library skeleton support various message transports, body structures, and data types (e.g., ESMTP RFC821, 1869 and MIME RFC1911, 1652). An RFC is a "request for comment," which is a method of sharing public technical issues over the Internet (see IETF), thus supporting a common ground for product development.

Mailbox Context[State] Transitions

Table 13.8 below introduces mailbox states in a limited messaging application (e.g., "CallProcSrvc"). The mailbox is a [temporary] container and management concept for zero or more messages. Operations on the mailbox are limited by its context state.

Message State Transition

Table 13.9 describes preliminary transitions in a message context. Currently, a message may not be associated with more than a single mailbox at one time. Outside the scope of a mailbox, a message is typically "parsed," or structured, with respect to a local [messaging] application. In the scope of a mailbox, the message is structured [contained], flagged, and managed with respect to the mailbox store and its access protocols. It is

Table 13.8   Mailbox States

Context State	Examples
Connected	A mailbox server is identified
Authenticated	Mailbox selection allowed
Selected	A mailbox is now identified
Disconnected	"Close" mailbox access
Not Authenticated	Limited access rights to mailbox server

Table 13.9　Transition States

Context State	Examples
In Mailbox Store	Message is in [remote [mailbox]] store
Transfer Out From Mailbox	Collecting message bodies
Transfer In To Mailbox	Waiting for storage confirmation
In Local Store	Message has a local "file" entry
Content Encode (-> Mailbox)	Edit message header
Content Decode (<- Mailbox)	S100 <- MIME
In Service	Message is now being played
Mailbox [Management] Ops	Delete, set flags, header attributes (other than transfer)

somewhat productive to recognize at least "Header" and "Body" parts structures in a message. Operations on a message may affect either of the parts.

Tech Talk

> **Since this is a preliminary text, simultaneous access policies to a message inside of a mailbox are deferred for later developments.**

[Mailbox] Message Flags

The following message flags are limited attributes, attached to a message while it is inside a scope of a mailbox. Other message attributes, which are irrelevant to a mailbox scope, are not considered at this time. An application context may include additional flags (e.g., see Table 13.10) or attributes as necessary (e.g., "AUDIO").

IMAP4 Mailbox Access

The following diagram demonstrates allowed access scenarios to an IMAP4 mailbox store. It is provided here for perspective on the protocol. Additional details are provided in RFC2060.

IMAP4, Functions and Evaluation

[Remote] mailbox store access is provided through a mailbox client application interface. IMAP4 "C" client functions and interfaces are described by Mark Crispin from the University of Washington. A limited IMAP4 client test fixture and source code are available on UNIX and NT.

Table 13.10 Message Flags

Context State	Examples
Seen	This message has been reviewed before[1]
Answered	A reply has been sent
Flagged	Urgent message. . . .
Deleted	Waiting for expunge (or flush)
Draft	Incomplete
Recent	Just arrived in this mailbox

[1]*The flag "Seen" may be set in the mailbox store once that message has been played to a subscriber, when it is prefetched from a [remote] mailbox store by a mailbox client!*

Mailbox [Client] Functions and Interfaces

Detailed discussions on the "C" client library utilization (see Figure 13-14) and services in the context of a [Voice] messaging application are somewhat premature at this time. In essence, a class of data structures, attributes, and request-response schemes will be defined in order to support an application-specific context (e.g., "call processing service").

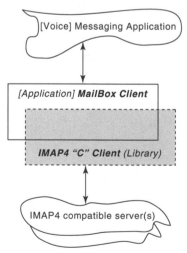

Figure 13-4
Client library example.

Mailbox Trades

It is possible to recognize two trades in mailbox access. In IMAP, a message is delivered between a mailbox client and server upon explicit dialog. In POP3, a message is "pushed" toward the mailbox client upon server access. Additional trades deal with storage policy and copying of a message between the mailbox client and its server.

In the IMAP4 protocol, a message is copied toward the client, while an original copy is retained by the server. Thus, explicit deletion of "old" messages is necessary. No update or "restore" is necessary for messages reviewed by the mailbox client.

Mailbox Content Exchange

In IMAP4, mailbox contents (e.g., message body) are exchanged between the client and its server in MIME, encoding a subtype registration scheme. It may utilize text-oriented encoding (e.g., "base64"), thus supporting host platform and transport media independence. A governing protocol between the mailbox client and its server is also text oriented (e.g., commands, responses).

Mailbox Functions

Preliminary mailbox client access supports the functions in Table 13.11.

Tech Talk

Currently, only one mailbox can be selected at a time. Simultaneous access to multiple mailboxes requires multiple connections!

Table 13.11   *Client Access Functions*

Function	Examples
Mailbox Server	Connect, authenticate, disconnect
Mailbox Selection	
Mailbox Management	Create, delete, get and set attributes, ping
Message Deposit	
Message Retrieval	
Message Management	Get and set attributes, get and set header, delete
Mailbox Events	Contents arrival and departure, attributes changes, ping

Message Encoding

A limited message [body] encoding scheme shall be supported for various media types (e.g. AUDIO). Within the mailbox context, MIME registration sub-types are expected. The current messaging application context expects an ECTF S100 container object for the message body.

Message [body] encoding shall be passed into message deposit or retrieval calls to the mailbox client as an *<AppEncDriver,AppEncContext>* arguments pair.

Application Encoding Driver *(AppEncDriver)*

<AppEncDriver> is a function for mapping a binary data stream and attributes to an application-specific container object and back, and for mapping an optional completion [callback] procedure.

Application Encoding Context *(AppEncContext)*

<AppEncContext> is a handle for access to essential application-specific resources (e.g., "container name").

References

RFC2060	Internet message access protocol (IMAP).
RFC2045	Multipurpose Internet mail.
RFC1911	MIME voice profile.
ECTF S100	"Container Management" section.

RFCs and Internet technology documents in general have a limited duration; thus, updates may follow. Good sources of information are the respective Internet bodies.

See http://www.ectf.org, for ECTF S100 topics, http://www.washington.edu/imap, for IMAP issues, ftp://ftp.cac.washington.edu/mail, and http://www.ema.org, for MIME issues.

Acronyms

IMAP4	Internet message access protocol (version 4).
MIME	Multipurpose Internet message exchange.
ECTF	Enterprise computer telephony forum.

S100	ECTF specification for media services.
IETF	Internet engineering task force.
RFC	Request for comment.
ESMTP	Extended simple mail transfer protocol.
POP3	Post Office [mail] protocol (version 3).
E-mail	Electronic mail.
base64	Binary data-encoding scheme.
c-client	IMAP client library nickname.

UOW MESSAGE STORE . . . .

A public domain, electronic mail server was introduced as a message store component. Such a server was developed and is being maintained by the University of Washington (UOW).

Introduction

An electronic message is a limited concept for information management, such as transporting and sharing. The term "electronic" is implied in further discussions. Typically, a message has attributes, such as storage size, delivery schedule, and membership in a "mailbox." A "mailbox" is a limited concept for message management, such as containment, ownership, and access protocols (e.g., retrieval).

The following text describes an implementation of a message store, based on file structures that reside in the operating environment (e.g., UNIX, NT) native file system. Such "mailbox" files can be observed through native file access utilities, such as listing directory content and attributes. A "mailbox" file structure enables compatible third-party mail tools to access, review, and manipulate its content. For further discussion, a "*flat*" file concept entitles this "mailbox" scheme, in contrast with a relational database, for example.

The logical representation in this section uses concepts such as "*bus*" and "*component*" to describe a system. The above message store scheme is now introduced as a component that interacts with other entities in the target [prototype] through several buses.

Reader Guidelines

The reader is encouraged to review relevant RFCs (i.e., requests for comments) as listed in the References section. Knowledge of basic concepts in electronic mail (e.g., delete, send) is also assumed. Familiarity with IMAP4 mailbox client interactions is assumed.

Application

The message store component may utilizing the buses shown in Table 13.12.

It is possible to describe the composition of a ["*flat*" file] message store component as follows:

The following text summarizes the concepts just discussed:

A message store based on the IMAP4 access scheme and a "flat" [UNIX] file structure is suggested. IMAP4 will manage both the content and the attributes of a mailbox scheme imposed on a native [UNIX] file entry. Although, it is possible to create nested mailboxes within mailboxes, it is not necessary at this time.

IMAP4 Mailbox File Structure

IMAP4 maintains a permanent message entry inside of a mailbox under its control. The permanent message content and structure is private to IMAP4 server process. The server maintains protocol, policies, and attributes for the whole mailbox inside of the permanent message. The following sentence demonstrates the above:

A mailbox file entry can be created through a native UNIX mail tool (as example of a "back door" access), or through the IMAP4 protocol and server. The following section demonstrates the content of an actual mailbox.

IMAP4, System Interface and Installation

An IMAP4 server is configured as a "daemon" process (i.e., system ownership). Interaction with the IMAP4 server is over a TCP/IP well-known service port #143. A session with the IMAP4 server is initiated by a client request on the well-known service port. Terminating the IMAP4 client will trigger an "exit" in the IMAP4 server

Table 13.12 Message Store IT/Buses

Bus	Note/Purpose
System Control	Operating system and IP network interactions
Message Control	Exchange of mailbox contents and attributes
Management (O&M)	Collect message traffic statistics
Service Control	Schedule a message deletion (i.e., expunge)

Table 13.13 Composition of Message Store

Element	Note/Purpose
Server/Policy	Mailbox size and message status updates
Protocol	Client commands are prefixed with identifier
Schedule/Periodic[1]	Expunge deleted messages
Driver(s)	Fetch message body from storage
Storage	A file entry on disk
[Back Door][2]	Optional third-party access [agent]

[1] *Timely interactions with the message store is considered as a message client application instance.*

[2] *Enables third-party mail tools to manipulate the message store. Maintains (e.g., Backup) message store contents through the operating environment file system.*

(i.e., "Cease"). Note that, for each IMAP4 client connection, a new copy of "imapd" is launched (i.e., a daemon process). It is possible to access an IMAP4 server without transmitting a "password" over the network by setting a ".rhost" file entry on the server and a link between "/usr/local/etc/imapd" (see above) and "/etc/rimapd". The mail spool directory should be protected with world write and sticky bit (i.e., 1777). Mail files should be protected with 600.

The user default "INBOX" is selected, unless an explicit mailbox entry is provided to the IMAP4 server.

IMAP4 Management Interface

Currently, an SNMP MIB interface is not implemented in the [public] IMAP4 source distribution from the University of Washington. Management entries are added to the source distribution by application developers, as necessary. SNMP entries (RFC1565 and 1566) typically are being provided in a commercial IMAP4 package.

IMAP4, Schedule and Periodic

A module for a mail-specific application like periodic operations (e.g., delete old mail) and timely operations (e.g., deliver now) can be included with a message store as a proprietary enhancement. Similar functionality can be achieved through a "Notification" agent or function and a mailbox client instance.

IMAP4 Message and Mailbox Interface

The IMAP4 message interface is documented in RFC 2060. For deposit or retrieval of the mailbox content and status, IMAP4 compatible e-mail clients set up a connection and authenticate to the server. The protocol is carried in text format, thus allowing system- and processor-independent protocol. The message body can be transported in binary (eight bits) form or encoded as text (e.g., base64). Encoding of the message body is done internally by the IMAP4 server or the client, as necessary. Voice messages are encoded in "base64" by the IMAP4 client library. Complex message body structures are partitioned and managed through MIME support (RFC 1521, 1522, 1864).

SMTP ("Back Door Access")

The use of a somewhat standard "mailbox" file structure enables message transport through SMTP. Other "mail tools" can deliver the messages in to and out of the mailbox directly, by passing the IMAP4 server. Such tools enable "off-line" e-mail delivery through queuing and scheduling. Access by SNMP agents to the mailbox is synchronized with the IMAP4 server, thus ensuring the integrity of the mailbox content. Yet, the permanent IMAP4 mailbox header is not maintained by SMTP agents. Subsequent access to the mailbox through IMAP4 will restore or update this header.

Mailbox Provision

Limited utilities are necessary for the target host server directory (i.e., /opt/imap/*). For example, empty mailboxes in the current directory can be created as follows:

```
alice% pwd
/home/slewis                          (<- Current Directory)
alice% /opt/imap/cpmbx "mbox1 mbox2"    (<- 2 Mailboxes ..)
New Subs: mbox1 mbox2
Is This Right (y/n) ? y
/opt/imap/mbx -> mbox1
/opt/imap/mbx -> mbox2
```

Acronyms

base64   Binary data-encoding scheme.

c-client   IMA client library nickname.

e-mail   Electronic mail.

ESMTP   Extended simple mail transfer protocol.

IETF   Internet engineering task force.

IMAP4   Internet message access protocol (version 4).

MIB   Message information base.

MIME   Multipurpose Internet message exchange.

POP3   Post Office [Mail] Protocol (version 3)

RFC   Request For Comment.

SNMP   Simple Network Management.

UOW   University of Washington.

References

RFC2060   Internet message access protocol.

RFC2045   Multipurpose Internet mail.

RFC1911   MIME voice profile.

RFC822,821   Message format, SMTP support.

RFC1521,1522,1864   IME support.

RFC1939   Remote mail access (POP).

Good sources of information are the respective Internet bodies:

http://www.washington.edu/imap, for IMAP issues, and http://www.ema.org, for MIME and e-mail.

Exporting Messages To A Wireless Message Service

This section explains how messages may be sent from a proprietary system to an Internet (generic) mail server by way of Internet message access protocol (IMAP4).

In addition, a brief write status on IMAP4 is provided, so that the reader can understand the implications of switching messaging kernels.

Simple Analysis

Figure 13-5 shows a processor diagram (type UML) showing the transfer of messages to an IMAP-POP message transfer agent (MTA):

Explanation of Processor Diagram

Table 13.14 explains the tasks performed by each of the processors shown in Figure 13-5.

Review of Processes for Transfer

Using Figure 13-5 and some analysis, four processes were identified for transferring messages:

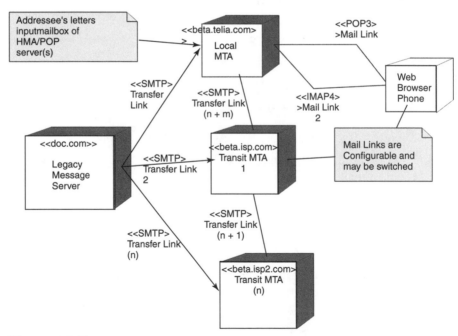

Figure 13-5
Exporting scenarios using a processor diagram.

Table 13.14 Tasks Performed by Each Processor

Processor	Task descriptions
Legacy message server	The conversion of messages from the proprietary format of the proprietary system to the Internet (generic) MTA would take place in the SMP process. This process is already part of the product, and its code is located in the SMP (user agent control) subsystem. The protocol between the proprietary system processor and the MTA processor is SMTP with MIME extensions. This is also called ESMTP. A shell script, or some other mechanism, is needed to mail subscriber messages over this route.
	Two scenarios can be encountered in the Intranets or Internets field, so, typically, the proprietary system is configured as an Intranet, in which the domain name is emx.ericsson.com and is contained in /etc/hosts. However, this convention is not true for sites connected to the Internet. Internet sites will have both a local domain name that reflects the customer's naming convention and, most likely, a DNS server.
	Lastly, this process can take place locally or remotely over the Internet.
	Tech Talk
	MIME extension is not currently deployed, but is under development. Options are available for having this work completed.
Local MTA(s)	The local MTA processor(s) will contain target accounts and associated mailboxes. The standard (E.164) telephone number identifies the proprietary system subscriber mailbox. Therefore, provisioning of these numbers is needed for SMTP to work properly.
	Tech Talk
	Provisioning the mailboxes is outside the scope of this text.
Transit MTA(s)	The transit MTA processor(s) can serve a number of local MTAs. Its primary task is to forward a message from one domain to another, regardless of subscriber or message content. Again, two scenarios arise: Internet and Intranet. Each has its own provisioning procedures. The Internet procedure requires the customer to register with the NIC (Network Solutions, Inc.)
Web-Browser Phone Device	This device is part of the local domain and has access to the local MTA(s) through IMAP/POP, or SMTP's sendmail. Storage is optional on the device itself.

1. *Off-line export of the messages from the proprietary system by way of UNIX application command utilities for import later by some off-the-shelf MTA.* This would entail breaking the mirrored pairs of the proprietary system, formatting the data on the demirrored drive, and moving disk drives from one machine to another in which the import takes place. Moving and formatting the data across the SCSI bus is an effective means for conversion. Less time is needed with faster bus speeds. Transaction-based file systems require more time, since the data conversion and the transaction commit time become a factor in the overall processing. If the University of Washington message store is used, then a proprietary system application program will need to output message heads and bodies into a UNIX flat file named *mbox*. This will need to be done for each subscriber, since IMAP requires an account for each. Furthermore, when a commercial-grade message store is selected, it may be desirable to conform to one of the import formats. For example, acceptable import formats for Microsoft's Exchange include MS Mail for PC Networks, Lotus CC:Mail, Novell GroupWise, and Collabra Share. What this means is that a company will need to modify the proprietary system application so that the data are presented in an acceptable format.

2. *Intranet transfer of messages by way of a local program.* The data flow would resemble something like this: MTA->SMP-EMD->local MTA. A shell script, or local application program, would then be used to route the messages over the link. However, the outbound transfer of messages from MHS to SMP requires more development. At this time, binary data transfer is not possible using user agent protocol (UAP). UAP is used between MHS and SMP. Furthermore, the proprietary system notify commands do not have the appropriate switches for sending a message out of the proprietary system. The only exception is the *notify* command. The switch that is required is–address, which represents the destination e-mail address.

3. *Internet transfer of messages by way of IMAP.* In this scenario, the subscriber has an existing account on the proprietary system. The user downloads his or her voice messages from the proprietary system. This implies that the proprietary system supports the IMAP4 or POP3 retrieve mailbox data function. The subscriber would then be instructed to change the parameters of the mail hub from the proprietary system to the new local MTA. This could be automated with the use of an e-mail containing a Java script to do the switch. In this case, local storage would be needed so that the messages would not be immediately lost, much like a laptop computer has disk drives.

4. *Replication of message transactions with an IMAP server.* In this case, each action is duplicated once on the proprietary system and once on the IMAP server. This would allow the IMAP server to synchronize, or become an exact replica, of the proprietary system. This replication process would last as long as the message aging function, which typically never exceeds 30 days. The switchover would occur instantly.

Frequently Asked Questions

1. How long will it take to transfer messages from a proprietary message store to an IMAP server?

It depends on the aforementioned process selected.

2. What happens to a voice-mail message when it is moved from proprietary system-Old to proprietary system-New?

It depends upon the aforementioned process selected, but in the worst case, a subscriber's message is marked as "not read."

3. Do the messages retain date and time?

In the worst-case scenario, the messages will have the date and time of the export.

4. Should there be media type conversion choices on a per-mailbox basis?

This should be left for the customer to decide. The files on the proprietary system are contained either in GSM or in ADPCM, both of which are standard to many browsers and mail retrieval clients. However, if the proprietary system owner has a subscriber base that does not have the software to process these encodings, he or she may choose to convert the messages to some other format, like .wav. Again, efficiency is the only concern.

5. Are we addressing FAX?

Again, it depends on the aforementioned process selected The proprietary system stores the message as a TIFF file. This may be converted, but the cost is in efficiency of the transfer (i.e., TIFF to GIF).

6. Would we allow "new" messages to come into the old mailbox, or should we block or "busy out" the old mailbox during the transfer?

This also depends on the process selected for transfer downtime—maybe a couple of hours, like that of an upgrade to Solaris. The SMTP transport requires only a switchover time of minutes, because as messages are exported, new arrivals can be forwarded. Naturally, the forwarding process will require some kind of manual intervention—that is the subject of further analysis.

Conclusion

Internet standards have made it easier to move messages between proprietary systems, since the web provides a common gateway for data transfers. Any company that produces messaging server software shall provide an interface that a company can adapt to. Efficiency is the only catch.

14 Wireless Network Management Service

ACCOUNT CONTROL—THE KEY STRATEGY ....

Manufactures of telecom and networking equipment position themselves in a customer account by supplying the network manager. They want to control the account, since a customer is less likely to purchase equipment that cannot be managed by the network manager.

Take, for example, a large manufacturer that makes routers and managers. Their routers support both a prioprietary protocol and SNMP. When they approach new accounts, they will instinctively push the prioprietary protocol, so that the unsuspecting customer is compelled to only buy their equipment.

BACKGROUND ....

This section explains why the previously mentioned services use the SNMP interface.

Overview

A system manager maintains an up-to-date image of an enterprise computer system. The system image and the actual system are kept in synchronization through the constant exchange of management information between the managed components (i.e., meter data repository and meter data server) and the system manager. This information is passed over the system manager interface (SMI).

An enterprise manager provides the platform on which the following management functions can be automated:

Configuration Management—A system manager can read and update components like meter data repository and CallProcSrvc management information to reconfigure the system. A system manager also enables remote provisioning of components, including remote program loading.

Performance Management—By collecting information from components, a system manager can generate statistics to identify performance problems. PBNM (policy-based network management) promises active QoS (quality of service) and network service-level agreement provisioning.

Fault Management—A system manager receives trouble notifications generated by the managed components, so that those events that cause faults can be correlated to facilitate fault detection, diagnostics, and automated correction.

Security Management—A system manager centralizes the administration of log-in IDs, passwords, encryption keys, and access control information.

Accounting Management—By collecting information from components reflecting resource consumption (e.g., number of files sent to applications), a system manager can allocate costs to users and implement accounting policies. One or more management applications will perform one of the five management functions. The system manager provides the platform on which management applications run. It is expected that the service provider will specify and implement many of these management applications.

Processor Diagram

The system manager consists of the hardware and the software necessary to provide integrated management of multivendor wireless components and services. Figure 14-1 shows a system manager processor connected to a service processor. The manager of manager shows the optional management of the manager processor (MgrOfMgr).

LARGE SYSTEMS . . . .

Management applications implement the management functions listed in Figure 14-1. They access, create, and modify management data and issue requests to managed components to accomplish their tasks. A company, the system manager supplier, or third-party independent software supplier, can create enterprise computer system management applications. The creation of management applications is facilitated by the system manager's application programming interface (API). The API provides a means for tailoring a system manager's evolving needs. Furthermore, the API enables management applications to be developed independent of the management protocols being used.

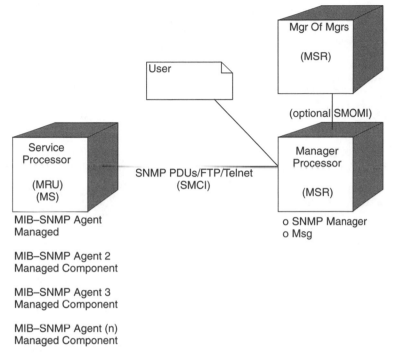

Figure 14-1
System manager processor diagram.

The system manager is not required to maintain a management information base (MIB). However, if a system manager maintains an MIB, it will be supported by ZFC mass storage of some kind.

A System Manager has three interfaces:

1. System Manager–Component Interface—enables a system manager to exchange management information with the system components that it manages.

2. User Interface—provides the means for a human user (e.g., system administrator) to locally access the system manager. This interface is intended to provide a user-friendly presentation.

3. System Manager–Manager Interface—enables coordination between multiple system managers. This interface, which is optional, provides the means by which the controlling and monitoring functions of network management can be distributed among multiple management stations. Such distribution accommodates growth in the number of managed

components and facilitates network management in an enterprise computer system composed of multiple interconnected administrations.

SIMPLE NETWORK MANAGEMENT PROTOCOL (SNMP) . . . .

The simple network management protocol (SNMP) is the Internet's standard protocol for exchanging management information between management consoles that use tools, such as HP Openview, Novell NMS, IBM NetView, or Sun Net Manager, and managed entities. The managed entities can include hosts, routers, bridges, and hubs.

ABOUT SNMP ON WINDOWS NT

SNMP uses a distributed architecture consisting of management systems and agents. The SNMP agent is responsible for retrieving and updating local management information based on the requests of the management system. The SNMP agent also notifies registered management systems when a significant event occurs. A Windows NT management system is any computer that has loaded the TCP/IP or IPX transport and is running third-party SNMP manager software. To use the Microsoft SNMP service, you need at least one management system. The primary function of a management system is to request information from an agent. The management system initiates Get, GetNext, and Set operations. The Get operation is a request for a specific value, such as the amount of hard-disk space available. The GetNext operation is a request for the value after a specified value in the conceptual database of management information that the agent maintains. The Set operation changes a value.

The primary function of an agent is to perform the Get, GetNext, and Set operations requested by a management system. The only operation initiated by an agent is the trap, which alerts management systems to an extraordinary event, such as a password violation. The SNMP service performs the duties of an SNMP agent on a computer running Windows NT.

SNMP SERVICE FEATURES

The SNMP service works with any computer running Windows NT and the TCP/IP protocol. With the SNMP service, a Windows NT computer can report its current status to an SNMP management system on a TCP/IP or IPX network. The service sends status information to a host in the following two cases:

- When a management system requests such information.
- When a significant event occurs on the Windows NT computer.

HOW SNMP WORKS

The following five steps outline how the SNMP service responds to management system requests:

1. The network management system uses either host names or IP addresses to initiate requests.
2. The request contains a Get, GetNext, or Set command involving one or more objects. The request also includes a community name and validating information.
3. The SNMP service receives the request. It verifies the community name and the source host name (or IP address) and selects the appropriate extension agent DLL by querying the registry to determine which extension agent DLLs have been installed and need to be loaded and initialized.
4. The extension agent DLL retrieves the requested information and passes it back to the SNMP service.
5. The SNMP service sends the completed request back to the SNMP manager.

TYPICAL SNMP ARCHITECTURE UNDER WINDOWS NT

Figure 14-2 shows how the Microsoft SNMP Extendible Agent (SNMP.EXE) works with the extension agent DLL under Window's NT. In this example, the extension is for T2W.

MEMORY MAPPING . . . .

MMF (memory-mapped files) used in sharing data. MMFs are usually attached to user-specified files. This is important, because the NTFS security plays a part in determining whether or not the service maps the memory. It will always work under an FAT partitioned OS. What this means is that interactive users that attempt to access

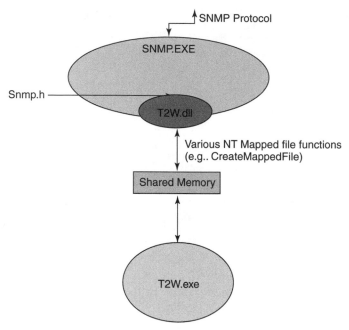

Figure 14-2
NT SNMP architecture.

the MMF will fail, because the user will more than likely have fewer rights than the system.[1]

ARCHITECTURE PROS AND CONS . . . .

PROS

- The MMF performance is very good.

CONS

- The level of complexity is relatively high.
- The developer is at the mercy of the TCP/IP stack vendor (i.e., Microsoft).
- The MMF implementation makes the T2W service Windows NT dependent.

[1]Grimes.

THE SNMP MANAGEMENT
INFORMATION BASE (MIB) . . . .

A management information base (MIB) describes a set of managed objects on an SNMP agent. A management system can manipulate the objects if the SNMP agent has associated an extension agent DLL with that MIB.

The entry for each managed object has a unique identifier. The entry also contains a description of the object's type (such as counter, string, gauge, or address), the object's access type (such as read or read or write), size restrictions, and range information.

The following MIBs ship with the Windows NT Resource Kit and the Microsoft Win32 Software Development Kit (SDK): MIB II (based on RFC 1213), LAN Manager MIB II, DHCP, WINS, FTP, HTTP, and Gopher. The extension agent DLLs for MIB II and for LAN Manager MIB II are installed with the SNMP service. The DLLs for the other MIBs are installed when their respective services are installed. At service start-up time, the SNMP service loads all of the extension agent DLLs that are listed in the Windows NT registry. Users can add or develop other extension agent DLLs that implement other MIBs, but they must remember to register the new MIB with the management system of their choice. For more information, see the documentation included with your management system.

MIB NAME TREE

The name space for MIB object identifiers is hierarchical. It is structured so that each manageable object can be assigned a globally unique name.

Authority for parts of the name space is assigned to individual organizations. This allows organizations to assign names without consulting an Internet authority for each assignment. For example, the name space assigned to Microsoft is 1.3.6.1.4.1.311. Microsoft has the authority to assign names to objects anywhere below that name space.

The object identifier in the hierarchy is written as a sequence of labels beginning at the root and ending at the object. Labels are separated with a period.

Tech Talk

The object names and object numbers are defined in each of the *.MIB files in the Win32 SDK. Refer to the Microsoft Windows Resource Kit for object names and numbers.

Table 14.1 shows the object identifier for each of the MIBs used in Windows NT.

Table 14.1   Object Identifiers for MIB in Windows NT

MIB	Contents
MIB_II.MIB	Internet MIB II defines 171 objects essential for either configuration or fault analysis. Internet MIB II is defined in RFC 1213.
LMMIB2.MIB	LAN Manager MIB II defines approximately 150 objects that include such items as statistical, share, session, user, and log-on information.

RELEVANT RFCS

TCP/IP standards are defined in requests for comment (RFCs), published by the Internet Engineering Task Force (IETF). The RFCs relevant to SNMP features are listed in Table 14.2.

WINDOWS NT FILES FOR SNMP

Table 14.3 describes the files that relate to the SNMP service. For complete installation instructions, refer to the Microsoft Windows Resource Kit.

SNMP UTILITIES

Table 14.4 summarizes the SNMP utilities and files that are available in the Microsoft Windows Resource Kit.

Table 14.2   SNMP RFCs

RFC number	Title
1155	Structure and identification of management information for TCP/IP-based internets. It defines SMI.MIB.
1157	Simple network management protocol (SNMP). It defines SNMP itself.
1213	Management information base for network management of TCP/IP-based internets: MIB - II. It defines MIB_II.MIB.

Table 14.3 SNMP Service Files for Windows NT

Filename	Description
DHCPMIB.DLL	DHCP SNMP agent (not in Windows NT 3.1). Only installed on DHCP servers.
INETMIB2.DLL	MIB II extension agent DLL.
LMMIB2.DLL	LAN manager MIB 2 extension agent DLL.
MGMTAPI.DLL	SNMP component; management API library.
WINSMIB.DLL	WINS SNMP agent (not in Windows NT 3.1). Only installed on WINS servers.
SNMP.EXE	SNMP agent service; proxy agent that listens for requests and hands them off to the appropriate network provider.
SNMPTRAP.EXE	Receives SNMP traps and forwards them to MGMTAPI.DLL.
SNMPAPI.DLL	SNMP utilities DLL.
MIB.BIN	SNMP component; SNMP service.

USING SNMP

This section contains information primarily of interest to network administrators:

- Turning SNMP on and off.
- SNMP service information.
- Configuring SNMP.
- Removing TCP/IP components.

Table 14.3 SNMP Utilities

Filename	Description
MIBCC.EXE	SNMP MIB compiler.
PerfMIB	SNMP to performance monitor.
SNMPUTIL.EXE	A very simple SNMP manager application that implements Get, Get Next, Walk, and Trap.
LMMIB2.MIB	Defines approximately 150 objects that include information on statistics, share, session, user, and log on.
MIB_II.MIB	Defines 171 objects essential for either configuration or fault analysis.

Turning SNMP On and Off

You can start and stop SNMP from the console window or through the Services icon in the Control Panel. Since SNMP starts when the computer is started, you will usually not need to start or stop SNMP. However, if you configure trap destinations or add a new community string, you will need to restart SNMP.

You will also need to restart SNMP after you install a new extension agent DLL. From the console window or from the Services application in Control Panel, type "Net Stop SNMP" and then "Net Start SNMP" (without the quotes).

You will have to start the SNMP trap service if you want to receive traps. From the console window or from the Services application in Control Panel, type "Net Start SNMPtrap" to start the SNMP trap service or "Net Stop SNMPtrap" to disable trap reception (without the quotes).

Stopping a service cancels any network connections the service is using. You must have administrative rights to stop the server service.

SNMP Service Information

On occasion, you may need to reconfigure SNMP (see the section entitled Configuring SNMP). In these instances, you need to know community names in your network, the trap destination for each community, and IP addresses or computer names for SNMP management hosts before you use or reconfigure SNMP services. You should always keep the following information available:

- Community names.
- Host names and IP addresses.
- Management systems and agents.
- UDP and IPX protocols.

Community Names

A community name identifies a collection of management systems and agents. The use of a community name provides primitive security and context checking for both agents and management systems that receive requests and initiate trap operations. An agent will not accept a request from a management system outside of the community.

Host Names and IP Addresses

If the Windows NT computer does not have access to a WINS server, the SNMP service uses the HOSTS file to resolve host names to IP addresses. The HOST file is merely a text file that lists explicit host names and IP addresses. If you use host names, be sure to add all host names and IP address mappings of the participating systems.

UDP and IPX Protocols

The information in this topic pertains only to a Windows NT server. Although the Windows NT server for SNMP service supports managing consoles over both the Internet package exchange (IPX) protocol and the user datagram protocol (UDP), SNMP must be installed in conjunction with the other TCP/IP services.

Configuring SNMP

The SNMP service is installed when you check the SNMP service option in the Windows NT TCP/IP Installation Options dialog box. After the SNMP service software is installed on your computer, you must configure it with valid information for SNMP to operate.

You must be logged on as a member of the administrator group for the local computer to configure SNMP.

The SNMP configuration information identifies communities and trap destinations.

- A community is a group of hosts to which a Windows NT computer running the SNMP service belongs. You can specify one or more communities to which the Windows NT computer using SNMP will send traps. The community name is included when a trap is sent.

  When the SNMP service receives a request for information that does not contain the correct community name or does not match an accepted host name for the service, the SNMP service can send a trap to the trap destination(s), indicating that the request failed authentication.

- Trap destinations are the names or IP addresses of hosts to which you want the SNMP service to send traps with the selected community name.

You might want to use SNMP for statistics, but you may not care about identifying communities or traps. In this case, you can specify the "public" community name when you configure the SNMP service.

Configuring SNMP Security

SNMP security allows you to specify the communities and hosts from which a computer will accept requests. It also allows you to specify whether to send an authentication trap when an unauthorized community or host requests information.

For details on how to configure security, refer to the Microsoft Windows Resource Kit.

Configuring SNMP Agent Information

SNMP agent information allows you to specify comments about both the user and the physical location of a computer and to indicate the types of service to report. The types of service that can be reported are based on the computer's configuration.

For details on how to configure SNMP agent information, refer to the Microsoft Windows Resource Kit.

Removing TCP/IP Components

If you want to remove the TCP/IP protocol, or any of the services installed on a computer, use the Network option in the Control Panel.

When you remove network software, Windows NT warns you that the action permanently removes that component. You cannot reinstall a component that has been removed until after you restart the computer.

For details on how to remove TCP/IP components, refer to the Microsoft Windows Resource Kit.

USING SNMP WITH OTHER WINDOWS NT TOOLS . . . .

The network administrator can monitor DHCP servers and use the performance monitor to look at TCP/IP, FTP, and WINS counters.

The DHCP manager and WINS manager are added to the Network Administrator group in Program Manager when you install DHCP and WINS servers. You can use these tools to view and change information for DHCP and WINS servers. Similarly, you can use the FTP server service to configure other FTP servers. The performance monitor can monitor WINS servers, FTP server service traffic, and each of the different elements that make up the TCP/IP protocol suite.

Some of the parameters for these functions cannot be changed except by either using SNMP or by editing the registry. You can set all of the WINS configuration parameters using SNMP. For information about additional monitoring tools, refer to the Microsoft Windows Resource Kit.

Tech Talk

You can impair or disable Windows NT if you make incorrect changes in the registry while using the Registry Editor. Whenever possible, use WINS manager or SNMP to make configuration changes rather than using the Registry Editor. If you make errors while changing values with Registry Editor, you will not be warned, because the Registry Editor does not recognize semantic errors.

SNMP FUNCTIONS . . . .

This section lists the SNMP functions and structures. These elements support SNMP for Windows NT.

SNMP functions support the development of both SNMP agent applications and SNMP manager applications. An SNMP agent application is an SNMP application entity that responds to queries from and generates traps to SNMP manager applications. An SNMP manager application is an SNMP application entity that generates queries to and receives traps from SNMP agent applications.

The manager functions allow multiple manager applications to simultaneously coexist. ISV-developed manager applications use the manager functions to perform SNMP manager operations. The SNMP manager functions are implemented as a Win32 DLL and as a single detached process. The DLL and the single detached process interact with one or more ISV-developed manager applications. Miscellaneous utility functions are also available to assist with comparing, copying, and freeing allocated data structures.

The SNMP functions are listed in three major categories.

Agent Functions

The agent functions define the interface between the extensible agent and the ISV-developed extension agent DLLs:

- SnmpExtensionInit.
- SnmpExtensionInitEx.
- SnmpExtensionQuery.
- SnmpExtensionTrap.

Manager Functions

The manager functions define the interface between ISV-developed manager applications and the management function dynamic-link library:

- MGMTAPI.DLL.
- SnmpMgrClose.
- SnmpMgrGetTrap.
- SnmpMgrOidToStr.
- SnmpMgrOpen.
- SnmpMgrRequest.
- SnmpMgrStrToOid.
- SnmpMgrTrapListen.

Utility Functions

The utility functions simplify the manipulation of SNMP data structures and perform other miscellaneous operations:

- SnmpUtilMemAlloc.
- SnmpUtilMemFree.
- SnmpUtilMemReAlloc.
- SnmpUtilOidAppend.
- SnmpUtilOidCmp.
- SnmpUtilOidCpy.
- SnmpUtilOidFree.
- SnmpUtilOidNCmp.
- SnmpUtilPrintAsnAny.
- SnmpUtilVarBindCpy.
- SnmpUtilVarBindListCpy.
- SnmpUtilVarBindFree.
- SnmpUtilVarBindListFree.

SNMP Structures

The following structures are used with SNMP:

- AsnAny.
- AsnObjectIdentifier.
- AsnOctetString.
- RFC1157VarBind.
- RFC1157VarBindList.

REFERENCES . . . .

TESTDLL: SAMPLE SNMP EXTENSION AGENT. Ontario, Canada. Microsoft Developers Network, 30 March 1998.

Mellquist, Peter Erik. *SNMP++ An Open Specification for Object-Oriented Network Management Development Using C++.* Chicago, Illinois. Hewlett-Packard Company, 31 March 1998.

Grimes, Dr. Richard. *Professional DCOM Programming.* San Francisco, California. Wrox Press, 1997.

SNMP CORRELATOR FOR LARGE-SCALE WIRELESS SYSTEMS . . . .

This section is a description of the network management agent (NMA) component for large-scale wireless systems. (See Figure 14-3).

Background

The NMA is the point of entry into the system from a management point of view. NMA makes it simple to operate and manage the system.

NMA exposes an SNMP-based management interface. At this time, SNMPv1 is used.

The management interface focuses on the high-level management and monitoring of the system. In other words, with this management interface, a network manage-

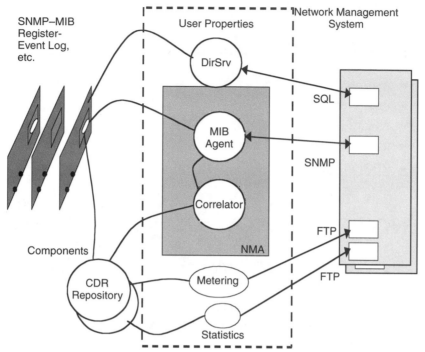

SNMP–MIB
Register-
Event Log,
etc.

Components

Figure 14-3
Network management agent.

ment system will know the overall operating status and performance of the system. The network management system may also order configuration changes, and so on, in order to remedy a fault situation, as well as prepare for maintenance (blocking a component, for example).

NMA is also instrumental in order to achieve component plug and play.

NMA integrates into a common view a number of sub-SNMP agents and other event information sources—for example, the Solaris and NT event and system logs. The sub-SNMP agents include both standard MIBs, such as MIBII, and enterprise MIBs, such as a component MIB.

All management information—traps or counters—are fed into the InCharge component. InCharge is a sourced component that allows management information to be filtered and correlated. InCharge is, at this time, part of the NMA. This is accomplished by describing the system in an InCharge proprietary language called Model. Model is a superset of the CORBA–IDL definition language.

With the right model, InCharge can pinpoint a problem with a certain probability. This problem will be reported by an SNMP–TRAP to a network management system.

To summarize, SNMP delivers a system with the following characteristics:

- SNMP will be used for connection to management systems.
- All components and nodes will be managed through open common interfaces.
- The operators' management administration systems will be used for OAM&P.

NMA deals mainly with O&M of the OAM&P. For the administration (A) and provisioning (P), other interfaces are used. For example,

- SQL and FTP will be used for connection to CAS.

No functions for administration and provisioning are included. This is also depicted in Figure 14-4

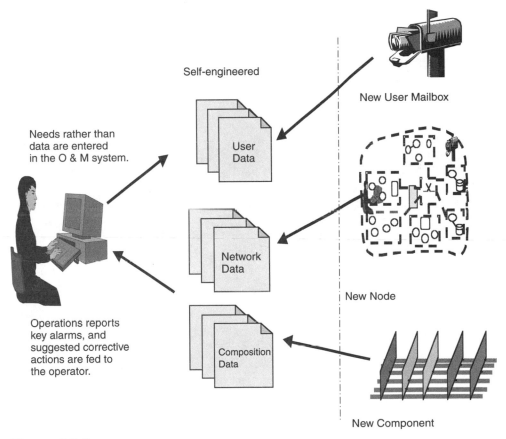

Figure 14-4
Plug and play self-configure system.

Network Management Agent Architecture

Figure 14-5 shows the generic O&M domain architecture. Here, we see a number of nodes interconnected in a LAN. Each node contains a number of sub-SNMP objects as well as event subagents. These subagents feed the NMA with management information.

Figure 14-6 depicts the application domain architecture. In this view, we see the involved components and the IT-buses used.

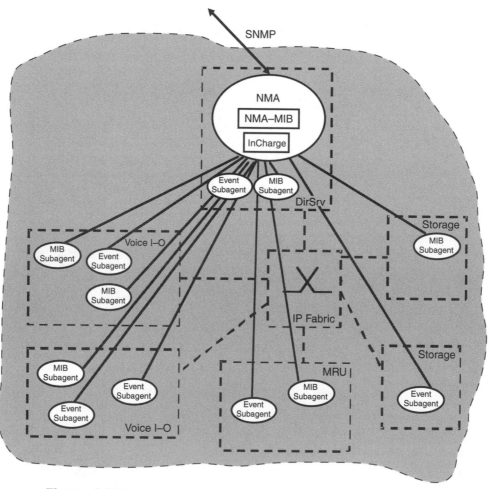

Figure 14-5
Operation and maintenance domain architecture.

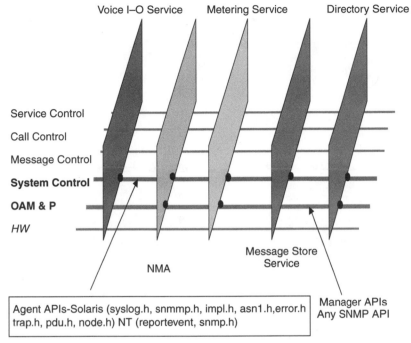

Figure 14-6
IT-bus monitoring.

Enterprise MIB

An enterprise MIB is defined to form the main O&M interface toward the system. A main interface is used by a network management system in order to manage the system.

The MIB (from now on called NMA–MIB) is mainly supporting application monitoring from a fault and configuration point of view. This means that the information contained in the NMA–MIB enables a network management system to monitor the system's overall performance and status. Some counters pertaining to certain key performance factors are also kept.

When something goes wrong (or well), a trap is emitted to the network management system. This system may then use any of the available SNMP agents within the system in order to remedy the situation.

NMA–MIB examples may be borrowed from RFC1566 and RFC2048.

OFF-THE-SHELF CORRELATOR . . . .

Before discussing how to build a correlator of events, this section presents an off-the-shelf solution, since it is better to buy than to build, in most instances.

Candle Command Center

Candle offers a suite of solutions designed for MQSeries, among other products. Their purpose is to simplify the broad, complex challenges of building, integrating and managing applications across many platforms.

- Candle Command Center® (CCC™) Management PAC for MQSeries provides advanced tools, such as prototyping and visual policy editing, that significantly enhance MQSeries network management capabilities and maintenance services.
- CCC Admin PAC makes MQSeries easier to test, configure, and monitor than the MQSeries network and applications. By combining Management PAC with Admin PAC, customers have a total solution that draws the most functionality and performance from MQSeries applications.
- CCC for MQSeries helps manage availability and performance by monitoring all resources in an MQSeries environment. CCC for MQSeries configuration is our integrated enterprise solution for simplifying configuration definition and management.
- MQSecure® protects valuable business information in MQSeries applications and defends networks against security breaches.
- A unique Candle application development tool, PQEdit™, speeds applications into production.

Candle Universal Agent SNMP

The Candle universal agent SNMP data provider uses universal agent metafiles produced from compiled SNMP–MIB files to introduce MIB applications into Candle Command Center. This site is a living repository for the latest metafiles that have been produced from MIB files. If you have a need to monitor MIB data and you do not have the associated metafile, look through this list for the associated metafile. If you do not find it within this list, send an e-mail message to snmpadm@Candle.com with the information requested at the end of the list.

This list also includes trap configuration files produced from definitions within an MIB file. Not all MIB files define traps, so not all MIBs will have a trapcnfg_enterpriseName file.[2]

BUILDING YOUR OWN CORRELATOR . . . .

It is possible to build your own correlator using SMARTS' InCharge[3] technology. This section explains NMA design.

InCharge was integrated into NMA. InCharge is a filter and correlation engine allowing NMA to keep an overall status of the messaging system, as well as identify and pinpoint the actual problem causing a disturbance. Through the system and control bus connection, InCharge will

Monitor MIB variables to

- Detect threshold violations.
- Trend them over time.
- Allow administrators to dynamically add policies. A system administrator is able to dynamically tune threshold values that better reflect the particular systems that they manage.

Receive traps from all management agents in the system to

- Process them.
- Send notifications indicating the result of the analysis. The processing of traps involves finding the root cause of a problem. The sending of notifications is done through an SNMP–TRAP to the network management system. This system may, among many things, involve sending a message, page, fax, and so on, to the responsible entity, or setting variables of the Ericsson message system MIBs.

While the problems discussed are specific to an application in a wireless messaging system, it would be desirable to include, in the model, generic problems common to application management in general. For example, if an application Y fails or is suffering performance degradation, then InCharge must indicate that Y might affect

[2]http://www.candle.com/support/softwarecenter/snmp/index.html
[3]http://www.incharge.com/incharge.html

the behavior of applications that rely on its services. That is, InCharge should identify the business impact caused by losing an application. In an analogous manner, if all applications that rely on the services of *Y* are suffering performance degradations, In-Charge should indicate that *Y* might be the root cause.

An InCharge model was developed. The class hierarchy and the class relation-ship of this model are illustrated in Figure 14-7 and Figure 14-8.

Service Traps and Events

The table that follows lists some of the states, and so on, that some classes may have. Traps and events are presented on a per-component-class basis (not complete).

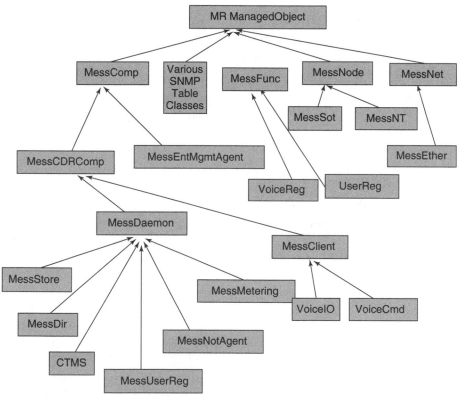

Figure 14-7
Class hierarchy for wireless message model.

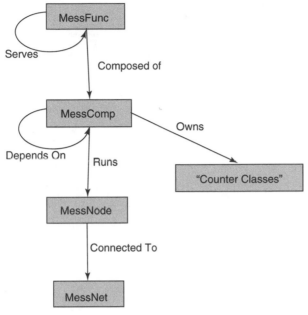

Figure 14-8
Class relationships.

Service	Event, Symptom, Trap, Problem
Call Processing service	Not a user Out of resources Local storage problem Communication lines Text-to-speech or Voice-recognition engine out of service
Call Processing service	Resources exhausted External T1/E1s UREs
Message Store	Lack of message file system space Could not bind Could not replicate Could not write to log file No activity (which could be a system control bus problem or an IP problem)

(continued)

Service	Event, Symptom, Trap, Problem
Directory Server	Lack of directory file system space Could not bind Could not replicate Could not write to log file No activity (which could be a system control bus problem or an IP problem)
User Register	Lack of user file system space Could not bind Could not replicate Could not write to the log file No activity (which can be a control bus problem or an IP problem)
Metering	Lack of meter data file system space Could not bind Could not replicate Could not write to log file No activity (which could be a system control bus problem or an IP problem) Could also cease billing, and inconsistency on the data could cause messages to be delivered to wrong entities
All Components	Routing problems Misconfigured or lack of registry information Exhausted resources (real time) Server is gone User registry information (asynchronous–nonreal time) (NA generates events) mistyped expired

Implementation

This subsection covers implementation beginning with the development environment and ending with the installation of the demo.

Development Environment Example

The making of NMA under Solaris should be as simple as this:

```
% make package.
```

The output should be an NMA.tar file. This file contains the component. In order to build the NT part, log on to an NT machine with access to the NMA directory. Go to the NMA directory and type (in an NT command shell)

```
G:\NMA> nmake -f ntevntpr.mak.
```

Example Install

The install is a simple unpack of a tar file in directory */opt* on a Solaris machine. Please observe that the */opt* directory must be used as base. Then, do the following:

```
% tar -xvf NMA.tar
% pkgadd -d pkg.
```

Follow the instructions. For the NT part, run the setup.exe and follow the instructions.

Example Service Start and Stop

The Solaris service is started and stopped using the standard Solaris methodology. In other words, a script is installed in the /etc/init.d directory. It is called NMA.agent. As a result, NMA is started at boot time etc.

In order to manually start NMA, the command issued is

```
% /etc/init.d/NMA.agent start.
```

In order to stop, issue the following command:

```
% /etc/init.d/NMA.agent stop.
```

The NT part (ntevntpr) is part of the standard NT service control manager (SCM). Start and stop is therefore performed by use of the SCM GUI.

Threads and Processes

SnmpNMAd

snmpNMAd runs on Solaris (thersls) and is the main process in this component. For example, it responds to SNMP requests from external network management systems delivering the NMA–MIB variables requested. It also emits SNMP traps to a network management system as a result of findings in InCharge.

snmpNMAd is built using the Sun Solstice Enterprise agents 1.0.2 developer tool kit. This tool kit contains all needed SNMP libraries, and so on. It also comes with a code generator (mibcodegen), based on your MIB, that will generate all needed SNMP agent code. The developer will have to add the "real variables," but all of the SNMP mechanics are there.

Therefore, snmpNMAd works together with the main component of Solstice Enterprise agent technology, snmpdx. Snmpdx runs as a daemon process and listens to the user datagram protocol (UDP) port 161 for SNMP requests. The master agent also opens another port to receive SNMP trap notifications from various subagents. These traps are forwarded to various managers, as determined by the configuration file.

Upon invocation, snmpdx reads its various configuration files and takes appropriate action by activating subagents, determining the subtree object identifier (OID) for various subagents, populating its own management information bases (MIBs), and so forth. The master agent invokes subagents, registers subagents, sends requests to subagents, receives responses from subagents, and traps notifications from subagents.

Example Files

/var/snmp/conf/NMAAgent.acl; is an agent access control file.

/var/snmp/conf/NMAAgent.rsrc; is an agent resource configuration file.

/var/snmp/mib/NMAAgent.reg; is an agent registration file.

NMAproxyd

NMAproxyd runs on Solaris (thersls) and acts as a proxy toward all of the sub-SNMP agents contained within the components. All traps received are fed into InCharge.

NMAproxyd also acts as a proxy towards the Solaris system event log. All events received are fed into InCharge. The entries are expected to follow the following format, that is they, contain at least the following string. If not, they will be ignored. For example,

```
"mcc=CallProcSrvc mcn=vp@dilbert.dilbertville, set=noResources
time=10"
```

is used to set (or create) an event, and mcc holds the name of the class. Allowed values are the class name from the above class diagram. mcn holds the name of the instance. This must be the name as stored in the directory server. The set contains a valid boolean-attribute name part of the given class. Finally, time specifies the time to live for this event, given in seconds. A time of –1 means forever. When time=-1 is used, the component must reset the event with the following log entry:

```
"mcc=CallProcSrvc mcn=vp@dilbert.dilbertville, reset=
noResources."
```

This is not fancy, but it works.

Log entries added to the NT event log shall also use the same format. This string shall be added to the first index ([0]) of the message array.

CODING EXAMPLES . . . .

Tech Talk

Will not compile.

Solaris

```
#include <syslog.h>
void *my_logger()
{
    syslog(LOG_USER|LOG_ERR,
              "mcc=CallProcSrvc mcn=vp@dilbert.dilbertville,
set=noResources time=10" );
}
```

NT

```
void *my_logger()
{
    HANDLE rsl
    eventstring = "mcc=CallProcSrvc mcn=vp@dilbert.dilbertville,
set=noResources time=10"
    rsl = RegisterEventSource( NULL, // server name for source,
NULL= Local host
                               "ABC" );  // source name for
registered handle
    str[0] = eventstring;
    ReportEvent( rsl,   // handle returned by Register
EventSource
```

```
                    EVENTLOG_WARNING_TYPE,   // event type to log
                    category,        // event category
                    eventid,              // event identifier
                    NULL,            // user security identifier
(optional)

                    1,   // number of strings to merge with message
                    0,   // size of binary data, in bytes
                    (LPCTSTR*)str, // array of strings to merge
with message

                    (void*) NULL )   // address of binary data
        }
```

Files

None.

nteventpr

nteventpr acts as a proxy towards the NT system event log. All events received are fed into InCharge through NMAproxyd.

Files

None.

InCharge

The InCharge system implements several processes. The following is worth mentioning:

- dmstart implements the model (i.e., it is the filter and correlation engine executing the NMA model).

InCharge Description

The fundamental building block of InCharge is a domain manager (DM), a software component that automates event management for a single domain. Each DM monitors observable events within its domain, correlates events to determine problems, and invokes predefined problem handlers. An InCharge system can consist of a single domain manager or may be a collection of cooperating domain managers.

The architecture of InCharge is recursive: Any domain, including the global networked system domain, can be partitioned into smaller domains. Partitioning a complex networked system into subdomains can be motivated by modularity and scalability concerns or to account for existing organizational boundaries.

Clients can subscribe to notifications of particular problems. Notifications are sent by the InCharge–DM server to the client, when the subscribed client has detected problems.

Many different applications can be designed as InCharge clients. For example, network management system graphic display applications can subscribe to an In-Charge–DM for problem notification and display results to the operator; trouble-ticketing systems can save InCharge–DM notifications to the trouble-ticket database.

InCharge/DM Internal Components

The modeler maintains a current model of the domain and its event information by polling data sources, such as network management MIBs, or by receiving asynchronous event notifications from SNMP traps. The correlator correlates domain events and operational data obtained from the modeler to analyze root cause problems and emits problem notifications to other processes. The modeler and correlator components are described in the following sections.

InCharge uses a modeling framework as its source of domain management information. This framework contains instrumentation enabling the following information to automated event analysis in a networked system: the classes and instances of managed objects in the managed domain, the problems that can originate in each object, the relationships among objects, and the propagation pattern of events along relationships. This information must be provided for all managed objects: network components, attached systems, and the services and applications that run on them. Information must also be provided about resources that do not directly participate in communication, such as power supplies or hardware.

Modeler classes are organized along an inheritance hierarchy. Inheritance is particularly valuable for modeling networked systems because typical networks contain numerous types of similar objects, such as computers, internetworking devices and databases. In addition, each generic type is represented by many different subtypes. Inheritance allows management applications to treat objects generically, ignoring their specific details when they are not relevant to the problem at hand.

The modeler emphasizes relationship properties, which capture the dependencies between managed objects. Relationship properties represent information such as a node connected to a particular link, a TCP connection layered over a particular IP link, a client using the services of a particular server, an application executed on a particular computer, and so on. Knowledge of such relationships is essential for automating problem management.

The modeler adds a layer of semantics to the data of standard MIBs. It provides a much higher level of abstraction than SNMP or CMIP MIBs and includes event management information that cannot be captured by SNMP or CMIP MIBs.

The MODEL-language compiler generates C++ code to implement classes defined in MODEL. When compiled, a codebook is created; this is the basis for the correlation.

InCharge's approach to correlation is based on coding techniques. The underlying idea of the coding approach is simple: Each problem causes many symptoms events. Symptom events can include local events in the object in which the problem originated and events propagated to related objects. We treat the set of events caused by a problem as a "code" that identifies the problem. Correlation is simply the process of "decoding" the set of observed symptoms by determining which problem has the observed symptoms as its code.

Event codes typically contain an enormous amount of redundancy, as typical systems tend to be overinstrumented. Since developers have no way to anticipate the troubleshooting processes that operators may apply, they make almost every device parameter queryable. Thus, a router can have over 5000 MIB variables. Typically, the information content of most variables is minimal; many events are symptoms of multiple problems and do not distinguish one problem from another.

The coding technique proceeds in two phases. In the codebook selection phase, a subset of events is selected for monitoring; the result of this process is called the codebook. The codebook is an optimal subset of events that must be monitored to distinguish the problems of interest from one another while ensuring the desired level of noise tolerance.

In a networked system, events can be lost or delayed, and spurious alarms can be generated. It is essential that the correlation algorithms correctly identify a problem, even in the case of "noise" in the event stream. In the decoding phase, the events in the codebook are monitored and analyzed in real time—that is, by finding the problems whose symptoms or "code" most closely match the set of observed symptoms. The coding approach reduces the complexity of real-time correlation analysis by preprocessing the event knowledge model, to optimize the number of events that must be monitored and analyzed, and by reducing correlation to a simple problem of minimal distance decoding.

To illustrate the MODEL language, the following specification provides a schematic of some of the classes in an enterprise domain. This model simply models some entities in an IP network.

```
interface Client : LogicalService {
event AbortedTransactions = #Aborted > AbortedThreshold;
attribute long #Aborted;
attribute long AbortedThreshold;
};
interface DBServer : LogicalService {
event SlowResponse = AvgResponse > ResponseThreshold;
attribute long AvgResponse;
attribute long ResponseThreshold;
};
interface TCP_Node : Node {
problem TCPPacketLoss = AbortedTransactions, SlowResponse;
propagate AbortedTransactions = Client, Underlying;
propagate SlowResponse = DBServer, Underlying;
};
interface IP_Node : Node {
problem PacketsLoss = IPDiscardedPackets, TCPPacketsLoss;
propagate TCPPacketsLoss = TCP_Node, Underlying;
event IPDiscardedPackets = DiscardedPackets > Discarded
Threshold;
attribute long DiscardedPackets;
attribute long DiscardedThreshold;
};
interface Router_Backbone : Link {
problem Failure = PacketsLoss;
propagate PacketsLoss = IP_Node, ConnectedTo;
export Failure;
};
```

The typical development life cycle of InCharge-based event management applications is as follows:

At Development Time

Event models of managed objects (when no models already exist) are written in the MODEL language. Libraries for collections of managed object classes are built by compiling MODEL specifications into C++. New class definitions can be added at any time and incorporated into a running InCharge system.

InCharge client application programs can also be developed. Examples of In-Charge clients include a graphical display of detected problems, a trouble-ticketing application, or a policy-based handler that invokes predefined handlers associated with each problem. A simple InCharge client is available as part of the basic system and can be specialized as needed.

At Runtime

Codebooks are automatically generated by the system. The codebook generation process requires as input

- The relevant class libraries.
- Specification of the current domain topology and configuration. This includes specification of all of the managed object instances in the current system, the class each object belongs to, and the values of its relationship attributes. These are used to build the modeler's management information repository.
- The current set of problem notifications to which clients of InCharge are subscribed. The causality matrix is computed and then reduced in the codebook reduction process. Once a codebook has been computed, the set of symptoms in the codebook is monitored in real time and matched against the current codebook using a minimal distance decoder. When a code is matched, InCharge notifies all clients that have subscribed to this problem. Whenever the set of relationships used to compute the current codebook changes, or the set of problems subscribed to changes, the codebook is automatically updated to reflect the current configuration.

To summarize and conclude, the InCharge system takes a different approach from other systems by combining

- A high-level specification language that extends CORBA IDL to specify event information per managed object class.
- A run-time modeler of managed object data, relationships, and event information compiled from MODEL specifications.
- A codebook correlation engine that uses observable events as problem codes to yield super fast and noise-insensitive correlation.
- A distributed architecture of cooperating domain managers that scale to arbitrarily complex systems.

Overview

Figure 14-9 shows the process overview depicted.

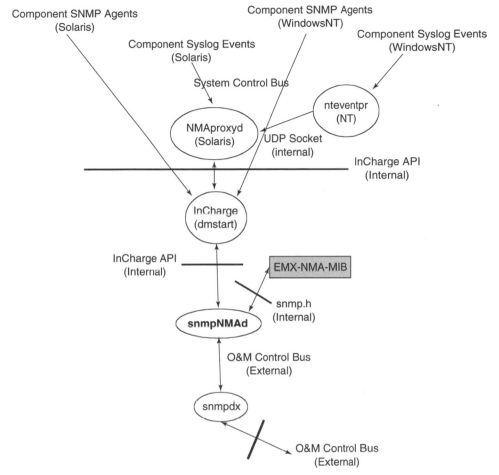

Figure 14-9
Example InCharge deployment diagram.

REFERENCES . . . .

- *Root Cause Analysis and its Role in Event Management.* SMARTS, Inc.
- *Event Modeling with MODEL Language: A Tutorial Introduction.* SMARTS, Inc.

15 Wireless Metering Service with MQI

BACKGROUND ·

This section describes a wireless metering service that uses MQI (message queue interface) within an IP architecture. Forthcoming is some background information on two kinds of metering.

Call Detail Recording

Call detail recording begins and ends with a circuit-switched telephone connection. This definition is consistent with that of the telephone industry.

In the SS7 world, this means that all Q.931 call setup information should generate events until the call is taken down. It also means all in-band signaling events are captured for engineering statistics and billing purposes.

As for the multifrequency networks, this means event records are generated for all A&B number analysis and all in-band signaling for the purpose of both billing and engineering statistics.

Message Detail Recording

Message detail recording begins when a message is committed for delivery to an MTA (message transfer agent). In terms of voice or fax mail, an event for these subsystems do not begin until someone successfully records and deposits a message to storage. After it is committed, the message may take several routes in the message handling system. For each route, the message could generate an event for recoding and billing purposes.

METERING SERVICE DESCRIPTION . . . .

The main functions of the metering service are to

- Interact with any and all components that produce meter data, specifically the call processing service.
- Interact with an external third party DPMS (data processing management system).
- Interact with the management agent or system administrator.

Essentially, metering service performs a protocol conversion from MRP (metering protocol) to FTP. If the FTP link fails, the component messages are stored by MRP. Once the FTP link is restored, MRP will continue to send messages. Lastly, the final processing, such as billing or statistical analysis, may occur on the DPMS.

PURPOSE . . . .

The metering service architecture should meet the goals of a cost-effective, effectual solution, as well as

- Achieve data integrity (i.e., ensure that CDR–AMA data has not been altered).
- Enable confidentiality (i.e., make the CDR–AMA data "unviewable without special commands").
- Be based on standards, with the exception of MRP.
- Be uniform across all system interfaces.

DEVELOPMENT ENVIRONMENT . . . .

Metering service was created with the Microsoft C++ 5.0 Enterprise edition, Microsoft Developer Studio 97, and MQSeries software.

A prototype of metering service was also created with CC WorkShop 4.2, RogueWave, & MQSeries libraries.

IT–BUS INTERFACES . . . .

Table 15.1 shows the IT–Bus interfaces used by the metering service.

LDAP

LDAP is used to obtain various configuration data from the directory server (please see "Wireless Directory" section for more information).

FTP

Metering service opens a file on the DPMS processor and writes the CDR records to that file as they arrive. If no data is received from the CPS component within an hour, an event message is generated.

SNMP

Metering service component has defined an SNMP MIB, MeterDll.mib.

MRP

The input and output connections to all event-generating services included in this system are through MRP.

The path this service is listening on is **ANY.TO.METER**.

The meter service expects a fixed-length message, but MRP is flexible and can handle messages of varying lengths.

Table 15.1   Metering Service IT–Bus

IT–Bus	Protocol	Service
System Control	LDAP	Directory lookup
	MRP	Metering service
OAM&P	SNMP	Management agent
	Report event (NT)	
	FTP	Data processing management system

Service Start Events

- Allocate and initialize internal structures and alert system manager of progress.
- Establish needed channel(s) with MRP.
- Establish link and log on as FTP agent for data server–DPMS interface.
- Generate a "component start event" in the event log.
- Open the session with the metering service (with itself) component and the SNMP component. Report any missing services at start-up in the event log.
- Tell any component that meter agent is in service.

Metering Service Events Stop

- Indicate that metering service is not in service through setting the operating status in the MIB.
- Unassign and deallocate any input channel(s).
- Unassign, deallocate, and log off any output channel(s).
- Generate a "service stop event" in the event log.
- Terminate the metering service component.

Crash

In the event of an uncontrolled stop (crash) of the service, the SNMP agent detects the absence of the service, which generates an SNMP trap (belly up) and logs an event in the event log file.

Alarm and Report Event Handling

When a persistent failure occurs and is remedied, alarms and alarm-ceasing instructions are generated and sent as SNMP traps. The following alarms are generated by the metering service:

- Failure to find resource.
- Failure to connect to resource.

Report Events

Report events are generated and sent as ReportEvents to the NT event log. The following report events are generated by the metering service.

- Service started.
- Service stopped.
- Failure to connect to SNMP agent.

Meter Data Handling

Metering service was configured to receive a message of 256 bytes. The content of the message may vary (text or binary). However, in the prototype, text messages were received from the following sources:

- CDR and MDR from the CPS (call processing service).

Directory Server

At start-up, the metering service component must fetch information in the component directory server. Below is an example of a metering service component entry in an LDAP directory server:

```
dn: mcn=MeteringAgent@peon.dilbertville, msn=Dilbertville,
o=MessagingSystem, c=US
objectclass: messagingcomponent
mcn: Meteringagent@peon.dilbertville
mcc: MeterDataRepos
rev-level: Beta 0.9
host: peon
port: 0
service: METERING-Service
patch-level: 0
component-path: c:\Meterservice\Meterservice.exe
control-bus-name: ANY.TO.METER
snmp-dll-path: c:\METERDLL\Meterdll.dll
smtp-wait-to: 40
description: Dilbertville Metering Service Services
dpmsname: wally
```

ARCHITECTURE FOR METER DATA TRANSFER . . . .

Figure 15-1 shows a unified modeling language (UML) processor diagram of the system for the metering service:

Tech Talk

It is possible to have one processor perform all of these tasks.

Explanation Of Processor Diagram

Table 15.2 explains the duties of each of the processors.

Acronyms

- CDR—call detail recording—A feature of a telephone system allowing the system to collect and record information on outgoing phone calls—who made them, to whom they were made, what time of day they were placed, how long they took, and so on. It is usually needed if you are to install a call accounting system on a DPMS. In North America, CDR is also referred to as AMA.

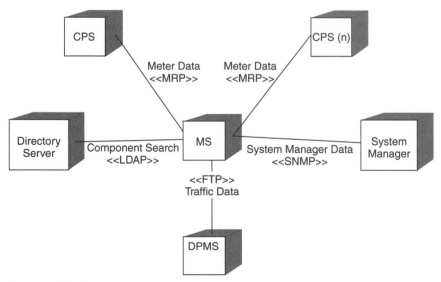

Figure 15-1
Metering service.

Table 15.2 Processors

Processor	Description
CPS	The Call Processing Service generates the call records. If the notification feature is active, the Notification Agent shall also generate records. Multiple nodes are supported.
MS	Metering Service consolidates the CDRs for delivery to the DPMS.
Directory	When metering is started, the Directory is consulted in order to obtain site-specific information about an interface of the other components.
DPMS	DPMS is where the final processing of the CDR takes place.
System Manager	The system manager listens for metering traps and events. It provides a real-time view of the metering component. For an example of a system manager, see the NMA service description.

- AMA—automatic message accounting—This is equivalent to CDR, but is specific to North America.
- CAS—call accounting system—This system is used to record information about telephone calls, organize that information, and, if requested, prepare reports or create bills.
- DPMS—data processing management system—Mainframe computer environment in which call accounting and statistics may be performed.
- FTP—file transfer protocol—This protocol is used between the metering service component and the DPMS processor.
- CPS—call processing service—This system deals with call processing and computer telephony standards, like S.100. The call processing service is a pure virtual base class of CPS.
- MEMA—messaging enterprise management agent.
- MDR—message detail recording—This data is produced by subsystems that process messages instead of calls. In the prototype, this data was generated by the CPS component.
- MRP—meter server protocol—This protocol is based on standard queuing API. IBM's MQSeries API was selected to transport the CDR.
- SNMP—simple network management protocol—This protocol is used between components and the system manager.
- LDAP—lightweight directory access protocol—This protocol is used when a component wishes to learn site-specific information in connection with its interfaces, among other things.
- Meter data—This data is the composite of MDR and CDR.

16 Media Conversion—An Exemplary Wireless Service

BACKGROUND ·························

Media conversion services are useful when converting between the various media types, as shown in Table 16.1 For example, this service is even used when converting a fax message to a voice message, as discussed later. Other media conversions such as voice to text are under consideration, but are not explored in this book.

What Is Media Conversion?

The MHS (message handling system) uses media conversion algorithms when converting between different types of encoded information and while following a fixed set of rules (format and coding aspects). Basically, all messages are converted to text for the purpose of converting to other formats. This is consistent with X.409. Text is the lowest common denominator for most networks.

Table 16.1 Possible Media Conversions

	SMS	Pager	Audio	Fax	CRT/NC	Video
Text	X	X	X	X	X	O
Numeric	X	X	X	X	X	O
Voice	X	X	X	X	X	O
Fax	X	X	X	X	X	O
Video	O	O	O	O	O	O

Legend: *X—Available*
O—Future Trend

What Kinds of Conversions Are There (X.409 Specification)?

- Explicit conversion—A conversion in which the originator selects both the initial and the final EITs (encoding information type).
- Implicit conversion—A conversion in which the MTA (message transfer agent) selects the final EITs based on the initial EITs and the capabilities of the UA (user agent).
- Conversion—with loss or loss-prohibited.

One type of conversion from the Internet domain is

- MIME—multipurpose Internet mail extensions, permits implicit conversion by the mail system.

What the Media Conversion Service Does

The media conversion service reads contents of a unified inbox to wireless subscribers, whether the message is voice (audio or wave), fax (TIF), or documents (text, RTF, DOC, etc.). This means that the conversions would be from fax to speech, text to speech, fax cover pages to speech (including handwriting conversion), GSM compressed audio to uncompressed audio, or ADPCM compressed audio to uncompressed audio.

What Media Conversions Are Covered

- Text to speech.
- Fax to speech.
- Handwriting to speech.

MULTILINGUAL CONVERSION . . . .

Another area of exploration is language conversion. Converting languages (i.e., English to Swedish) is necessary, since E-mail may arrive using a different character set or language inappropriate for the speech engine. Naturally, if you were to supply Swedish text to an English text-to-speech engine, the end result would be noise. This leaves a developer two options for conversion: either convert text from one language to another with a language translator (language-to-language) engine or use a speech engine that expects English text as input and produces audio output in some other language. Furthermore, the process then becomes text-to-text conversion followed by text to speech, which is a good thing when it comes to distributing the processing. One book worth reading is *Multilingual Text-To-Speech Synthesis: The Bell Labs Approach*, by Richard Sproat.

Table 16.2 contains an example matrix of possible conversions, as of the end of 1998. To complete the matrix would require engines from L&H, Telia, University of Austria, and others. Some conversions may require an interim translation to English before completion. A table such as this would be useful for keeping track of the development of new conversions.

E-MAIL CONVERSION ·

E-mail has its own nuisances that require conversion in order for them to become audible to the wireless terminal or cellular phone. Take, for example, the smiley face ":-)"; the text-to-speech engine would have to produce a wave file containing an au-

Table 16.2 Example Language-Conversion Matrix

	En-glish	Span-ish	French	Portu-guese	Ger-man	Italian	Man-darin	Swe-dish	Aust-ralian	Brit-ish
English	X	X	X	X	X	X	X	X	X	X
Spanish	X	X	N/A	TBD	TBD	TBD	TBD	TBD	TBD	TBD
French	X	N/A	TBD	TBD	TBD	TBD	TBD	TBD	TBD	TBD
Portuguese	X	TBD	TBD	TBD	TBD	TBD	TBD	TBD	TBD	TBD
German	X	TBD	TBD	TBD	TBD	TBD	TBD	TBD	TBD	TBD
Italian	X	TBD	TBD	TBD	TBD	TBD	TBD	TBD	TBD	TBD
Mandarin	X	TBD	TBD	TBD	TBD	TBD	TBD	TBD	TBD	TBD
Swedish	X	TBD	TBD	TBD	TBD	TBD	TBD	TBD	TBD	TBD
Australian	X	TBD	TBD	TBD	TBD	TBD	TBD	TBD	TBD	TBD
British	X	TBD	TBD	TBD	TBD	TBD	TBD	TBD	TBD	TBD

Legend: TBD—To be determined. N/A—Not available. X—Available

dible smiley face. Companies like L&H provide add-on packages to support this type of conversion.

TEXT-TO-WAV FILE SERVICE . . . .

This section explains integrating the host-based text-to-wav file service into the IP Architecture. Text-to-wav file service is used to enhance the TUI (telephone user interface) through a text-to-speech engine. The service interaction is as follows:

- Services that need text-to-wav file conversion, specifically the CPS.
- Interact with a system manager.
- Interact with the LDAP server for configuration information.
- Interact with the MS server to provide traffic information for billing, among other things.

Tech Talk

The SNMP interface supports a subset of the CCITT X.208 (ASN.1) and encoding using CCITT X.209 Basic Encoding Rules (BER).

Input File Format

ASCII text file is expected by T2W.

Output File Format

Essentially, this service performs a media conversion from a text-to-wav file, specifically, an output file with these characteristics:

- PCM,22.050 kHz.
- 16 bit.
- Mono.
- Windows NT WAV RIFF (resource interchange file format) chunk encoded.

Tech Talk

This is configurable by way of Windows NT–Control Panel–Multimedia icon.

Speech Command Option

The output of the speech engine has these characteristics:

- Female.
- English.
- 135 words per minute.
- Engine configurable.
- If the media conversion fails, an audible error message is returned in place of the message.

Last, the media conversion can take place either locally on the MRU or distributed onto another NT server.

IT–Bus Interfaces

Table 16.3 shows the IT-Bus interfaces used by the T2W Service.

LDAP

LDAP is used to obtain various configuration data from the directory server.

MDP

The details of the conversion are output to the MS service.

Table 16.3   IT–Bus

IT–BUS	Protocol	Service
System Control	LDAP MDP System call/BMQ IPC	Directory lookup Meter data protocol (CPS to T2W) (T2W to Speech engine)
OAM&P	SNMP Report event (NT)	Management agent

SNMP

T2W service has defined an SNMP MIB, txt2wavDll.mib.

System Call and BMQ

The T2W service receives as input a text file name, in string form, and returns the same file name with the "wav" extension.

System Call

The file to be converted was passed to T2W through a system call parameter list.

Distributed Processing

Distributed computing was tried using MQSeries. CPS and T2W exchange remote procedure calls through the MQ software infrastructure, ergo the new protocol BMQ. This is the same infrastructure used by the MS service.

IPC (COM API)

IPC (interprocess communications) is the exchange of data between two or more processes or applications.

During the conversion process, the T2W accesses the text-to-speech engine component through IPC, which the COM API supports automatically.

On the same machine, secure IPC is used by T2W. (See Figure 16-1.)

SERVICE START LIST OF EVENTS . . . .

Here is a list of the events that occur at the start of T2W:

- Internal structures are allocated and initialized.
- System manager is alerted of progress.
- Needed channel(s) with text-to-speech engine are established.
- Input file and format are validated.

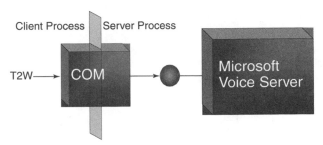

Figure 16-1
Interprocess communications.

- A "service start event" is generated in the event log.
- The session with the meter data repository service and the SNMP service is opened. Any services missing at start-up are recorded in the event log. Any service is told that T2W is in service.

SERVICE STOP LIST OF EVENTS . . . .

Here is a list of the events that occur when T2W stops:

- Indicate that T2W is not in service by setting the operating status in the MIB.
- Any input channel(s) are unassigned and deallocated.
- Any output channel(s) arc unassigned, deallocated, and logged off.
- A "service stop event" is generated in the event log.
- The T2W service is terminated.

CRASH . . . .

In the event of an uncontrolled stop (crash) of the service, the SNMP agent detects the absence of the service, generating an SNMP trap (belly up) and logs an event in the event log file.

ALARM HANDLING . . . .

Alarms and alarm ceasing are generated and sent as SNMP traps when persistent failures occur, and when they are remedied. The following alarms are generated by T2W:

- Failure to find resource.
- Failure to connect to resource.

REPORT EVENT HANDLING . . . .

Report events are generated and sent as ReportEvents to the NT event log. The following report events are generated by T2W:

- Service started.
- Service stopped.
- Failure to connect to SNMP agent.

Text-to-Speech Media Handling

T2W was configured to receive a message as large as the heap space on the machine executing the program. The content of the message may be only text!

Directory Server

At start-up, the T2W service must fetch the information from the directory server. Figure 16-2 shows an example of a T2W service entry in an LDAP directory server.

ARCHITECTURE FOR TYPICAL TEXT-TO-SPEECH . . .

Figure 16-3 shows the architecture of a typical text-to-speech engine. The conversion process begins when the application hands the engine a string of text—such as, "The man walked down 56th St." The text analysis module converts numbers into words, identifies punctuation—such as commas, periods, and semicolons—converts

```
dn: mcn=T2WAgent@peon.dilbertville, msn=Dilbertville,
o=MessagingSystem, c=US
objectclass: messagingcomponent
mcn: tdragent@peon.dibertville
mcc: Text2WavFile
rev-level: Beta 0.9
host: tina
port: 0
service: T2W-Service
patch-level: 0
component-path: c:\txt2wavService\txt2wav.exe
control-bus-name: ANY.TO.TRAFFIC
snmp-dll-path: c:\TXT2WAVDLL\txt2wavdll.dll
snmp-wait-to: 40
description: Dilbertville Text To Wav File Services
```

Figure 16-2
Service entry in LDAP.

abbreviations to words, and even figures out how to pronounce acronyms. Some
acronyms are spelled out (MSJ), whereas others are pronounced as a word (FEMA).
The sample sentence would be converted to something like

```
<beginStatement>
The man walked down fifty sixth street
<endStatement>.
```

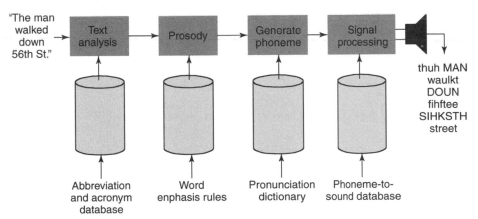

Figure 16-3
Typical text-to-speech architecture.

Text analysis is quite complex, because written language can be so ambiguous. A human has no trouble pronouncing "St. John St." as "Saint John Street," but a computer, in typically mechanical fashion, might come up with "Street John Street," unless a clever programmer gives it some help. Once the text is converted to words, the engine figures out what words should be emphasized by making them louder or longer, or giving them a higher pitch. Other words may be deemphasised. Without word emphasis, or "prosody," the result is a monotone voice that sounds robotic, like something out of a 1950s sci-fi flick. After adding prosody, the sample sentence might end up like this:

```
<beginStatement>
<de-emphasize>the <emphasize>man walked
<emphasize>down fifty <emphasize>sixth street<pause>.
<endStatement>.
```

Next, the text-to-speech engine determines how the words are pronounced, either by looking them up in a pronunciation dictionary or by running an algorithm that guesses the pronunciation. Some text strings have ambiguous pronunciations, such as "read." The engine must use context to disambiguate the pronunciations. The result of this analysis is the original sentence expressed as phonemes: "Th-uh M-A-Nw-au-l-k-tD-OU-Nf-ih-f-t-eeS-IH-K-S-TH s-t-r-ee-t."

Next, the phonemes are parsed and their pronunciations are retrieved from a phoneme-to-sound database that numerically describes what the individual phonemes sound like. If speech were simple, this table would have only 44 entries, one for each English phoneme (or whatever language is used). In practice, each phoneme is modified slightly by its neighbors, so the table often has as many as 1600 (or more) entries. Depending on the implementation, the table might store either a short wave recording or parameters that describe the mouth and tongue shape. Either way, the sound database values are finally smoothed together using signal processing techniques, and the digital audio signal is sent to an output device (such as a PC sound card), then to speakers, and finally to your ears.

ARCHITECTURE FOR MEDIA CONVERSION . . . .

This section explains both the T2W client and the text-to-speech engine.

Inside T2W Client

The text-to-wav file processes and procedures occuring inside the T2W client program are explained here.

Tech Talk

This program is written mainly in the "C" language, since no class libraries were available, other than the notification class, at the time this program was made. However, now with SAPI 4.0, it should be possible to produce a complete C++ product. In fact, it was tried, but there were some conflicts with the audio compression libraries. This problem lead to the creation of the complementary program _wav2vox_.

Apartment Thread

The rules of COM apply when working with this text-to-speech engine. The first rule is to create an apartment thread model. This is necessary for the message pump. Figure 16-4 shows the necessary steps for starting the model, and of course, there is an EndOle function.

Tech Talk

OLE is the precursor of COM.

FIND AND SELECT ENGINE MODE . . . .

T2W provides a way for the user to select or change the sound of the computer voice by using the FindAndSelect function.

```
BOOL BeginOLE (void)
{
   DWORD     dwVer;
                        // Initialize OLE
   SetMessageQueue(96);
   dwVer = CoBuildVersion();         //check if free thread
                                     //allowed
   if (rmm != HIWORD(dwVer)) return FALSE;
                     // error
   if (FAILED(CoInitialize(NULL))) return FALSE;
                     //new thread to enter apartment
   return TRUE;
}
```

Figure 16-4
Apartment thread model.

Tech Talk

There is another function, called voice text, that uses whatever the user has selected as the system default.

Most people want their computers to always speak with the same voice. The voice quality (male or female, the pitch, and so on) is specified through a Control Panel applet, called Microsoft Voice, installed as part of the Microsoft Voice setup (for more information, see the sidebar). It is possible to programmatically change the voice with a low-level API. It is not advisable for most applets; it might annoy users who have taken the trouble to select their ideal cybervoice.

Next is the mechanics, selection of the text-to-speech engine mode using the TTSMODEINFO structure and specifications. For this specific function, shown in Figure 16-5, the desired mode is passed as a parameter. The function then returns a pointer to the interface, the desired TTS engine object.

WAVE AND AUDIO DESTINATION . . . .

At this point, the engine is aware of the client thread, since we created an OLE COM object that supports these three interfaces: IUnknown, IAudioDest, and IAudioDestFile.

Next, we defined and used IAudioFile custom interface to specify which file should receive the audio output. To clarify, when speaking of COM, we speak in terms of Class IDs and Interface IDs; both are unique.

After the engine selects a wave format, it generates the engine object and returns from the call to the ITTSFind::Select member function (See Figure 16-6.)

FEATURES OF AUDIODEST AND AUDIODESTFILE . .

This custom audio destination permits us to perform the following tasks:

- Send speech output to an audio file for processing at a later time.
- Mix the outgoing audio with another signal, such as sound effects or audio from another text-to-speech engine. (Currently, multimedia does not support the sharing of a wav device.)
- Play audio on hardware that does not support a multimedia driver.
- Apply special effects to the text-to-speech voice, such as reverberation, echo, or distortion.
- "Fool" the text-to-speech engine into thinking that the audio is playing several milliseconds before it is actually being played to give animated graphics time to draw.

```
PITTSCENTRAL FindAndSelect (PTTSMODEINFO pTTSInfo)//i.e. "Female"
{
   HRESULT          hRes;
   TTSMODEINFO         ttsResult;
   WCHAR            Zero = 0;
   PITTSFIND        pITTSFind;
   PITTSCENTRAL     pITTSCentral;


   hRes = CoCreateInstance(CLSID_TTSEnumerator, NULL, CLSCTX_ALL, IID_ITTSFind,
                                        (void**)&pITTSFind);

   if (FAILED(hRes)) return NULL;

   hRes = pITTSFind->Find(pTTSInfo, NULL, &ttsResult);

   if (hRes)
      {
      pITTSFind->Release();
      return NULL;      // error
      }


   hRes = CoCreateInstance(CLSID_AudioDestFile, NULL, CLSCTX_ALL,

                                        (void**)&gpIAF);
   if (hRes)
      {
      pITTSFind->Release();
      return NULL;
      }



      hRes = pITTSFind->Select(ttsResult.gModeID,
&pITTSCentral, gpIAF);



         pITTSFind->Release();
         return NULL;
         };

// free random stuff up
   pITTSFind->Release();
   return pITTSCentral;} //End of Find & Select
```

Figure 16-5
Find and select engine mode.

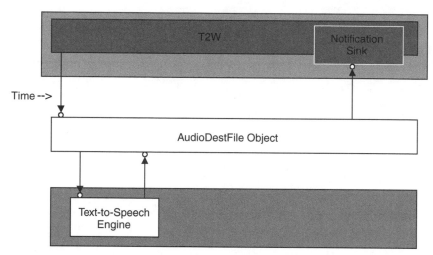

Figure 16-6
TTS objects.

REGISTRATION OF NOTIFICATIONS CLASS . . . .

Since our client application T2W needs to know when the text is finished processing, we must register a sink to receive notifications. This activates the notification object CtestNotify. (See Figure 16-7.)

TEXTDATA AND THE MESSAGE PUMP . . . .

The media conversion takes place when gpITTSCentral->TextData is issued from within the callback function DialogProc. (See Figure 16-9.)

Once TextData is called, notification messages are delivered to the T2W. Therefore, a message pump is needed to process the notifications. Figure 16-8 shows a list of messages that arrive over the notification interface.

```
gpIITSCentral->Register((void*)&gNotify,        // notify global class
                        IID_ITTSNotifySink,     //notifysinkIID
                        &dwRegKey,              // flags
                    );                          // VTSITEINFO* not used
```

Figure 16-7
Register.

```
TextData function call
1 AudioStart
2 Visual
3 Visual
4 Visual (loop continues until text-to-wav process is complete)
5 AudioStop
Release
```

Figure 16-8
Message pump.

CALLBACK . . . .

TextData is called from within a Callback function named DialogProc(HWND hWnd, UINT uMsg, WPARAM wParam, LPARAM lParam). This is a special kind of function with the following characteristics:

- Callback functions provide a way for the server to execute code on the client.
- Callbacks are special cases of remote calls that execute as part of a single thread.
- Callbacks are used in place of FAR PASCAL in application callback routines, such as window procedures and dialog procedures.
- Only the connection-oriented and local protocol sequence support the callback attribute.

Tech Talk

SAPI 4.0 supports object Callback. Object specifies the name of a class module containing methods that receive notifications from the voice–text automation object. This is an alternative implementation. The class module must contain a SpeakingStarted method and a SpeakingDone method (i.e., *Vtxt.Callback = "TESTVCMD.VTxtSink"*).

The call to TextData happens asynchronously; that is, control returns immediately—the application does not need to wait for the computer to finish speaking (but when it does, its notification is from an ITTSNotifySink Command). The thread of execution returns to DialogProc. T2W has two threads (WndMain, and DialogProc).

Like other Win32 API functions, ITTSCentral::TextData accepts ANSI or Unicode, as determined by the compile-time #define symbol UNICODE.

```
char szSpeak[10240]="";                // TEXT buffer
SDATA data;                            //
int ifh;
strcpy(oname,gszFile);
slth-strlen(oname);
for(sidx=0;sidx<slth;++sidx)           /* get the prefix*/
     if(oname[sidx]=='.')
        break;
oname[sidx]=0;                         // convert to asciz
strcat(oname,".wav");                  // attack on our suffix
                                       // open the TEXT file
if((ifh=_open(gszFile,_O_TEXTI_O_RDONLY))!=3){
     MessageBox(hWnd,"input file not found",NULL,MB_OK);
     gpITTSCentral->AudioReset();
     EndDialog (hWnd, WM_QUIT);
     return FALSE;
}
                                       // read in the TEXT file
strcpy(gszFile,oname);
if (_read(ifh,szSpeak,10240)==0) {
     MessageBox(hWnd,"read input file error or empty",NULL,MB_OK);
     gpITTSCentral->AudioReset ();
          EndDialog (hWnd,WM_QUIT);
     return FALSE;
}
                                       // classes use Wide Char instead of char ptr
MultiByteToWideChar (CP_ACP, 0, gszFile, -1,
     gwszFile, sizeof(gwszFile) / sizeof(WCHAR));

if (gpIAF->Set(gwszFile, 1)) {         // open the file WAV file.
          MessageBox (hWnd, "usage: destfile -[fn].txt", NULL, MB_OK);
          gpITTSCentral->AudioReset ();
          EndDialog (hWnd, WM_QUIT);
          return FALSE;
}
                                       //This starts the TTS engine and
                                       //notification. The text conversion begins.
data.dwSize = strlen(szSpeak) + 1;
data.pData = szSpeak;
gpITTSCentral->TextData (  CHARSET_TEXT,
                   TTSDATAFLAG_TAGGED,
                   data, NULL,
                   IID_ITTSBufNotifySink);
```

Figure 16-9
Speech API (AudioDestFile,TTSEnumerator).

INSIDE THE TEXT-TO-SPEECH ENGINE . . . .

What follows in this section are the events occurring behind the scenes from the programmer within the Microsoft source code, which we do not possess.

When an engine first receives the address of the IUnknown interface for the audio destination file, it calls the QueryInterface member function for a variety of interfaces, such as those that control specific hardware. If the engine cannot find any of these custom interfaces, it eventually tries the IAudioDest and IAudioDestFile interfaces. The engine then calls the IAudioDestFile::Set file member function. After that, the engine calls the IAudio::WaveFormatSet member function with several different wave formats, starting with custom formats and working its way down to pulse code modulation (PCM), if none of the earlier formats are supported. (The application must determine which formats are acceptable.) If the engine cannot find any interfaces or formats that it can use, it fails to create an engine object.

Architecture for T2W Data Transfer

Figure 16-10 shows the unified modeling language (UML) processor diagram of the system for the T2W:

Tech Talk

It is possible to have one processor perform all of these tasks.

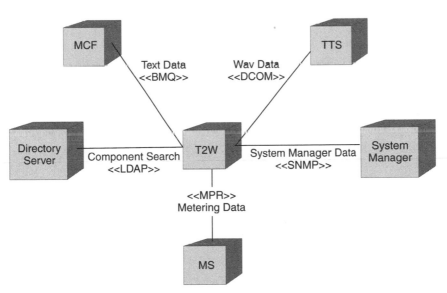

Figure 16-10
T2W processor diagram.

Explanation of Processor Diagram

Table 16.4 explains each processor's duties:

How to Obtain the API

The Microsoft Research Area hosts the SAPI 4.0 SDK Suite. The URL is
http://www.research.microsoft.com/research/srg/download.htm.

Acronyms

- BMQ—Batch MQSeries protocol for remote procedure calls.
- ASCII—American standard code for information interchange.
- COM—Component object model interface.
- MEMA—Messaging enterprise manager agent.
- TTS—Text-to-speech process.
- W2V—Wave-to-vox program. VOX is defined as voice-operated exchange file format.
- T2W—Text-to-wav file program.
- RIFF—Resource interchange file format; the Microsoft preferred format for multimedia files. The RIFF file I–O functions work with the basic

Table 16.4 Processor Descriptions

Processor	Description
CPS	The CPS retrieves the text data and sends it to T2W. T2W then consumes the text data and produces the wave data. Multiple nodes are supported by way of BMQ.
MS	Metering service records the conversion events for creating billing or charging records.
Directory	When T2W is started, the directory is consulted in order to obtain site-specific information about an interface of the other services.
TTS	TTS is the text-to-speech engine.
T2W	T2W is where the text-to-speech engine performs the conversions.
System Manager	The system manager listens for T2W traps and events. It provides a real-time view of the T2W service.

buffered and unbuffered file I–O services. It is possible to open, read, and write RIFF files in the same way as other file types. For detailed information about RIFF, see AVIFile functions and macros.

- MS—Meter data repository protocol.

References

"MSDN CD-ROM" article, Talk to Your Computer and Have It Answer Back with the Microsoft Speech API.

"MSDN CD-ROM" article, Custom Audio-Destination Object.

AUDIO COMPRESSION SERVICE . . . .

This section explains the work performed to integrate the host-based wav-to-vox file service into the IP architecture.

More importantly, this report explains how to interface the audio compression manager and explains certain aspects of streaming technology within the Windows NT environment.

Last, a conclusion was drawn regarding how practical it would be to use the audio compression manager of Microsoft in a product.

Tech Talk

Dialogic and APEX use VOX files and their format was found to be proprietary. Therefore, it was necessary to reverse-engineer VOX files and the CODEC of Dialogic. This document explains that effort.

Wav-to-Vox Conversion Description

The main functions of the wav-to-vox (W2V) service are to

- Interact with any and all services that need wav-to-vox file conversion, specifically the CPS.
- Interact with any and all services that need audio compression, specifically the CPS.
- Interact with the management agent or the system administrator.
- Interact with the LDAP server for configuration information.
- Interact with the MS server to provide billing information.

Furthermore, the SNMP interface supports a subset of the CCITT X.208 (ASN.1) and encoding using CCITT X.209 basic encoding rules (BER).

Input Wav File Format

This service expects a wave file with these characteristics:

- PCM.
- 22.050 kHz.
- 16 bit.
- Mono.
- Windows NT WAV RIFF (resource interchange file format) chunk encoded.
- Size is limited to available virtual memory (it worked with an 18-Mbytes file).

Tech Talk

This is configurable through the Windows NT–Control Panel–Multimedia icon.

Output Vox File Format

VOX is defined as voice-operated exchange file format.

Essentially, this service performs a compression and file format conversion, specifically an output file with these characteristics:

- Without header fields and information.
- Microsoft CCITT G.711 u-Law CODEC.
- 8000 kHz.
- 8 bit.
- Mono.

Tech Talk

This is configurable through the Windows NT–Control Panel–Multimedia icon.

CONSOLE OUTPUT ·

Figure 16-11 Shows the output from the wav2vox executable file.

Reverse-Engineering Effort

APEX (service creation and call flow tool) supports these four rates of encoding:

1. ADP6—ADPCM 6-bit sample.
2. ADP8—ADPCM 8-bit sample.
3. PCM6—PCM 6-bit sample.
4. PCM8—PCM 8-bit sample.

It was learned, through trial and error, that Dialogic (MRU) supports the same four rates of encoding, but with these exceptions:

Tech Talk

This was not a trivial task, given the fact that there are an infinite number of frequencies.

```
Driver found (hadid: 142AE8H)
  Short name: Microsoft CCITT G.711
  Long name: Microsoft CCITT G. 711 A-Law and u-Law CODEC
  Copyright: Copyright (c) 1993-1996 Microsoft Corporation
  Licensing:
  Features: Compresses and decompresses CCITT G.711 A-Law and
  u-Law audio data.
Dest. Driver format: 8 bits, 8000 samples per second
PCM format: 16 bits, 8000 samples per second
Converting to intermediate PCM format...
Converted OK
Converting to final format...
Converted OK
output file f:scott.vox already exists
Ok to replace (y or n)? y
Source wave had 116270 bytes
Converted wave has 21092 bytes
Compression ratio is 5.512517
```

Figure 16-11
Example console output.

1. PCM8 – 8-bit ulaw at 8-kHz frequency. Meets CCITT standards.
2. The other three APEX formats are supported by the Dialogic DSPs. No host-based processing is needed.

Tech Talk

ADP8 does not conform exactly to the ADPCM standard, resulting in distorted audio output. Therefore, use of this format is not recommended.

Compression Option

The audio compression manager (ACM) from Microsoft supports 12 CODECs at any one time. Adding and removing a CODEC is performed through WINDOWS NT–Settings–Multimedia Properties–Devices. The enumeration can also be changed. Table 16.5 is from a typical NT workstation.

IT–Bus Interfaces

Table 16.6 shows the IT–Bus interfaces used by the W2V Service.

Table 16.5 Audio Compression CODEC Enumeration

Audio Compression CODEC	Name
1	Microsoft CCITT G.711 Audio CODEC
2	Microsoft PCM converter
3	Microsoft ADPCM audio CODEC
4	IMA ADPCM audio CODEC
5	Microsoft GSM 6.10 audio CODEC
6	DSP Group TrueSpeech™ audio CODEC
7	Lernout and Hauspie CODECs
8	msg723.acm
9	VivoActive audio CODEC version 2.0.0
10	Voxware audio CODECs (VDK32118)
11	Fraunhofer IIS MPEG Layer-3 CODEC
12	Indeo® audio software

Table 16.6   W2V IT-Bus Interfaces

IT-BUS	Protocol	Service
System Control	LDAP MDP System Call and BMQ IPC	Directory lookup Metering data protocol (T2W to W2V) (W2V to ACM)
OAM&P	SNMP Report event (NT) SMTP	Management Agent

LDAP

LDAP is used to obtain various configuration data from the directory server.

SNMP

W2V service has defined an SNMP MIB, wav2voxDll.mib.

System Call and BMQ

The W2V service receives as input a wave file name, in string form, and returns the same file name with the "vox" extension.

System Call

The file to be converted was passed to W2V through a system call.

Distributed Processing

Distributed computing was tried using MQSeries. T2W and W2V exchange remote procedure calls through the MQ software infrastructure, ergo the new protocol BMQ. This is the same infrastructure used by the MS service.

IPC (COM API)

IPC (interprocess communications) is the exchange of data between two or more processes or applications.

During the conversion process, the W2V accesses the ACM component through the IPC, which the COM API supports automatically.

On the same machine, secure IPC is used by W2V. (See Figure 16-12.)

SERVICE START EVENTS . . . .

- Allocate and initialize internal structures.
- Alert system manager of progress.
- Establish needed channel(s) with ACM.
- Validate input file and format.
- Generate a "service start event" in the event log.
- Open the session with the metering service and the SNMP service. Report any missing services at start-up in the event log. Tell any service that W2V is in service.

SERVICE STOP EVENTS . . . .

- Indicate that W2V is not in service by setting the operating status in the MIB.
- Unassign and deallocate any input channel(s).
- Unassign, deallocate, and log off any output channel(s).
- Generate a "service stop event" in the event log.
- Terminate the W2V service.

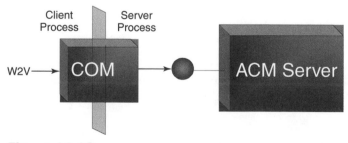

Figure 16-12
W2V interprocess communications.

CRASH ·······························

In the event of an uncontrolled stop (crash) of the service, the SNMP agent detects the absence of the service, generating an SNMP trap (belly up) and logging an event in the event log file.

ALARM HANDLING ························

Alarms and alarm ceasing are generated and sent as SNMP traps when a failure occurs and is persistent, and when it is remedied. The following alarms are generated by W2V:

- Failure to find resource.
- Failure to connect to resource.

Report Event Handling

Report events are generated and sent as ReportEvents to the NT event log. The following report events are generated by W2V:

- Service started.
- Service stopped.
- Failure to connect to SNMP agent.

Audio Compression Handling

W2V was configured to receive a wave file of size equal to the system memory, which includes total available memory after applications are loaded, plus swap space.

Playing small .wav files with W2V requires little buffer management; the entire sound can be loaded into memory and played. With larger ewav files, though, you should be more efficient in your memory usage, especially if you will be playing multiple sounds simultaneously.

Streaming is the recommended technique for W2V. This technique uses a small buffer to play a large file by filling the buffer with data from the file at the same rate that data is taken from the buffer and played.

DIRECTORY SERVER ....

At start-up, the W2V service must fetch information in the directory server. Figure 16-13 shows an example of a W2V service entry in an LDAP directory server.

ACM SERVER ....

An ACM server is accessed with a set of API functions that allow a client to perform compressions, decompressions, format conversions, and filtering operations on waveform file data.

The ACM is implemented as a dynamic-link library, named *msacm32.dll*. Applications that link with the ACM can call its API functions. The ACM is also used by the Windows NT® wave mapper, *msacm32.drv*, so applications that specify the wave mapper as an input or output device make indirect use of the ACM. To view a diagram that illustrates the relationship of the ACM to other Windows NT audio software, please see Figure 16-14.

Descriptions of the ACM API functions are provided in the Win32 SDK. ACM API functions begin with a prefix of **acm.**

The ACM calls installable, user-mode drivers to perform conversions. Most ACM drivers can be installed with the Control Panel's Multimedia applet and are

```
dn: mcn=W2VAgent@carol.dilbertville,
msn=Dilbertville, o=MessagingSystem, c=US
objectclass: mediacomponent
mcn: W2Vagent@carol.dilbertville
mcc: Wave2Vox
rev-level: Beta 0.9
host: carol
port: 0
service: W2V-Service
patch-level: 0
component-path: c:\Wav2VoxService\Wav2vox.exe
                control-bus-name: ANY.TO.TRAFFIC
snmp-dll-path: c:\WAV2VOXDLL\wav2voxdll.dll
snmp-wait-to: 40
description: Dilbertville Wave to Vox File Services
acmSrcFormat: 22KHZ_PCM_16BIT_MONO
acmDestFormat: MULAW_8BIT_MONO
```

Figure 16-13
Service entry in LDAP.

available in all Win32-based applications. Individual applications can also load ACM drivers for their own private use.

ACM Architecture

Figure 16-14 shows an illustration of the relationship of the major Windows NT audio software components.

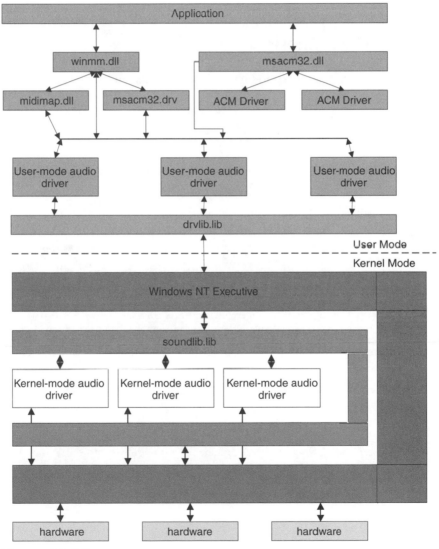

Figure 16-14
Windows NT audio compression architecture.

AUDIO COMPRESSION COMPONENT LIST . . . .

Table 16.7 is a list of the ACM components.

ARCHITECTURE FOR CONVERSION . . . .

This section explains both W2V client and the ACM.

Inside W2V Client

The wav-to-vox processes and procedures are explained here.

Table 16.7 ACM Component List

Component	Description
Application	Any user-mode, Win32-based application that calls the audio API functions described in the Win32 SDK.
winmm.dll	A dynamic-link library that exports the waveform, MIDI, mixer, and auxiliary audio functions described in the Win32 SDK.
msacm32.dll	A dynamic-link library that contains the ACM. For information about the ACM and ACM drivers, see the MSDN document entitled *Audio Compression Manager Drivers*.
midimap.dll	The Windows NT MIDI mapper.
msacm32.drv	The Windows NT wave mapper.
User-mode drivers	Dynamic-link libraries that communicate with kernel-mode drivers (or sometimes other user-mode drivers).
ACM drivers	Dynamic-link libraries under the control of the ACM. See msacm32.dll above.
drvlib.lib	A library used as a basis for user-mode audio drivers.
Kernel-mode drivers	Kernel-mode code that communicates with the Windows NT executive in order to access device hardware.
Soundlib.lib	A library used as a basis for kernel-mode audio drivers.

NMake Details

The W2V program was written mainly in the "C" language since there were no class libraries available. It should be possible to build a C++ implementation of streaming using the new Microsoft DirectSound SDK. It compiles in both Visual C++ 5.0 and C++ 6.0. The *nmake* command may be used in place of Visual Studio.

The specific libraries used included these paths:

- Microsoft Visual Studio\VC98\INCLUDE.
- Microsoft Visual Studio\VC98\MFC\INCLUDE.
- Microsoft Visual Studio\VC98\ATL\INCLUDE.
- Microsoft Visual Studio\VC98\LIB.
- Microsoft Visual Studio\VC98\MFC\LIB.

Here are the specific library files:

- odbc32.lib, odbccp32.lib, kernel32.lib, user32.lib, gdi32.lib, winspool.lib, comdlg32.lib, advapi32.lib, shell32.lib, ole32.lib, oleaut32.lib, uuid.lib, msacm32.lib, vfw32.lib, winmm.lib, spchwrap.lib.

Apartment Thread

The rules for COM apply when working with the ACM. The first rule is to create an apartment thread model. This is necessary for a Windows NT message pump; however, at the time this program was written, this feature had not been added, since notification was not necessary. Figure 16-15 shows the code necessary for starting the model. Of course, there is an EndOle function.

```
BOOL BeginOLE (void)
{
   DWORD     dwVer;
                                   // Initialize OLE
   SetMessageQueue(96);
   dwVer = CoBuildVersion();      //check if free thread allowed

   if (rmm != HIWORD(dwVer)) return FALSE;
                                   // error

   if (FAILED(CoInitialize(NULL))) return FALSE;
                                   //new thread to enter apatment

   return TRUE;
}
```

Figure 16-15
Apartment thread model.

Tech Talk

OLE is the precursor to COM.

PROCESS FOR USING CODEC
TO COMPRESS WAVE AUDIO . . . .

The W2V process follows these steps:

1. Open the sample wave file data produced by T2W.
2. Load it into heap.
3. Locate suitable CODEC.
4. Create a structure of the final converted data.
5. Convert to an intermediate form.
6. Convert it to the required form.
7. Write it out in VOX format, which means with no header information.
8. Go to Step 1.

Tech Talk

Step 1 also creates a suitable structure for conversion.

Open Wave File

The easiest way to read wave files is to use the Microsoft multimedia libraries and software development kit (SDK). My reason for saying this has to do with the fact that most companies had libraries that were able to read wave files. But these libraries, over time, quickly became obsolete. Resource interchange file format (RIFF) services have newer wave format structures to support the newer functions and features.

The mmioOpen function shown in Figure 16-16, is used to open a file for buffered I–O. The file is a standard file. The handle returned by mmioOpen is not a standard file handle; it is not used with any file I–O functions other than multimedia file I–O functions (i.e., mmioFOURCC, mmioDescend, etc.).

```
HPSTR OpenAndLoad(char onameLoc[12])
{

            long i;
            MMIOINFO                        mmioinfo;
                                                    //Get the filename
   szFileName[0]  = 0;
   i=strlen(onameLoc);
             onameLoc[i+1]=0;
   if(!(hmmio = mmioOpen((LPSTR) &iname, NULL, MMIO_READ I MMIO_ALLOCBUF)))
   {
      printf("Failed to open file./n");
      return NULL;
   }
                                          //Locate a 'RIFF'chunk with a 'WAVE' form type
                                                    //to make sure it's a WAVE file.
   mmckinfoParent.fccType = mmioFOURCC('W','A','V','E');
   if (mmioDescend(hmmio, (LPMMCKINFO) &mmckinfoParent, NULL, MMIO_FINDRIFF))
   {
      printf("This is not a WAVE file.\n");
      mmioClose(hmmio, 0);
      return 0;
   }
                                                    //Now, find the format chunk
(form type 'fmt').
                       //It should be a subchunk of the 'RIFF' parent chunk.
   mmckinfoSubchunk.ckid = mmioFOURCC('f','m','t','');
   if (mmioDescend(hmmio, &mmckinfoSubchunk, &mmckinfoParent,
      MMIO_FINDCHUNK))
   {
      printf("WAVE file is corrupted.\n");
      mmioClose(hmmio, 0);
      return NULL;
   }
```

Figure 16-16
Open the wave file.

Load Buffer Area

Furthermore, Win32 memory management allows the user to create huge buffers, a convenience when dealing with these applications. (See Figure 16-17.) The GlobalAlloc function allocates the specified number of bytes from the heap. Win32 memory management does not provide a separate local and global heap.

This function guarantees that the memory allocated is aligned on 8-byte boundaries. All memory is created with execute access; no special function is required to execute dynamically generated code.

When GlobalAlloc succeeds, it allocates at least the amount of memory requested. If the actual amount allocated is greater than the amount requested, the process can use the entire amount.

```
                                     //Get the size of the format chunk, allocate and lock
                                            //memory for it.
dwFmtSize = mmckinfoSubchunk.cksize;
hFormat = GlobalAlloc(LMEM_MOVEABLE, LOWORD(dwFmtSize));
if (!hFormat)
{
    printf("Out of memory");
    mmioClose(hmmio, 0);
    return NULL;
}                                                    //Lock the heap space
pFormat = (WAVEFORMATEX*) GlobalLock(hFormat);
if (!pFormat)
{
    printf("Failed to lock memory for format chunk.\n");
    LocalFree(hFormat);
    mmioClose(hmmio, 0);
    return NULL;
}
```

Figure 16-17
Allocate the buffer area.

DESCENDING THE WAVE FILE . . . .

Figure 16-18 shows a sample of the code for descending the wave file and for loading the buffer area.

FINDING A SUITABLE CODEC . . . .

In the ideal world, compressing some data would be simply a case of saying to the system, "Here's some data, compress it in this format, please." Unfortunately, the Windows programming world is far from ideal, and, as usual, we get to do a lot of the grunt work ourselves. The first and most important problem to solve arises because of the fact that any given CODEC may not be able to compress the data format in which you just happened to be working. In our example, it is the output of the txt2wav command—which is PCM, 22.050 kHz, 16 bit, and mono. First, convert the source data into an intermediate PCM format (i.e., Microsoft CCITT G.711 u-Law CODEC), then have the Microsoft ACM convert the intermediate data to the final format that we need.

Converting one PCM format to another can be done using a different CODEC that also ships with Windows, so you need to use one CODEC to convert the data to a

```
                                                            // Read the format chunk.
if (mmioRead(hmmio, (HPSTR) pFormat, dwFmtSize) != (LONG) dwFmtSize
   { printf("Failed to read format chunk.\n");
     LocalUnlock(hFormat);
     LocalFree(hFormat);
     mmioClose(hmmio, 0);
     return NULL;
   }
   mmioAscend(hmmio, &mmckinfoSubchunk, 0);        //Ascend out of the format subchunk.
   mmiockinfoSUBchunk.ckid = mmioFOURCC('d','a','t','a');   //Find the data subchunk.
   if (mmioDescend(hmmio, &mmckinfoSubchunk, &mmckinfoParent,
      MMIO_FINDCHUNK))
   {   printf("WAVE file has no data chunk.\n");
       LocalUnlock( hFormat );
       LocalFree( hFormat );
       mmioClose(hmmio, 0);
       return NULL;
   }
   dwDataSize = mmckinfoSubchunk.cksize;                   //Get the size of the data
                                                           subchunk.

   if (dwDataSize ==0L)
   {   printf("The data chunk has no data.\n");
       LocalUnlock( hFormat );
       LocalFree( hFormat );
       mmioClose(hmmio, 0);
       return NULL;
   }
   wBlockSize = pFormat->nBlockAlign;                      //Save block allignment info
                                                           for later use.

   hData = GlobalAlloc(GMEM_MOVEABLE , dwDataSize);        //Allocate and lock memory for
                                                           the waveform data.
                                                           // GMEM_SHARE is not needed on
                                                           32 bits */

   if (!hData)
   {   printf("The data chunk has no data.\n");
       mmioClose(hmmio, 0);
       return NULL;
   }
   lpData = (char*)GlobalLock(hData);
   if (!lpData)
   {   printf("Failed to lock memory for data chunk .\n");
       GlobalFree (hData);
       mmioClose(hmmio, 0);
       return NULL;
                                                           // Read the waveform data
   }                                                       subchunk.
if(mmioRead(hmmio, (HPSTR) lpData, dwDataSize) != (LONG) dwDataSize)
{ printf("Failed to read data chunk.");
   GlobalUnlock( hData );
   GlobalFree( hData );
   mmioClose(hmmio, 0);
   return NULL;
if (mmioGetInfo(hmmio, &mmioinfo, 0)) {
  printf("Failed to get I/O buffer info.\n");
  mmioClose(hmmio,0);
  return NULL;
}
i=0;                                                       //Read backwords
mmioSetinfo(hmmio, &mmioClose(hmmio, 0);

return lpData;                                             //Return a pointer to the heap
                                                           data
```

Figure 16-18
Descending the wave file.

format that the other CODEC can handle. Given that we know how to enumerate the CODECs and their supported formats, this looks reasonable. (See Figure 16-19.)

CREATING A FINAL STRUCTURE . . . .

Shown in Figure 16-20 is the assignment of a WAVEFORMATEX structure that describes the source data format of 22-kHz, 16-bit, mono PCM wave files.

The find_driver function enumerates all of the drivers until it finds one that supports the given tag. This means that the format is unknown until the program is run, but more often than not, it is some variant of PCM. I will not show the details because it is very similar to the enumeration code we looked at earlier. You can examine how it works for yourself later.

Once we have WAVEFORMATEX structures built to describe the source format (22KHZ PCM 16BIT MONO 4), the intermediate PCM format and the final compressed format (MULAW 8BIT MONO), it is time to start converting the data. Conversion is done using ACM streams. We open the stream by passing a description of the source and then the destination format, and then we ask the stream to convert them.

CONVERTING TO AN INTERMEDIATE FORM . . . . . .

Figure 16-21 shows the first conversion step, which converts the source format to the intermediate format.

```
BOOL CALLBACK find_format_enum(HACMDRIVERID hadid, LPACMFORMATDETAILS
pafd, DWORD dwInstance, DWORD fdwSupport)
{
            FIND_DRIVER_INFO* pdi = (FIND_DRIVER_INFOR*) dwInstance;
                                                //loop through the pdi to
find
                                                //the matching
dwFormatTag
            if (pafd->dwFormatTag == (DWORD)pdi->wFormatTag) {
                        pdi->hadid = hadid;
                            return FALSE;
                                                // stop enumerating
            }
            return TRUE;                         // continue enumerating
}
```

Figure 16-19
Find format.

```
WORD wFormatTag = WAVE_FORMAT_MULAW;

// Now we locate a CODEC that supports the destination
format tag HACMDRIVERID hadid = find_driver(wFormatTag);
if (hadid == NULL) {
            printf("No driver found\n");
            exit (1);
}
printf("Driver found (hadid: %4.4IXH)\n", hadid);
```

Figure 16-20
Final structure.

Registration of Notifications Class

In this case, the conversion is done synchronously and may take quite some time. Fortunately, the CODEC algorithm is not complex. "Synchronously" means that the application waits until it completes the conversion. The notification is done by the callback function and the console output.

Tech Talk

CODECs can work asynchronously, when progress notification has made a message to a window, *a call to a callback function,* or set an event.

When W2V opens the conversion streams, we specify the **ACM_STREAMOPENF_NONREALTIME** flag. If you omit this flag, some drivers will report error 512 (not possible). This error means that the conversion you asked for cannot be done in real time. This is not an issue in W2V, but it would be when attempting to convert a lot of data at the same time that it was being played.

Having located the driver, it is time to construct a **WAVEFORATEX** structure for the final compressed data format that the driver will generate and also one for the intermediate PCM format that the driver needs as input.

Tech Talk

If the CODEC that will create the compressed format supports several input formats, choose the first enumerated PCM format that the CODEC supports. While this is very easy to implement, it can lead to some loss of data fidelity. Consider that the CODEC has some algorithm for almost lossless compression and can accept 8- or 16-bit PCM data at 11.025 or 22 kHz. In the case of 44.1-kHz, 16-bit stereo, we are trying to reduce the data volume, but not at the expense of quality. When enumerating with the first one, 11 kHz, 8 bit, and mono, it will certainly have lost some quality because the intermediate format that we chose was not good enough. In the case of a 16-bit, 22 kHz system, the result would have been much better.

```
HACMSTREAM hstr = NULL;
mmr = acmStreanOpen(&hstr,
                         NULL,              // any driver
                         &wfSrc,            // source format
                         pwfPCM,            // destination format wBitsPerSample
                         NULL,              // no filter
                         NULL,              // no callback
                         0,                 // instance data
                         ACM_STREAMOPENF_NONREALTIME); // flags
if (mmr) }
                         printf("Failed to open a stream to do PCM to PCM
                         conversion\n");
                         exit(1);
}
                                            // allocate a buffer for the result of the
conversion.
                                            // Don't use DWORD here or you will get
truncated
float dwDst1Samples = (float) dwDataSize * (float) pwfPCM->SamplesPerSec / (float)
wfSrc.nSamplesPerSec;
                                            //Ignore compiler warnings here
DWORD dwDst1Bytes = dwDst1Samples * pwfPCM->wBitsPerSample / 16; //In coming wave file
was 16 bits
BYTE* pDst1Data = new BYTE [dwDst1Bytes];
                                            // fill in the conversion into
ACMSTREAMHEADER strhdr;
memset(&strhdr, 0, sizeof(strhdr));
strhdr.cbStruct = sizeof(strhdr);
strhdr.pbSrc = (unsigned char*) pSrcData    // the source data to convert
                                            //strhdr.cbSrcLength = dwSrcBytes;
strhdr.cbSrcLength = dwDataSize;
strhdr.pbDst = pDst1Data;
strhdr.cbDstLength = dwDst1Bytes;
                                            // prep the header
mmr = acmStreamPrepareHeader(hsr, &strhdr, 0);
                                            // convert the data
printf("Converting to intermediate PCM format...\n");
mmr = acmStreamConvert(hstr, &strhdr, 0);
if (mmr) {
          printf("Failed to do PCM to PCM conversion");
          exit(1);
}
printf("Converted OK\n");
                                            // close the stream
acmStreamClose(hstr, 0);
```

Figure 16-21
Convert the source wave to the PCM format supported by the CODEC.

Streaming

When the stream is opened, the second parameter is set to NULL, indicating that we will accept any driver to perform this conversion. The only complexity is computing how much buffer space is needed for the output data. Because a PCM-to-PCM conversion involves no compression or decompression, the computation is straight-forward.

Tech Talk

> The call to *acmStreamPrepareHeader* is actually a convenience for the driver, allowing it to lock memory before conversion begins.

The Final Step

Figure 16-22 shows the final step in converting the intermediate format to the final compressed format.

This is very similar to the PCM-to-PCM conversion, but in this case, we supply the handle to the driver we want to use when we open the stream. Actually, we could also supply NULL here, because we already ascertained that the driver exists, but supplying the handle helps the system avoid wasting time finding the driver for us.

Computing the buffer size for the compressed data is a little tricky and requires some slight guesswork. The *nAvgBytesPerSec* field of the WAVEFORMATEX structure indicates the average rate at which bytes are read during playback. We can use this estimate to see how much data we need in order to store the compressed wave. Some drivers give data that is truly average and not the worst case, so I chose to add 50 percent more to the buffer. This works well in practice, even if it is a little wasteful.

Statistics

Once the conversion is complete, the *cbDstLengthUsed* field of the ACMSTREAM-HEADER structure contains the actual number of bytes used in the buffer. Figure 16-23 uses this field to compute the compression ratio.

Advantage of Using ACM

Compressing waveform data using the CODECs that ship with the Windows operating systems is easy to do and results in data that occupies less disk space and takes less time to transmit.

```
HACMDRIVER had = NULL;
mmr = acmDriverOpen(&had, hadid, 0);
if (mmr) {
            printf("Failed to open driver\n");
            exit(1);
}
// open the conversion stream and note ACM_STREAMOPENF_NONREALTIME flag.
//Without this some software
// compressors will report error 512 - not possible
mmr = acmStreamOpen(&hstr,
                    had,                          // driver handle
                    pwfPCM,                       // source format format wBitsPerSample
                    pwfDrv,                       // destination format OK
                    NULL,                         // no filter
                    NULL,                         // no callback
                    0,                            //instance data (not used)
                    ACM_STREAMOPENF_NONREALTIME);//flags
if (mmr) {
                    printf("Failed to open a stream to do PCM to driver format
                    conversion\n");
                    exit(1);
}
// allocate a buffer for the result of the conversion. Compute the output buffer size based on
the average
// byte rate and add a bit for randomness. The IMA_ADPCM driver fails the conversion without
this extra
// space
                                        //This calculation applies to MULAW
DWORD dwDst2Bytes = dwDst1Samples / 2;
dwDst2Bytes = dwDst2Bytes *9  /8;// add a little room
BYTE* pDst2Data = new BYTE [dwDst2Bytes];
                                        // fill in the conversion info
ACMSTREAMHEADER strhdr2;
memset(&strhdr2, 0, sizeof(strhdr2));
strhdr2.cbStruct = sizeof(strhdr2);
strhdr2.pbSrc = pDst1Data;                      // the source data to convert
strhdr2.cbSrcLength = dwDst1Bytes;
strhdr2.pbDstLength = dwDst2Data;
strhdr2.cbDstLength = dwDst2Bytes;
                                        // prep the header
mmr = acmStreamPrepareHeader(hstr, &strhdr2, 0);
printf("Converting to final format...\n");
mmr = acmStreamConvert(hstr, &strhdr2, 0);              // convert the data
if (mmr) {   printf("Failed to do PCM to driver format conversion\n");
            exit(1);
}
printf("Converted OK\n");
if((ofh=_open(oname,_O_RDONLY))>0){
            printf("output file f:%s already exits\n",oname);_close(ofh);}
if((ofh=_open(oname,_O_WRONLYI_O_BINARYI_O_CREATI_O_TRUNC,_S_IWRITE))<0){
            printf("output file f:%s.vox not opened\n",oname); exit (99);}
_write(ofh,strhdr2.pbDst,strhdr2.cbDstLengthUsed);     // close the stream and driver
_close(ofh);
mmr = acmStreamClose(hstr, 0);
mmr = acmDriverClose(had, 0);
```

Figure 16-22
Convert the intermediate PCM format to the final format.

```
printf("Source wave had %lu bytes\n", dwDataSize);
printf("Converted wave has %lu bytes\n", strhdr2.cbDstLengthUsed);
printf("Compression ratio is %f\n", (double) dwDataSize / (double)
strhdr2.cbDstLengthUsed);
```

Figure 16-23
Show the conversion statistics.

Using Proprietary Compression Formats in ACM

If you have a proprietary compression format, it is possible to create your own CODEC to install and use in the same way shown here.

Architecture for W2V Data Transfer

Figure 16-24 shows the unified modeling language (UML) processor diagram of the system for W2V.

Tech Talk

It is possible to have one processor perform all of these tasks.

Explanation of Processor Diagram

The following table explains the duties of each of the processors shown in Figure 16-24.

How to Obtain the API

The MSDN CD-ROM hosts the multimedia SDK for ACM. Here are the instructions for finding the working code and SDK.

1. Search in either of the articles mentioned in the reference section.
2. Click on the hotlink to open or copy the files in the CODEC sample application for the article.

Tech Talk

This file is required: DevStudio\samples\sdk\mm\aviedit\muldiv32.h.

Processor	Description
CPS	The call processing service retrieves the VOX data from W2V and sends it to the Dialogic card. It uses the NT distributed file system. The Dialogic card then consumes the VOX data and produces an audible message. Multiple nodes are supported by BMQ.
MDR	Metering data recorder keeps the metering events for creating, billing, or charging records.
Directory	When T2W is started, the directory is consulted in order to obtain site-specific information about an interface on the other components.
W2V	W2V is where the audio compression and conversion are performed. ACM is shown sharing the same processor, but it is possible to distribute this task.
System Manager	The system manager listens for W2V traps and events. It provides a real-time view of the W2V component.

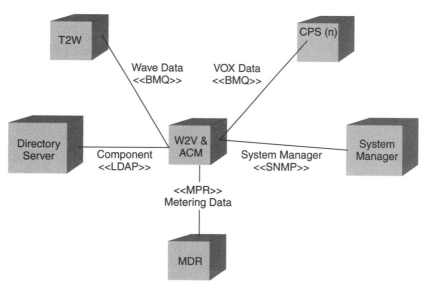

Figure 16-24
W2V processor diagram.

CONSTRAINTS . . . .

The W2V component has what I believe are the following constraints:

- A virtual memory constraint, which restricts the size of the input and output file.
- NT 4.0 file system is small in file size and capacity (i.e., 32 Gbytes).
- ACM interface is proprietary since it requires COM. However, cross-platform software does exist.
- W2V only works with files. Streams are not handled at this time.

CONCLUSION, RECOMMENDATION, AND COMMENTARY . . . .

What Microsoft has done to the printer driver in Windows 3.1 is now what they are attempting to do with CODECs in Window 95 and NT, which is to distribute the most widely used manufacturer's CODECs for both audio and video devices (i.e., Audio compression CODEC enumeration types). This strategy makes more devices accessible for all kinds of applications including, in this case, text-to-speech and fax-to-speech media conversion for the Dialogic cards, among other things.

Over a six-month period, the component never failed, except when a bug was introduced into the client program. Even under an adverse condition such as this, the ACM performed well, but produced a corrupt file. Given how flexible and well-documented the ACM API is, I can only say it is far better than working with the UNIX tool set for audio compression.

The ACM is efficient in comparison to other processes. Consider the following table, which shows processing times in milliseconds of the various processes.

Audio Length (sec)	T2W (ms)	W2V (ms)	CPS (ms)
25	26919	190	151288

REFERENCES . . . .

- "Streaming Wav Files with DirectSound," MSDN CD-ROM, 1 October 1998.

- "Using CODECs to Compress Wave Audio," MSDN CD-ROM, 1 July 1998.
- "Microsoft Multimedia Standards Update: New Multimedia Data Types and Data Techniques," Microsoft ftp site, 15 April 1994.

ACRONYMS . . . .

- ACM—Audio compression manager.
- BMQ—Batch MQSeries protocol for remote procedure calls.
- CODEC—Coder–decoder is software that converts digital voice or video signals from one format to another and is acceptable to the digital video or audio transmission systems.
- COM—Component object model interface.
- DSP—Digital signal processor is a specialized computer chip designed to perform speedy and complex operations on digitized waveforms.
- ASCII—American standard code for information interchange.
- MEMA—Messaging enterprise manager agent.
- TTS—Text-to-speech process.
- T2W—Text-to-wave file program.

OPTICAL CHARACTER RECOGNITION SERVICE . . . .

This section explains the work performed to integrate the host-based TIFF file to TEXT file service into the IP architecture. More importantly, this section explains how to interface the Xerox text bridge image and character recognition server within the Windows NT environment. Lastly, this section explains certain aspects of optical character recognition for a fax-to-speech application.

TIFF-to-Text Conversion

TIFF to TEXT (T2T) main service functions are as follows:

- To interact with any and all services that need TIFF file to TXT file conversion, specifically the CPS; any image data (black and white, halftone, dithered, or grayscale) can be converted to text.

- To interact with the management agent or system administrator.
- To interact with the LDAP server for configuration information.
- To interact with the TDR server to provide billing information.

Input Image File Format

Input image file format expects a TIFF file with any of these characteristics:

- Document types—Facsimiles, photocopies, and documents with complex layouts.
- Language support—English, Danish, Dutch, Finnish, French, German, Italian, Norwegian, Portuguese, Russian, Spanish, or Swedish.
- Text from 5 to 72 points in virtually any typeface.
- Fax, dot matrix, or other degraded documents.
- Process documents in two-page mode for open-faced books and magazines.
- File support—TIFF. However, support exists for these file types: Windows PCX, DCX, BMP, CCITT group 3, CCITT group 4, or XDOC.
- Image resolution—100 by 200, 200 by 100, 200 by 400, 400 by 200, or within the range 70 dpi to 900 dpi.
- Image type—Black and white, halftone, dithered, or grayscale.
- Compression—Black and white.

Tech Talk

The input file name can be defined by an environment variable INFILE.

Additional Optical Recognition Feature

These features go beyond the scope of T2T; however, they are listed here for completeness:

- Photometric interpretation—Inversion or rotation, or inverted image (white text on black background).
- Region specification—Text, image, any, unused, overlapping, columns, stacking.

- Interactive text verification—Documents with noise (dirt, smudges, hand-written notes in the margin); documents that are too dark or too light; multiple-generation photocopies; documents with ornate, thin-stroke type-faces—that is, character segments that do not always connect; documents with special symbols that are not part of the standard character set supported by the API; low-resolution images (i.e., fax).
- Increase recognition accuracy with built-in lexical classes and user-defined lexicons.
- Output confidence values and categories of lexical information for post-recognition processing.
- Delineate areas of a document page and specify treatment for those areas; up to 2000 different areas per page.
- Generate a scaled version of any portion of the current image loaded into memory for display in a window.
- Generate miniature thumbnail images of scanned pages.

Output Text File Format

The T2T service can output the following:

- ASCII text files—The output file name can be defined by an environment variable OUTFILE or by the BMQ interface.
- XDOC files—A Xerox markup file format for eventual conversion to other formats.
- ISO marked-up paragraphs and tables.

Console Output

Figure 16-25 is the output from the tif2txt executable.

IT–Bus Interfaces

Table 16.8 shows the T2T IT–Bus.

LDAP

LDAP is used to obtain various configuration data from the directory server.

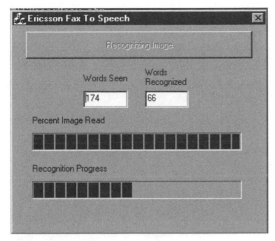

Figure 16-25
T2T console output.

SNMP

T2T service has defined an SNMP MIB, wav2voxDll.mib.

System Call and BMQ

The T2T service receives a "tif" file name as input and returns the same file name with the "txt" extension, if so desired. It is configurable.

System Call

The file to be converted was passed to T2T by a system call.

Table 16.8   T2T IT–Buses

IT–BUS	Protocol	Service
System Control	LDAP	Directory lookup
	MDP	Meter data protocol
	System Call and BMQ	(CPS to T2T)
	IPC	(T2T to ICR)
OAM&P	SNMP	Management agent
	Report Event (NT)	

Distributed Processing

Distributed computing was tried using MQSeries. CPS and T2T exchange remote procedure calls through the MQ software infrastructure, ergo the new protocol BMQ. This is the same infrastructure used by the TDR service with the exception of the NT distributed file system. The file system is used to move the files around.

IPC (COM API)

IPC (interprocess communications) is the exchange of data between two or more processes or applications.

During the conversion process, the T2T accesses the ICR component through the IPC, which the COM API supports automatically. On the same machine, secure IPC is used by T2T.

SERVICE START EVENTS . . . .

- Allocate and initialize internal structures.
- Alert system manager of progress.
- Establish needed channel(s) with ICR.
- Validate input file and format.
- Generate a "service start event" in the event log.
- Open the session with the meter data repository service and the SNMP service. Report any missing services at start-up in the event log. Tell any service that T2T is in service.

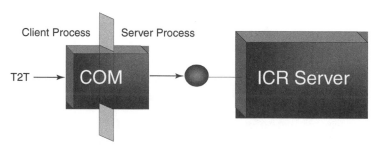

Figure 16-26
T2T interprocess communications.

SERVICE STOP EVENTS ....

- Indicate that T2T is not in service by setting the operating status in the MIB.
- Unassign and deallocate any input channel(s).
- Unassign, deallocate, and log off any output channel(s).
- Generate a "service stop event" in the event log.
- Terminate the T2T service.

CRASH ....

In the event of an uncontrolled stop (crash) of the service, the SNMP agent detects the absence of the service generating an SNMP trap (belly up) and logging an event in the event log file.

ALARM HANDLING ....

Alarms and alarm ceasing are generated and sent as SNMP traps when a failure occurs, is persistent, and is remedied. The following alarms are generated by T2T:

- Failure to find resource.
- Failure to connect to resource.

REPORT EVENT HANDLING ....

Report events are generated and sent as ReportEvents to the NT event log. The following report events are generated by T2T:

- Service started.
- Service stopped.
- Failure to connect to SNMP agent.

DIRECTORY SERVER FETCH . . . .

At start-up, the T2T service must fetch information in the directory server. Figure 16-27 shows an example of a T2T service entry in an LDAP directory Server.

ARCHITECTURE FOR OPTICAL CHARACTER RECOGNITION . . . .

ICR provides a set of API functions that allow a client to perform optical recognition services on an image file.

The TextBridge is implemented as a static-link library, named *icr32.li*b, or a dynamic-link library, *icr32.dll*. Applications that link with the ICR can call its API functions.

The language packs (*.LC files) must reside in the same directory as that of icrsrv.exe.

Descriptions of the ICR API functions are provided in the SDK. ICR API functions begin with a prefix of ICR. The functions are written in C, must be compiled with Microsoft C 6.0, and include MFC.

The ICR calls installable, user-mode drivers to perform conversions. Most ICR drivers can be installed with the setup.exe program found on CD-ROM.

```
Service entry LDAP
dn: mcn=T2TAgent@carol.dilbertville, msn=Dilbertville,o=MessagingSystem, c=US
objectclass: mediacomponent
mcn: T2Tagent@carol.dilbertville
mcc: tif2txt
rev-level: Beta 0.9
host: carol
port: 0
service: T2T-Service
patch-level: 0
component-path: c:\Tif2txtService\Tif2txt.exe
control-bus-name: ANY.TO.TRAFFIC
snmp-dll-path: c:\TIF2TXTDLL\tif2txtdll.dll
snmp-wait-to: 40
description: Dilbertville Image to Text File Services
mimeSrcFormat: IMAGE
mimeDestFormat: Text
```

Figure 16-27
T2T LDAP entry.

CLIENT/SERVER INTERACTION . . . .

TextBridge API is not a network-level product. The client and server must run on the same machine at this time.

Most communications between the applications and the ICR server are application requests for service. Standard application requests for service include

- Sending data to the ICR server.
- Starting a recognition operation to process the data.
- Asking for the status of the ICR server or ongoing operations.
- Retrieving processed data from the ICR server.

If the ICR server needs data for processing or needs to dispose of processed data, it raises a blocked condition and waits for the application to clear the condition by making the necessary I–O request.

The ICR server can communicate with the application to inform it that the ICR task has entered a blocked state. In some cases, the API interface code that is linked with the application will resolve the block on behalf of the application.

In simple terms, an application accesses recognition in the following manner:

1. Sets initial conditions.
2. Starts processing.
3. Responds to changes in server status.

It is very important that an application respond to changes in server status, especially with regard to blocked conditions. Blocked conditions are an indication that recognition cannot continue until the condition is resolved.

Setting Parameters

The API uses tagged values to set parameters that modify certain aspects of the ICR server's data processing. These parameters have a persistent effect across multiple API function calls. They are often set only once per session.

The API associates each parameter with a defined constant, which is specified symbolically in the appropriate include file. When an application sets a parameter or retrieves its value, the application specifies the defined constant, or tag, and a value, as the arguments to a function call.

The API uses tagged values in two contexts: to set general system parameters for the ICR server and to associate properties with defined areas of the page, also known as regions.

Tagged values for system parameters begin with the prefix V_ (meaning value); tagged values that set parameters for regions begin with the prefix R_ (meaning region).

Recognition Technologies

Xerox document recognition software provides unsurpassed recognition accuracy for a variety of documents, including facsimiles, photocopies, and documents with complex layouts.

To ensure this accuracy, the recognition system software uses cooperating experts that contribute to the analysis and recognition of characters and words, as well as to the underlying page.

Here are the three experts that provide document understanding:

1. Fax and degrade document subsystem—provides recognition accuracy for facsimile documents and other low-resolution TIFF images.
2. Confidence subsystem—helps answer the question, "Can I trust what I am being told, and how dependable is the recognized result?" Using proprietary Neural Network technology, the confidence subsystem calculates confidence values for recognition results on a scale of 0 to 999, where 0 indicates no confidence and 999 indicates extremely high confidence. The software can output these values to an XDOC file, in which they can be used in further processing. (See Figure 16-28 for the range of interest.)
3. Lexifier—is a Xerox patent-pending technology that can verify and recognize strings of characters. It goes beyond simple dictionaries of English words by working with any string of ISO characters, including numbers, alphanumeric, or mixed case. It also classifies strings into categories or types, such as, date, time, and currency.

By increasing accuracy and reducing false positive results in the output (fewer substitution errors), the cost of processing is reduced.

INSIDE T2T CLIENT . . . .

The TIFF file-to-text processes and procedures are explained in this section.

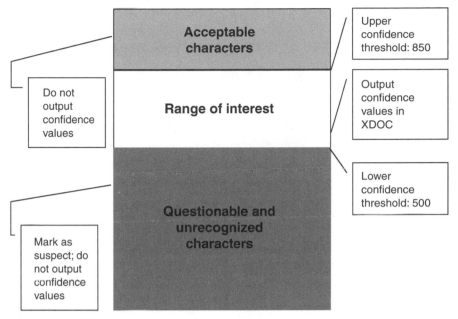

Figure 16-28
Range of interest.

NMake Details

The T2T program was written mainly in the "C++" language; however, the ICR API is "C." It compiles in Visual Studio C++ 6.0. The *nmake* command may be used in place of Visual Studio.

The specific libraries included use the following paths:

- \TXBRDG45.32\LIB.
- \TXBRDG45.32\INCLUDE.
- \TXBRDG45.32\SOURCE.
- Microsoft Visual Studio\VC98\INCLUDE.
- Microsoft Visual Studio\VC98\MFC\INCLUDE.
- Microsoft Visual Studio\VC98\ATL\INCLUDE.
- Microsoft Visual Studio\VC98\LIB.
- Microsoft Visual Studio\VC98\MFC\LIB.

Here is the specific library file:

icr32.lib.

T2T Classes CMainFrame

The T2T class was derived from the CFrameWnd class, which encapsulates the functionality of a Windows single document interface (SDI) frame window. A frame window is a window that frames an application.

```
class CMainFrame : public CFrameWnd
{
protected:                         // create from serialization only
         CMainFrame():
         DECLARE_DYNCREATE(CMainFrame)
                                 // Attibutes
public:
                                 // Operations
public:
                                 Overrides
         // ClassWizard generated virtual function overrides
         //{{AFX_VIRTUAL(CMainFrame)
         virtual BOOL PreCreateWindow(CREATESTRUCT& cs);
         //}}AFX_VIRTUAL
                                 // Implementation
public:
         virtual ~CMainFrame();
#ifdef_DEBUG
         virtual void AssertValid() const;
         virtual void Dump(CDumpContext& dc) const;
#endif
                                 // Generated message map functions
protected:
         //{{AFX_MSG(CMainFrame)
                 // NOTE - the ClassWizard will add and
                 remove member functions
here.
                 // DO NOT EDIT what you see in these
                 blocks of generated code!
         //}}AFX_MSG
         DECLARE_MESSAGE_MAP()
};
```

Figure 16-29
CMainFrame class.

CMFCRecogApp

The CMFCRecogApp was derived from CwinApp. CwinApp class is the base class from which you derive a Windows application object. An application object provides member functions for initializing your application (and each instance of it) and for running the application.

This is the one and only CMFCRecogApp object. Here is how it is defined:

- CMFCRecogApp theApp.

This class handles no messages from the ICR server.

CMFCRecogDlg

The CMFCRecogDlg dialog class does almost all of the work in this application. All ICR server communication is done here, as well as keeping track of state and attempting to protect against dangerous situations. The "Recognize Image" button has been disabled. Two environment variables (INFILE, OUTFILE) are used to indicate the file to be processed and generated. The BMQ protocol is the alternate method for sending this information. A dialog box will appear on the console while the image is read in and preprocessed.

During this time, the "Percent Image Read" status and "Preprocessing . . ." will show the current progress. Once the image is read and preprocessed (preprocessing

```
class CMFCRecogApp : public CWinApp
{
public:
        CMFCRecogApp();          // Overrides
        // ClassWizard generated virtual function overrides
        //{{AFX_VIRTUAL(CMFCRecogApp)
        public:
        virtual BOOL InitInstance();
        //}}AFX_VIRTUAL
                                // Implementation - No messages are
                                directly handled by
this
                                // simple implementation
        //{{AFX_MSG(CMFCRecogApp)
        //}}AFX_MSG
        DECLARE_MESSAGE_MAP()
};
```

Figure 16-30
CMFCRecogApp class.

includes autosegmentation and autoorientation), the process ends. Whenever an image is read into memory, preprocessed, or recognized, it is necessary to call icr_get_status until either the state returns to ICR_WAITING or an error occurs. This is handled in the timer, when needed.

Preprocess Image

The function icr_set_preprocessing() indicates the type of image preprocessing to be performed on page images before recognition.

```
class CMFCRecogDlg : public CDialog
{
// Construction
public:
          void ProcessNextState();          // go to the next state in the process
          BOOL AsynchActive();              // Do we need asynchronous
                                            processing?
          CMFCRecogDlg(CWnd* pParent = NULL);  //standard constructor

                                            // Dialog Data
          //{{AFX_DATA(CMFCRecogDlg)
          enum { IDD = IDD_MFCRECOG_DIALOG};
          CStatic      m_StaticPreproc;     // The 'Preprocessing...' status
message
          CButton      m_ButtonRecog;       // The 'Recognize Image' button
          CProgressCtrl m_ReadProgress;                  // The 'Percent Image
Read' progress bar
          CProgressCtrl m_RecProgress;                   // The 'Recognition
Progress' progress bar
          int                    m_iWordsSeen;                      // The
'Words Seen' status box
          int                    m_iWordsRec;          // The 'Words
Recognized' status box
          CString      m_sPreprocStat;                  // The 'Preprocessing...'
status message
          //}}AFX_DATA

          // ClassWizard generated virtual function overrides
          //{{AFX_VIRTUAL(CMFCRecogDig)
          public:
          virtual BOOL DestroyWindow();                 // Called when the
                                                        window is going away
          protected:
          virtual void DODataExchange(CDataExchange* pDX);  // DDX/DDV support
          //}}AFX_VIRTUAL
//End of public. Private begins on the next page.
```

Figure 16-31
CMFCRecogDlg class.

```
// Implementation
protected:
          void InitIcr();
          void ResetStatus();              // Reset the processing status indicators
          CString GetUserImageFile();      // Prompt the user for an output image file
          void ReadUserImage( CString sImageFileName );      // Read the specified image

          void PreprocessImage();          // Run preprocessing on a loaded image
          void GetUserOutputFile();        // Prompt the user for file to output to
          void RecognizeImage();           // Start recognition
          void error_message ( CString sErrorMessage, BOOL bFatal );

          HICON m_hicon;
          int m_iPreprocCalls;             // How many times has the timer
                                           // been called during preprocessing? Used
                                           for status.
          UNIT m_nTimer;                   // Indentifier for our time function

          // State flags
          BOOL m_bRecognizing;
          BOOL m_bPreprocessing;
          BOOL m_bReadingImage;

          // ICR Server interaction
          ICR_H m_hlcr;                                    // Handle to the ICR server
          BOOL m_bServerValid;             // True only if m_hlcr is still valid
          IO_TOKEN_T m_ImageToken;                         // Image input token
          IO_TOKEN_T m_UserTextToken;      // Text output token

          // Generated message map functions
          //{{AFX_MSG(CMFCRecogDlg)
          virtual BOOL OnInitDialog();      // Do special initialization here
          afx_msg HCURSOR OnQueryDragIcon(); // For dragging the app icon around
          afx_msg void OnRecognize();                      // Called when 'Recognize
                                                           Image' is pressed
          afx_msg void OnTimer(UINT nIDEvent); // Called regularly to do any processing

          //}}AFX_MSG
          DECLARE_MESSAGE_MAP()
};
```

Figure 16-31
CMFCRecogDlg class (continued).

Preprocessing Flags

Icr_h parameter (the last one in 0) is the handle to the ICR server. The flags command is some OR combination of the following list of preprocessing flags shown in Table 16.9.

Tech Talk

The recognizer will fail if these flags are not set correctly. For example, if a fax is upside-down, the recognizer will interpret it wrongly unless it is rotated 180 degrees.

```
void CMFCRecogDlg::PreprocessImage()
{
        // Set the preprocessing flags for the image
        // here we'll run auto segmentation and auto orientation
        //if ((icr_set_preprocessing(m_hlcr, PP_AUTOSEG I PP_FULLORIENT)) < 0)

           if ((icr_set_preprocessing(m_hlcr, PP_AUTOSEG I PP_FULLORIENT I
                               PP_TXTORIENT_CIPP_FAX)) < 0)
        {
                error_message("icr_set_preprocessing: failed\n", FALSE);
                return;
        }


        if ((icr_read_image(m_hlcr, ICR_IMPP, 1)) < 0)
                error_message("icr_read_image: failed\n", FALSE);
}
```

Figure 16-32
PreprocessImage method.

Table 16.9   T2T Preprocessing Flags

Constant	Description
PP_AUTOFAX	This turns on combined time stamp filter–detector and sets ICRMODE_DEGRADED, if header information indicates low resolution, automatic low-resolution detector indicates rescanned low-resolution document, or if the fax time stamp is detected.
PP_AUTOSEG	This enables automatic segmentation of the page. Automatic segmentation identifies the columns and images, including detection of reverse video and line art on the page, so that a user need not use a preview and mouse operation to do so.
PP_AUTOSETDEGRADE	This turns on ICRMODE_DEGRADED, if the automatic low-resolution detector indicates low resolution or a rescanned low-resolution document.
PP_DOT_DETECT	This turns on the PP_DTMTRIX dot-matrix filter, if necessary.
PP_DO_RIGHT	This turns on the PP_DOT_DETECT, PP_ORIENTATION_ C, PP_FAX, PP_SKEW_C, and PP_AUTOSEG.
PP_DTMTRIX	This enhances recognition of documents produced by dot matrix.
PP_FAX	This improves recognition of faxed documents.
PP_FULLORIENT	This turns on PP_ORIENTATION_C and PP_ TXTORIENT_C

(continued)

Table 16.9 T2T Preprocessing Flags (continued)

Constant	Description
PP_HTREM	This filters halftones out of the page image. This speeds up text recognition, but actually removes the halftones from the page image in memory, so that they cannot be output as images.
PP_INVRT	This inverts the image in memory, turning black to white and vice versa.
PP_LINEART	This detects line art during preprocessing and sets the region subtype as such. These regions are then output as graphics in formats that support them.
PP_NEWSPAPER	This improves segmentation on scanned newspapers.
PP_NONE	This clears any previously set flags. Preprocessor flags remain in effect until you explicitly clear them. This flag must be set alone.
PP_ORIENT	This enables automatic detection of page orientation by line; that is, portrait vs. landscape.
PP_ORIENTATION_C	This enables automatic detection and correction of orientation (landscape vs. portrait).
PP_REVVIDEO	Detects reverse video during preprocessing.
PP_RP90,PP_RM90, & PP_R180	This rotates the image in memory the given number of degrees in a clockwise direction before performing any other special preprocessing or recognition. You can select one rotation flag at a time.
PP_SKEW_C	This enables automatic detection and correction of document skew angle.
PP_TXTORIENT_C	This enables automatic detection and correction of orientation (upside down, right side up).

CMFCRecogDOC

This class was derived from the MFC CDocument class, which provides the basic functionality for user-defined document classes. A document represents the unit of data that the user typically opens with the "File/Open" command and saves with the "File/Save" command. In addition, it acts as a wrapper around the Serialize, Dump, AssertValid, and OnNewDocument exceptions.

```
class CMFCRecogDoc : public CDocument
{
protected:                                      // create from serialization only
          CMFCRecogDoc();
          DECLARE_DYNCREATE(CMFCRecogDoc)
                                                // Attributes
public:
                                                // Operations
public:
                                                // Overrides
          // ClassWizard generated virtual function overrides
          //{{AFX_VIRTUAL(CMFCRecogDoc)
          public:
          virtual BOOL OnNewDocument();
          virtual void Serialize(CArchive& ar);
          //}}AFX_VIRTUAL
                                                // Implementation
public:
          virtual ~CMFCRecogDoc();
#ifdef_DEBUG
          virtual void AssertValid() const;
          virtual void Dump(CDumpContext& dc) const;
#endif

protected;
                                                // Generated message map functions
protected:
          //{{AFX_MSG(CMFCRecogDoc)
             // NOTE - the ClassWizard will add and remove member functions here.
             //  DO NOT EDIT what you see in these blocks of generated code!
          //}}AFX_MSG
          DECLARE_MESSAGE_MAP()
};
```

Figure 16-33
CMFCRecogDoc class.

CMFCRecog View

The CView class provides the basic functionality for user-defined view classes. A view is attached to a document and acts as an intermediary between the document and the user: The view renders an image of the document on the screen or printer and interprets user input as operations upon the document. It wraps other exceptions. The on-draw function was not implemented.

ARCHITECTURE FOR T2T DATA TRANSFER . . . .

Figure 16-35 shows the unified modeling language (UML) processor diagram of the system for the T2T.

```
class CMFCRecogView : public CView
{
protected:                                              // create from serialization only
        CMFCRecogView();
        DECLARE_DYNCREATE(CMFCRecogView)
                                                        // Attributes
public:
        CMFCRecogDoc* GetDocument();
                                                        // Operations
public:
                                                        // Overrides
        // ClassWizard generated virtual function overrides
        //{{AFX_VIRTUAL(CMFCRecogView)
        public:
        virtual void OnDraw(CDC* pDC);                  // overridden to draw this view
        virtual BOOL PreCreateWindow(CREATESTRUCT& cs);
        protected:
        //}}AFX_VIRTUAL
                                                        // Implementation
public:
        virtual ~CMFCRecogView();
#ifdef_DEBUG
        virtual void AssertValid() const;
        virtual void Dump(CDumpContext& dc) const;
#endif
protected:
                                                        // Generated message map functions
protected:
        //{{AFX_MSG(CMFCRecogView)
                // NOTE - the ClassWizard will add and remove member functions here.
                //  DO NOT EDIT what you see in these blocks of generated code !
        //}}AFX_MSG
        DECLARE_MESSAGE_MAP()
};
```

Figure 16-34
CMFCRecogView class.

Tech Talk

It is possible to have one processor perform all of these tasks.

Explanation of Processor Diagram

The following is a table that explains the duties of each of the processors.

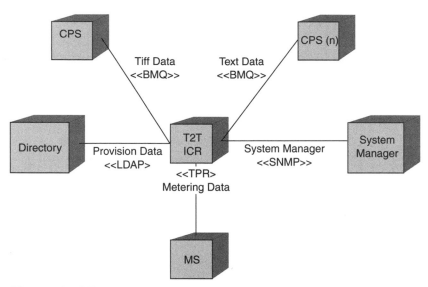

Figure 16-35
T2T processor diagram.

Processor	Description
CPS	The CPS server retrieves the TIFF data from the message store. It then notifies T2T through a media-conversion BMQ. T2T then performs the conversion. T2W and W2V are not shown, but are necessary for the fax-to-speech process. Multiple nodes are supported through BMQ.
MS	Metering server records the conversion events for creating billing or charging records.
Directory	When T2T is started, the directory is consulted in order to obtain site-specific information about the other services' interface.
T2T	T2T is where the optical character recognition is performed. ICR is shown sharing the same processor., At this time, it is not possible to distribute this task.
System manager	The system manager listens for T2T traps and events. It provides a real-time view of the T2T.

CONSTRAINTS . . . .

The T2T service has what I believe are the following constraints:

- ICR (OCR server) is not capable of handwriting recognition.
- A virtual memory constraint restricts the size of the input and output files.
- ICR interface is proprietary, since it requires COM. Xerox has not implemented DCOM, so T2T and ICR must reside on the same box.
- Examples use the Microsoft foundation classes instead of Java.
- ICR API is in "C" and is not standard; therefore, a C++ wrapper should be used.
- T2T only works with files. Streaming fax data and text are not handled at this time.
- NT 4.0 file system file size and capacity (i.e., 32 Gbytes) are restricting.

Tech Talk

Other APIs to consider include Kodak, Caere, and Cognitive Technology.

CONCLUSION, RECOMMENDATION, AND COMMENTARY . . . .

The TextBridge API, documentation, and samples were excellent. A person familiar with COM can get an application running in under a week.

Furthermore, the performance of the OCR process was surprisingly fast (4817 ms, or about 5 seconds) for a fax with these characteristics:

- Various fonts.
- A table.
- Header and footer.
- Line count: 128.
- Word count: 172.
- Character count: 2284.

HOW TO OBTAIN THE API . . . .

The Xerox ScanSoft, Inc. TextBridge API Programmer's tool kit on CD-ROM contains everything needed to interface the ICR server. ScanSoft Inc. is at 9 Centennial Drive, Peabody, Massachusetts, 01960. For Sales, call (978)977-2000, and for Technical Support call (800)248-6550, extesion 2174.

REFERENCES . . . .

TextBridge API Programmers Guide. ScanSoft Inc: Peabody, MA, 1998.

Acronyms

- ASCII—American Standard Code for Information Interchange.
- BMQ—Batch MQSeries protocol for remote procedure calls.
- COM—Component object model interface.
- ICR—Image-to-character recognizer.
- MEMA—Messaging enterprise manager agent.
- TTS—Text-to-speech process.
- T2W—Text-to-wave file program.
- W2V—Wave-to-vox program.
- TIFF—Tagged image file format. TIFF provides a way of storing and exchanging digital image data. Major scanner vendors developed TIFF to help link scanned images with the popular desktop publishing applications. It is now used for many different types of software applications, ranging from medical imagery to fax modem data transfer, CAD programs, and 3D-graphics packages. The current TIFF specifications support three main types of image data: black and white data, halftones or dithered data, and grayscale data.

HANDWRITING-TO-TEXT SERVICE . . . .

This section explains the work performed to integrate the host-based handwriting-to-text file service into the IP architecture. Furthermore, the work applies to mobile terminals that are beginning to embrace this technology.

The key distinction between TIFF-To-Text service is the use of forms. Forms are used for defining the regions in which the handwritten text is expected.

More importantly, this service explains how to interface the MITEK Quick-Strokes intelligent character recognition server within the Windows NT environment.

Finally, this service explains certain aspects of intelligent character recognition for the purpose of converting handwritten fax cover sheets to speech application; specifically, the application determines the contents of the handwriting in the TO field, the FROM field, and the SUBJECT field on a fax cover sheet. The purpose of this effort is to enable a cellular phone user to hear whom the fax is from and what it is about, so that he or she may respond accordingly.

HAND-TO-TEXT CONVERSION DESCRIPTION . . . . .

The main functions of the handwriting-to-text (H2T) service are to:

- Interact with any and all services that need handwriting-to-text file conversion, specifically the CPS; any legible image data (black and white, halftone, dithered, or grayscale) can be converted to text.
- Interact with the management agent or system administrator.
- Interact with the LDAP server for configuration information.
- Interact with the TDR server to provide billing information.

INPUT IMAGE FILE FORMAT . . . .

The input image file format expects a TIFF file with any of the characteristics explained in this section.

Industry Standard Image Formats

- TIFF (Revision 5): binary, 4-bit and 8-bit grayscale, all compression formats, all sizes, all resolutions.
- Resolution of fax 200 by 200, or 200 by 100.
- Group 3 and Group 4 fax images.
- Plain bitmaps (binary or grayscale).
- JPEG compressed.

Types of Text

- Hand-printed text: touching, even overlapping, digits or letters (both uppercase and lowercase).
- Machine-printed text: all fonts, all sizes, multiline fields.
- European handwriting styles (e.g., a seven with a crossbar) and European language characters are also supported.

Segmentation

- Constrained: characters in individual boxes.
- Unconstrained: characters anywhere in a given area.
- Machine-printed fields: single-line, multiline, proportional, or fixed-pitch fonts.
- Separation of touching or overlapping characters.

Recognition

- Multiple character sets (digits only, letters only, etc.).
- Choice of neural classifier (standard or custom trained for application) on a per-field or per-character basis.
- Automatic distinction between hand-printed and machine-printed text.
- Several modes of using multiple experts.

Tech Talk

The input file name can be defined by an environment variable INFILE.

ADDITIONAL OPTICAL RECOGNITION FEATURE . . .

Here are features that go beyond the scope of H2T; however, they are listed here for completeness:

- Deskewing.
- Line removal.
- Background-noise removal.

- Contrast enhancement.
- Registration.
- Dilation and erosion of images.
- Box and comb removal.
- Filtering.
- Courtesy amount and special financial document recogition modalities.
- ZIP code (postal code) processing.
- Neural classifier-based recognition provides greater advantages and accuracy over conventional techniques.
- Neural classifier-based recognition of low-resolution or poor-quality documents, such as facsimile, with much higher accuracy than competitive products.

FORM FILE FORMAT AND TEMPLATES . . . .

A form file is needed to specify views, align text define objects (characters, fields, registration targets, etc.). It is made on top of a template bitmap or a fax.

Templates

The template bitmap allows the recognition process to compare the original image with the image to be recognized.

Registration Targets

Registration targets are special markings that align the scanned form with the form image that contains the character and field definitions in the form definition (DEF) file. All scanners skew and rotate forms as they travel through the scanner's feeder mechanism. These distortions, however small, can cause recognition problems. The system uses registration targets (i.e., registration marks) to compensate for some of the skewing. An example is provided in Figure 16-36.

Defining a Form

A form is the logical collection of all elements that make up a single form, which most often corresponds to a single page of paper.

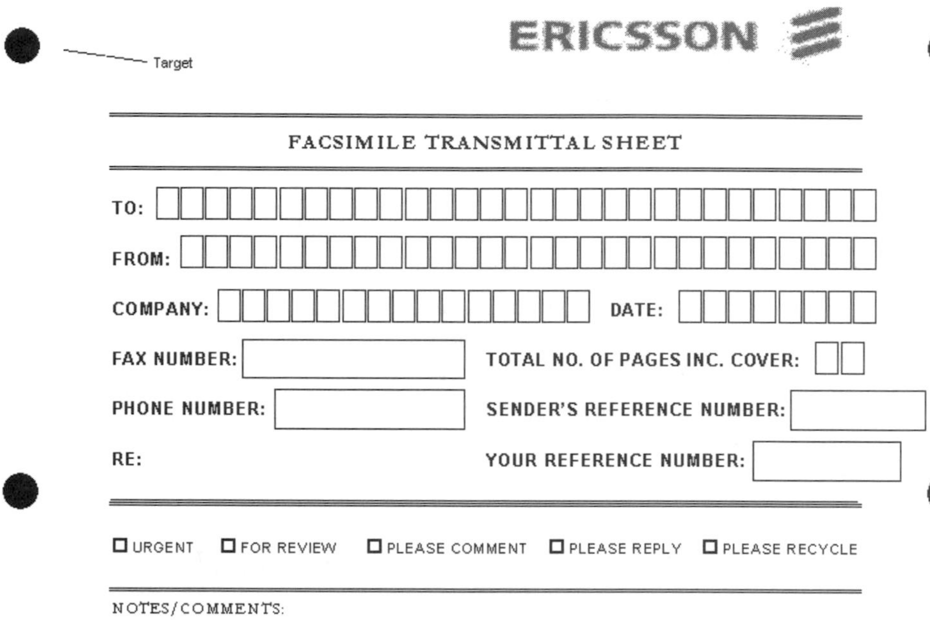

ERICSSON ≋

Target

FACSIMILE TRANSMITTAL SHEET

TO: ⬜⬜⬜⬜⬜⬜⬜⬜⬜⬜⬜⬜⬜⬜⬜⬜⬜⬜⬜⬜⬜⬜⬜⬜⬜⬜⬜

FROM: ⬜⬜⬜⬜⬜⬜⬜⬜⬜⬜⬜⬜⬜⬜⬜⬜⬜⬜⬜⬜⬜⬜⬜⬜⬜⬜⬜

COMPANY: ⬜⬜⬜⬜⬜⬜⬜⬜⬜⬜⬜⬜⬜⬜⬜   DATE: ⬜⬜⬜⬜⬜⬜⬜

FAX NUMBER: [＿＿＿＿＿]   TOTAL NO. OF PAGES INC. COVER: ⬜⬜

PHONE NUMBER: [＿＿＿＿＿]   SENDER'S REFERENCE NUMBER: [＿＿＿＿]

RE: YOUR REFERENCE NUMBER: [＿＿＿＿]

☐ URGENT   ☐ FOR REVIEW   ☐ PLEASE COMMENT   ☐ PLEASE REPLY   ☐ PLEASE RECYCLE

NOTES/COMMENTS:

Figure 16-36
Example cover sheet with targets.

Defining Fields on a Form

A field is a natural grouping of characters (i.e., letters or numbers). A field is a set of data located in a particular region of the form that the recognition engine is to read as a whole, such as a name or a telephone number. For isolated or semiconstrained fields, the length of the field is equal to the maximum number of characters that make up the field. (See Figure 16-36).

Field Properties

Each character and field is defined in order for the recognition engine to work.

- Field name— (e.g., To, From, Re).
- Classifier—A classifier specifies the type of characters the system can expect for this field (e.g., handprint numbers and letters).
- Segmentation— (e.g., semiconstrained characters).
- Maximum Characters in Field—This option is only available with semiconstrained characters.
- Modes—Special instruction for the recognition engine (e.g., deslant field).

OUTPUT TEXT FILE FORMAT · · · · · · · · · · · · · · ·

The H2T service can output the following:

- ASCII text files—the output file name can be defined by an environment variable OUTFILE or by the MQI interface.

POSTPROCESSING ·

- Suppression (or preservation) of blanks and punctuation.
- Conversion of lowercase to uppercase letters.
- Intelligent selection of letters vs. digits in alphanumeric fields.
- Lexicon-enhanced recognition.

INPUT EXAMPLE ·

Figure 16-37 shows the input to the H2T program.

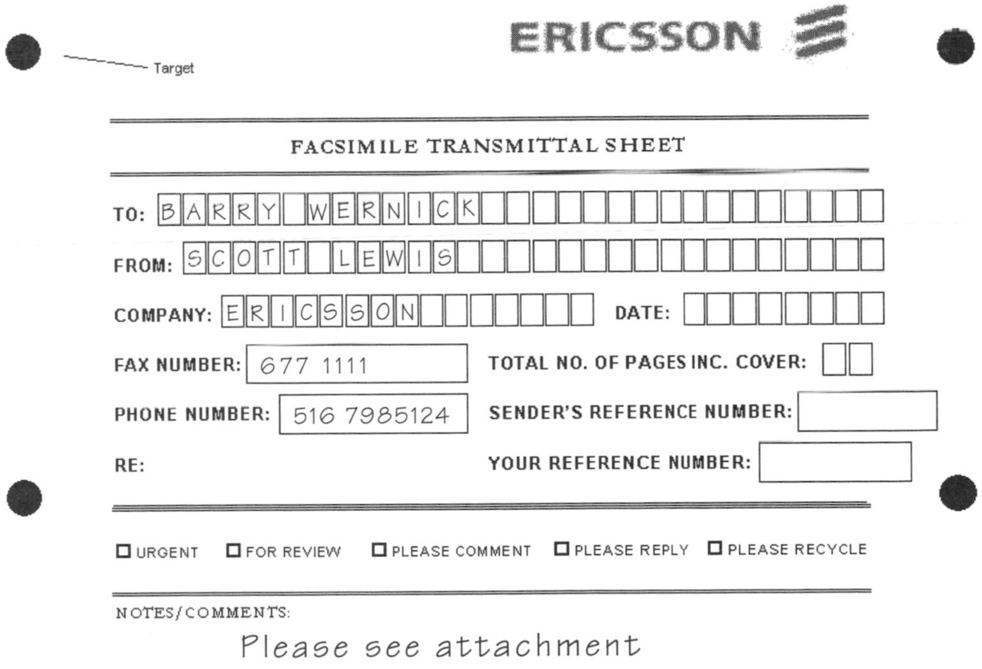

ERICSSON

Target

FACSIMILE TRANSMITTAL SHEET

TO: BARRY WERNICK

FROM: SCOTT LEWIS

COMPANY: ERICSSON   DATE:

FAX NUMBER: 677 1111   TOTAL NO. OF PAGES INC. COVER:

PHONE NUMBER: 516 7985124   SENDER'S REFERENCE NUMBER:

RE: YOUR REFERENCE NUMBER:

☐ URGENT   ☐ FOR REVIEW   ☐ PLEASE COMMENT   ☐ PLEASE REPLY   ☐ PLEASE RECYCLE

NOTES/COMMENTS:

Please see attachment

Figure 16-37
Handwriting Input to H2T.

Console Output

Figure 16-38 shows the output from the H2T executable with "debug" turned on. Nothing is output when "debug" is turned off.

IT–BUS INTERFACES . . . .

Table 16.10 shows the IT–Bus interfaces used by the H2T service.

MQI

Metering service is used for billing, among other things.

LDAP

LDAP is used to obtain various configuration data from the directory server.

SNMP

H2T service has defined an SNMP MIB, hand2txtDll.mib.

Figure 16-38
H2T console output.

Table 16.10   IT-Bus

IT–BUS	Protocol	Service
System control	LDAP MQI System Call and MQI IPC	Directory lookup Metering service (CPS to H2T) (H2T to ICR)
OAM&P	SNMP Report Event (NT)	Management agent

System Call and MQI

The H2T service receives as input a "tif" file name and returns the same file name with the "txt" extension, if so desired. It is configurable.

System Call

The file to be converted was passed to H2T by a system call.

Distributed Processing

Distributed computing was tried using MQSeries. CPS and H2T exchange remote procedure calls through the MQ software infrastructure, ergo the new protocol MQI. This is the same infrastructure used by the TDR service with the exception of the NT distributed file system. The file system is used to move the files.

IPC (COM API)

IPC (interprocess communications) is the exchange of data between two or more processes or applications.

During the conversion process, the H2T accesses the ICR component through the IPC, which the COM API supports automatically.

On the same machine, a secure IPC is used by H2T. (See Figure 16-39).

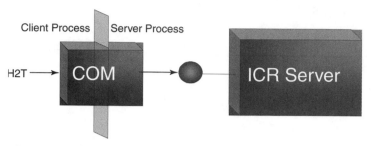

Figure 16-39
Interprocess communications.

SERVICE START EVENTS . . . .

- Allocate and initialize internal structures.
- Alert system manager of progress.
- Establish needed channel(s) with ICR.
- Validate input file and format.
- Generate a "service start event" in the event log.
- Open the session with the meter data repository service and the SNMP service. Report any missing services at start-up in the event log. Tell any service that H2T is in service.

SERVICE STOP EVENTS . . . .

- Indicate that H2T is not in service by setting the operating status in the MIB.
- Unassign and deallocate any input channel(s).
- Unassign, deallocate, and log off any output channel(s).
- Generate a "service stop event" in the event log.
- Terminate the H2T service.

CRASH . . . .

In the event of an uncontrolled stop (crash) of the service, the SNMP agent detects the absence of the service generating an SNMP trap (belly up) and logging an event in the event log file.

ALARM HANDLING . . . .

When a persistant failure occurs and when it is remedied, alarms and alarm ceasing instructions are generated and sent as SNMP traps. The following alarms are generated by H2T:

- Failure to find resource.
- Failure to connect to resource.

REPORT EVENT HANDLING . . . .

Report events are generated and sent as ReportEvents to the NT event log. The following events are generated by H2T:

- Service started.
- Service stopped.
- Failure to connect to SNMP agent.

DIRECTORY SERVER . . . .

At start-up, the H2T service must fetch information in the directory server. Figure 16-40 shows an example of an H2T service entry in an LDAP directory server.

ARCHITECTURE FOR OPTICAL HANDWRITING RECOGNITION (OHR) . . . .

This subsection explains the architecture for OHR.

How It Works

H2T handles image files from any source, cleaning up the image, deleting lines, boxes, and combs, and removing noise while reading broken characters. In addition, it can process distorted or skewed images by segmenting individual characters within

```
dn: mcn=H2TAgent@carol.dilbertville, msn=Dilbertville,o=MessagingSystem, c=US
objectclass: mediacomponent
mcn: H2Tagent@carol.dilbertville
mcc: H2T
rev-level: Beta 0.9
host: carol
port: 0
service: H2T-Service
patch-level: 0
component-path: c:\hand2txtService\hand2txt.exe
control-bus-name: ANY.TO.TRAFFIC
snmp-dll-path: c:\H2TDLL\H2Tdll.dll
snmp-wait-to: 40
description: Hand Written Image to Text File Services
mimeSrcFOrmat: IMAGE
mimeDestFormat: TEXT
```

Figure 16-40
Service entry in LDAP server.

each field, using its large collection of image processing tools. Highly sophisticated neural network–based recognition engines are used to recognize the characters—machine printed, handprinted, alpha, numeric, alpha-numeric, special national or regional characters or symbol sets, and grayscale images. Lastly, regular upgrades are made to its large family of character classifiers, so that more and more characters are accurately recognized.

H2T's unique recognition engines assign multiple confidence levels to each recognized character, so that the system can be configured to tightly control the acceptance of forms and error levels in the application.

H2T Processing

Table 16.11 shows the steps for image processing.

SCALABILITY . . . .

You can run the H2T on many different processor configurations, depending on the application's cost and performance requirements.

Low End

A software-only version will run directly on a slower PC.

Table 16.11 Image Processing Flow

Step	Action	Description
1	Image Input	Input of these file types: • Scanned (TIFF or JPEG) • Faxes (Group 3, 4) • Stored (TIFF or JPEG)
2	Preprocessing	Preprocessing includes these actions: • Form identification • Form cleanup and removal • Registration • Line removal • Field deskew • Repair broken characters • Separate touching characters • Background removal
3	Segmentation	Segments include • Hand print • Machine print • Change of address detection
4	Recognition	Things to recognize include • Hand print • Machine print • Mark sense (check box) • Alternate recognition • Voting classifiers • Multilanguage full-page OCR (LITRE)
5	Postprocessing	Final post-processing actions include • Force alpha or numeric • Force uppercase • Find punctuation • Remove punctuation • Suppress characters • Spell check • Space recognition and insertion

High End

Multiple proprietary coprocessor boards (even of different types) are available from Mitek, or more powerful CPUs may be combined to achieve the needed throughput. The recognition results will in all cases be identical—only the speed will differ.

RECOGNITION AND CONFIDENCE VALUES . . . . . .

H2T's multiple recognition engines are based on a neural network, which recognizes specific sets of characters and assigns a set of confidence levels to each recognized character. The confidence values are used to determine whether or not to present the recognized character to an operator for manual verification.

Tech Talk

Extensive tests have shown that the confidence values directly correlate with accuracy. Automated processing then occurs more quickly with less chance of substitution errors.

CLIENT/SERVER INTERACTION . . . .

QuickStroke API is not a network-level product. The client and server must run on the same machine at this time. Most communications between the applications and the ICR server are application requests for service. Standard application requests for service include

- Sending data to the ICR server.
- Starting a recognition operation to process the data.
- Asking for the status of the ICR server or ongoing operations.
- Retrieving processed data from the ICR server.

If the ICR server needs data for processing or needs to dispose of processed data, it raises a blocked condition and waits for the application to clear the condition by making the necessary I–O request.

The ICR server can communicate with the application to inform it that the ICR task has entered a blocked state. In some cases, the API interface code, linked with the application, will resolve the block on behalf of the application.

In simple terms, an application accesses recognition in the following manner:

- Set initial conditions.
- Start processing.
- Respond to changes in server status.

It is very important that an application respond to changes in server status, especially with regard to blocked conditions. Blocked conditions are an indication that recognition cannot continue until the condition is resolved.

INTERFACE LIBRARY

This subsection explains the interface library.

Offsets and Extents

Figure 16-41 shows how the various offsets and sizes (extents) are measured.

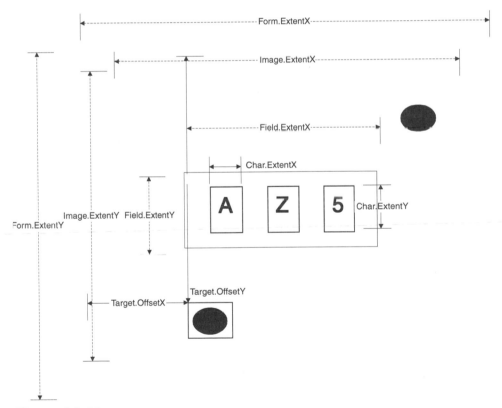

Figure 16-41
Offsets and extents.

LIBRARY FUNCTIONS DATA STRUCTURE RELATIONSHIPS ·················

The API uses hierarchic data structures implemented with dynamic linked lists. The following topics show the relationships of the various lists.

RECOGNITION RESULTS LIST ················

Figure 16-42 shows the results of the reading process (H2T). Depending on the parameter passed to the function idept_get_results, it returns the results for just one field or for a list of fields.

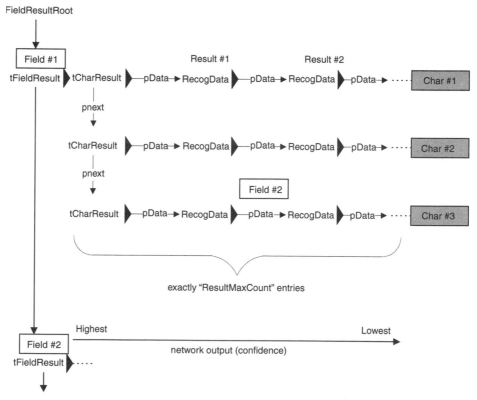

Figure 16-42
Recognition results list.

READING THE LIST SAMPLE SOURCE . . . .

Figure 16-43 shows a useful code snippet for reading a list in order to ascertain the characters.

FORMS LIST . . . .

Figure 16-44 shows the relationship between the various data elements. The calling application is not required to store the information in any particular form. The calling application only needs to store "Ids."

DATA DEFINITIONS . . . .

Table 16.12 contains a list of standard, predefined data types used to communicate with the API. All definitions listed in this section are contained in either ICRLIB.H or MTKTYPES.H, which are both part of the API distribution.

```
tpChar          pFieldBuffer  =NULL;
tpCharResult    pCharResult   =NULL;
tpRecogData     pRecogData    =NULL;
tpFieldResult   pFieldResultList=NULL;

pFieldResultList = ppFieldResult;
while (pFieldResultList != NULL) {

 pCharResult = pFieldResultList->pCharList;
 while (pCharResult != NULL) {

        /* loop through all results for current character */
        /* and collect all the characters */
        //pRecogData = pCharResult->pData;
   OutMsg[n++]=pCharResult->pData->Char;

        pCharResult = pCharResult->pNext;

}/*End while CharResult*/
OutMsg[n++]='\n';
```

Figure 16-43
Reading the list sample code.

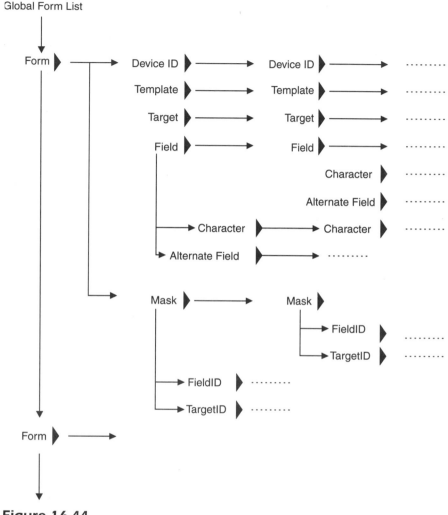

Figure 16-44
Forms list.

FIELD-SPECIFIC OPTIONS . . . .

Each field has options. Therefore, to optimize each field, it is necessary to define each field for the type of data expected in it. Each option is a single bit set using a bit flag in a 32-bit mask and referred to by its symbolic name. The options are set using one of two modes.

Predefined bit masks are stored with the formIdepth_set_value.

Table 16.12   Field-Specific Options

Field Name	Description
Field_mode_alt_recog	If the main field and alternate field specified different groups, one hand print and the other machine print, then the software will determine whether to use the hand-print or the machine-print classifier.
Field_mode2_auto_dilate	This option attempts to automatically dilate broken characters.
Field_mode2_best_oracle Field_mode_multiple_oracles	These control the output of the results list by returning the result from the best classifier, or all of the results. If multiple_oracles is specified, the results returned by each classifier are left together as a unit and concatenated.
Field_mode_broken_characters	The segmentation code for unconstrained hand-printed fields will attempt to recombine disjointed fragments of characters into the original character(s).
Field_mode_char_recog	Each character within the field definition can contain a list of recognition values; in addition to the main value specified for the field, this becomes the default when set. This character-specification recognition classifier will then be applied to the character, independently of which classifiers are specified for the other characters. To define such a field, set this flag and pass a linked list of recognition values for each character.
Field_mode2_check_box_hand_find	This is used to detect the presence of handwriting in a machine printed field. This is especially useful for change of address detection in machine-printed address blocks.
Field_mode2_check_box_pix_count	This is used to detect the presence of handwriting in a machine printed field. This is especially useful for change of address detection in machine-printed address blocks.
Field_mode2_clear_left Field_mode2_clear_lower Field_mode2_clear_right Field_mode2_clear_upper	The system removes the intrusions of certain height and area.

(continued)

Table 16.12   Field-Specific Options (continued)

Field Name	Description
Field_mode2_deskew_machineprint	The skew of the extracted field is computed and compared against the global field skew threshold.
Field_mode2_enhance_case	This algorithm is used to improve the chance that the case of letters will be correct inside of words (e.g., USA, Andromeda). This option only applies to letters and not to digits, punctuation marks, and so on.
Field_mode_enhance_probable	This algorithm raises the confidence value of a character's first result, if the second result belongs to the same ambiguity class, and raises it again, if the third result belongs to the same class as well.
Field_mode_find_colons Field_mode_find_commas Field_mode_find_dashes Field_mode_find_periods	Corresponding characters are found when these flags are set. Only the "commas," "dashes," and "periods" flags apply to handwritten text (i.e., not the "colons" flag).
Field_mode2_find_umlauts Field_mode2_find_diacritics	Recognize some characters containing diacritical marks, such as the German umlaut or the Scandinavian characters.
Field_mode_force_uppercase	Any character recognized as a lowercase letter will be converted to its uppercase equivalent.
Field_mode_insert_blanks	Blank characters are returned only from fields using isolated and semiconstrained segmentation types. This option allows you to retrieve the spaces from all other fields as well. All spaces found in the field at the appropriate position relative to the nonblank characters are returned to the results list.
Field_mode_laplacian	An edge-enhancement filter improves the appearance and segmentation of characters and thus helps the recognition process. The filter works on each gray pixel by modifying its value depending on the value of its 8 neighbors and using two global values.
Field_mode_multiple_oracles	Same as field_mode2_best_oracles.
Field_mode_no_remove_orphan Field_mode_no_remove_stalactite	Useful when character is touching the boundaries of the defined character box. It allows the developer to specify the side that is touching.

Table 16.12 Field-Specific Options (continued)

Field Name	Description
Field_mode_no_remove_stalagmite Field_mode_no_remove_window	
Field_mode2_reject_cursive	Detects cursive handwriting. It is used to reject it.
Field_mode2_remove_boxes Field_mode2_remove_combs	Removes boxes that inhibit the recognition of characters.
Field_mode_remove_lines	Removes lines that are part of the form. These lines could be long lines reaching completely across the field, or boxes around each character.
Field_mode_remove_lines_autosiz	All horizontal and vertical lines found in the field that satisfy certain conditions are removed from the field bitmap before the character segmentation takes place. If field_mode_remove_lines is set, then the minimal horizontal and vertical lengths of lines to be removed are defined by global values. If field_mode_remove_Lines_autosiz is set, the minimal horizontal length is the distance from the left edge of the left-most character and the right edge of the right-most character; the minimal vertical length is the largest character Y extent in the field.
Field_mode2_remove_noise	Removes all pixel groups in the field whose pixel count lies outside of a specified range. This is useful on dirty images of photocopies, fax copies, or colored or patterned paper. It is good for imperfections, such as spurious pixels, during the binarization process.
Field_mode2_save_box_info Field_mode2_save_comb_info Field_mode2_save_line_info	Retrieves the coordinates of the lines, combs, and boxes that are removed during prepocessing.
Field_mode_save_char_bitmap	Retrieves the bitmaps of the individual recognized characters.
Field_mode_save_field_bitmap	Retrieves the bitmaps of the individual recognized fields.
Field_mode_sloppy_registration	The field floats to the text. It applies to semiconstrained hand printed fields.

(continued)

Table 16.12   Field-Specific Options (continued)

Field Name	Description
Field_mode_spatial_filter	Filters background pixels that are part of patterns running across the field. This allows the segmentation process to achieve better performance on the resulting image.
Field_mode_suppress_unusual	The segmentation code for unconstrained hand-printed fields will reduce the number of both words falsely containing digits or punctuation and of numbers falsely containing letters or punctuation.
Field_mode_test_for_commas Field_mode_test_for_dashes Field_mode_test_for_periods	Search for punctuation in unconstrained hand-printed fields.
Field_mode2_update_image	Updates and removes images from fields that have spurious pixels or characters out of alignment with the other characters.

FORM STUDIO EXAMPLE . . . .

The Mitek form tool allows the user to define fields, as shown in Figure 16-45.

Choosing a Segmentation Type

Next to recognition, segmentation is the most important part of performing text reading. There are many types (see 16.13). Segmentation is the method of extracting each individual character from the field. The different methods available are split into three main categories: for hand-printed text, for machine-printed text, and special purpose methods (i.e., reading checks).

Semiconstrained Segmentation

This segmentation combines the speed of isolated segmentation with some of the flexibility of unconstrained segmentation. The algorithm will search outside the original character area if the text seems to go beyond it, and will thus expand the original box, if necessary.

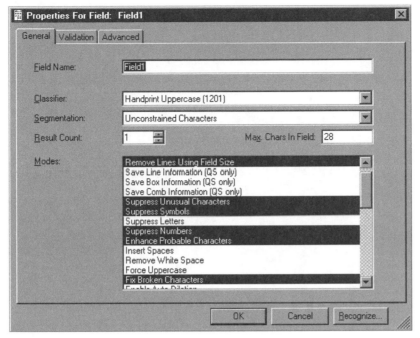

Figure 16-45
Field-specific options within form studio.

Table 16.13 Segmentation Types

Segmentation	Handprinted Text	Machine-Printed Text
ISOLATED	Used when characters are known in advance and are not expected to violate the character box boundaries	N/A
SEMICONSTRAINED	Suitable for a characters that are contained within an individual box. It allows for some characters to protrude outside of those boundaries.	N/A
UNCONSTRAINED	Used for fields in which location of characters is unknown. Best for single-line fields.	Used for fields in which location of characters is unknown. Works on multiline and proportional texts.

(continued)

Table 16.13 Segmentation Types (continued)

Segmentation	Handprinted Text	Machine-Printed Text
MONOSPACED	N/A	Used for fields made up of monospaced characters; works on multiple lines, and character columns need not be aligned; marginal tolerance for field skew (rotation).
MONOSPACED_LABEL	N/A	Used for fields on a form containing the same font (of the same size) throughout. Works on multiline fields with straight, separated lines of text.
MACH_FONT	N/A	Same as MONOSPACED_LABEL, but works well on single fields.
CHECK CHECK_1 CHECK_2 CHECK_3 CHECK_4	Used on courtesy amount fields on checks containing a currency symbol. The field must include the "$."	N/A
ZIP	Used for postal ZIP code images—both the regular 5-digit and the 5 + 4 digit varieties.	N/A
MACH_FIELD	N/A	Same as MACH_FONT, but works well on single fields
BLOBS	Used for both handprinted text and machine-printed text, but for single fields only. Will automatically insert breaks in words. Corresponds roughly to UNCONSTRAINED segmentation for handprint and MAC_FIELD segmentation for machineprint.	
GROUPS (Page Reader Option)	Used for multiline fields in which text could be hand printed or machine printed. It will automatically insert breaks between words. Is a more general machine-print segmentation than MONOSPACED_LABEL; this is the only segmentation for multiline, handprinted text.	

Table 16.13 Segmentation Types (continued)

Segmentation	Handprinted Text	Machine-Printed Text
GROTESQUE	N/A	Used for special stylized fonts such as CMC7. The characters in these fonts are composed of single isolated vertical or horizontal bars. These fonts are a combination of bar codes and regular fonts such as OCR-B.

Machine-Printed Segmentation

This segmentation considers the information collected from other fields and applies only to text printed using the same font of the same size. However, all machine fonts and sizes are allowed.

Automatic Form Identification

It is possible to determine the form automatically on the fly, which is useful when dealing with many different forms. The form must satisfy the following requirements:

- Horizontal or vertical lines must be present.
- Each form's line pattern must be distinct.

The form identification itself is a two-step process of teaching the API what each form type looks like and splitting form recognition and text recognition.

Settable Parameters

It is possible to tune the API's functionality using of the *idepth_set_value* function. It changes various parameters at run time. There are global and field-specific parameters.

Query Parameters

It is possible for applications to retrieve various real-time parameters from the ICR engine. These include

- Available memory on a device.
- Registration results.
- Version number and date of device software.
- Version number and date of recognition network (classifier).

CAR (Courtesy Amount Reading)

CAR is the ability of the ICR engine to interpret personal checks, business checks, and other financial documents. Features included with this option are

- Currency cut-off distance (i.e., $).
- Adjustable currency symbol confidence interval.
- Star confidence (i.e., ***VOID***).
- Stipulated currency symbol location.
- Disabling special (neural) classifiers.

INSIDE H2T CLIENT . . . .

The handwriting-to-text process is explained in this subsection.

NMake Details

The H2T program was written mainly in the "C" language, because the ICR API is in "C." It compiles in Visual Studio C++ 6.0. The nmake command may be used in place of Visual Studio.

The specific libraries used include these paths are as follows:

- \OC\LIB.
- \OC\INCLUDE.
- \OC\SOURCE.
- Microsoft Visual Studio\VC98\INCLUDE.
- Microsoft Visual Studio\VC98\ATL\INCLUDE.
- Microsoft Visual Studio\VC98\LIB.

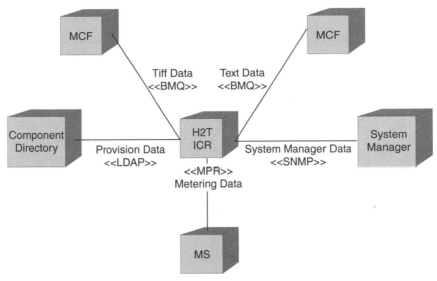

Figure 16-46
H2T processor diagram.

Here are the specific library files:

- IDUTIL.lib.
- ICRUISL.lib.

ARCHITECTURE FOR H2T DATA TRANSFER ......

Figure 16-46 shows the unified modeling language (UML) processor diagram of the system for the H2T.

Tech Talk

It is possible to have one processor perform all of these tasks.

EXPLANATION OF PROCESSOR DIAGRAM ....

The following table 16.14 explains the duties of each of the processors:

Table 16.14 Processor

Processor	Description
CPS	The call processing server retrieves TIFF data from the message store. It then notifies H2T through a media-conversion MQI. H2T then performs the conversion. T2W and W2V are not shown, but are necessary for the fax-to-speech conversion process. Multiple nodes are supported through MQI.
MS	Metering server records the conversion events for creating billing or charging records.
Directory	When H2T is started, the directory is consulted in order to obtain site-specific information about the other services' interface.
H2T	H2T is where the optical character recognition is performed. ICR is shown sharing the same processor. At this time, it is not possible to distribute this task.
System Manager	The system manager listens for H2T traps and events. It provides a real-time view of the H2T service.

CONSTRAINTS . . . .

The H2T service has what I believe are the following constraints:

- Training is required for fax cover letters that do not have a form. This means that an operator pool is needed, or the person sending the fax must be instructed ahead of time to use a specially designed cover sheet.
- A missing "Undo" key in the form tool makes editing forms difficult.
- Adding new fields to an existing form is annoying, since the field number cannot be changed; thus, the output is in the wrong order.
- When letters touch, the engine interprets them as new letters; this may be rectified with field-specific options.
- Names get concatenated, so special directory searches using concatenated names may be useful in determining the TO and FROM fields of a fax.
- Field labels are not in the results list, so it becomes necessary to read the forms file to create a match and then output the appropriate text (i.e., FROM + RECOGNIZED NAME = RESULT).

- Uppercase and lowercase handwriting makes a significant difference in the recognition results. Much more intelligence is needed in the engine or the client program to provide a high-quality service.
- Plain text messages are fine, but HTML documents are not. There is no provision for this.

CONCLUSION AND COMMENTARY · · · · · · · · · · ·

The Mitek API was somewhat difficult to use, since the resulting data structure was a three-dimensional, double-linked list. Once one becomes familiar with the addressing and indirection syntax, wireless services are just a keystroke away.

The documentation and sample code was good. A person familiar with C can have an application running in under one month. The reason it takes three to four times longer than Xerox's TextBridge has to do with the learning curve involved with the form tool. This tool defines the handwriting recognition fields, since free-floating handwriting recognition engines have another five years to go before they are ready for integration into wireless products.

In summary, this technology is ready for wireless applications and terminals! Quality of service is a risk. Spell checkers can improve the accuracy of the handwriting recognition for conventional sentences. Improvements to subscriber name recognition are possible by dipping into the directory server to verify the accuracy of the recognized result.

The recognition was excellent when the fields were well defined and the parameters were set correctly. Finding the optimal setting for a particular fax can be time consuming.

Furthermore, the performance of the OCR process was surprisingly fast (4817 ms, or about 5 seconds) for a fax with these characteristics:

- Various fonts.
- A table.
- Header and footer.
- Line count: 128.
- Word count: 172.
- Character count: 2284.

HOW TO OBTAIN THE API . . . .

Mitek Systems, Inc. 10070 Carroll Canyon Road, San Diego, California 92131, (619) 635-9500, (619) 635-5908 [fax], E-mail: support@miteksys.com, http://www.miteksys.com.

REFERENCES . . . .

QuickStrokes Application Development Manual. Mitek Systems, Inc.: San Diego, CA, 1998.

ACRONYMS . . . .

- ASCII—American Standard Code for Information Interchange.
- MQI—Batch MQSeries protocol for remote procedure calls.
- COM—Component object model interface.
- ICR—Image-to-character recognizer.
- MEMA—Messaging enterprise manager agent.
- TTS—Text-to-speech process.
- T2W—Text-to-wave file program.
- W2V—Wave-to-vox program.
- TIFF—Tagged image file format. TIFF provides a way of storing and exchanging digital image data. Major scanner vendors developed TIFF to help link scanned images with the popular desktop publishing applications. It is now used for many different types of software applications, ranging from medical imagery to fax modem data transfer, CAD programs, and 3D graphics packages. The current TIFF specifications support three main types of image data: black and white, halftones (or dithered), and grayscale data.

17 Distributed Batch Processing for Wireless Communications

INTRODUCTION ·

This section examines how to best handle batch processing on one machine or in a distributed computing environment. The trial application was media conversion, but the concepts can be applied to other applications. Several infrastructures were tested in order to learn which is robust and efficient.

Here is a list of the alternative batch processing approaches examined:

- Simple synchronous system calls on one platform.
- DLL server on one platform.
- DLL server that crosses multiple servers.
- EXE server on one platform.
- EXE server that spans multiple platforms using a proxy and DCOM.
- Queuing as an alternative to the aforementioned approaches.

A prototype with a timer was used to quantify most of the approaches. The results are documented and a conclusion reached.

By using an IP architecture in a computer lab, it was possible to prototype six different configurations for media conversion.

Media Conversion

Following are the two steps that constitute media conversion in this case:

- Convert a text file to a wave file.
- Convert a wave-to-vox file.

This media conversion was necessary in order to produce an audible output of an e-mail message on a mobile phone.

What the Distributed Tests Have in Common

The distributed batch processing tests have a datagram in common; UDP was used instead of TCP over IP. This is essentially an investigation of protocols that are connection oriented (vs. connectionless), as well as an exploration of programming techniques.

SYSTEM CALL ON ONE PLATFORM . . . .

In this case, the client used a system call to a program that performed the media conversion. This was fine in single platform environments in which requests for media conversion were few. But, system calls use resources, like memory, and do not share them. When the system call is made, the cmd.exe (shell) environment plus the program are loaded into memory and disposed of upon completion of the request. This is very costly in terms of performance.

Furthermore, the system call was to a BAT file containing a list of commands (set, t2w, w2v, move, and del). Attempts were made to improve the time in the batch file, but each step was needed in the specified sequence.

Pros

- Simple C-hook or _system call is useful for prototypes.
- System call offers more protection to the client application than do DLLs, since they have their own memory address space.

Cons

- Single thread of execution means that nothing can connect to the program issuing the call.
- There is no facility to return messages to the calling program, since the function status information is returned instead (i.e., out of memory to launch command interpret).
- You must explicitly flush (using flush or _flushall) or close any stream before calling the system.
- It is memory intensive, since the cmd.exe is invoked with associated environment.

DLL SERVER ON ONE PLATFORM . . . .

Pros

- If multiple client processes create objects from the DLL, the in-process server is loaded into each process. Code from the DLL is shared between the processes, but the data is not.
- DLL servers are efficient in terms of clients accessing their interfaces' methods. In the best case (which this was), no proxy will be used to access the object's interfaces; compared with creating a C++ stack-based object, there is just one extra level of indirection to get to the object.
- DLL servers can delay creating their class objects until DLLGetClass-Object() is called for that particular class object. This makes a client "lightweight."
- Clients use pointers to the server's class objects from (indirect) calls to *DllGetClassObject*().
- DLL servers run in the security context of the client process; the objects from the DLL have the same security clearance and identity as the client process. This is fine for trusted objects, but if the object has been written by an unknown third party, the preferred method is to run under a less-privileged account.

Cons

- DLLs are platform dependent, but the concepts are still applicable across any platform.
- DLL servers are risky. They are loaded into the memory space of the client, so they have complete access to the client's memory. A badly written server could write over the client's memory, causing the process to crash. A malicious server can wreak havoc.

CLIENT-BATCH PROCESSING USING IPC . . . .

IPC (Interprocess communications) is the exchange of data between two or more processes or applications. This exchange takes place solely through software, without any human intervention.

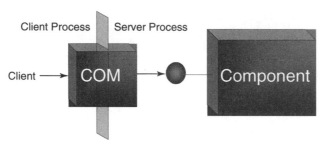

Figure 17-1
IPC.

During the conversion process, the T2W accesses the text-to-speech engine component through IPC, which the COM API supports automatically.

On the same machine, secure IPC is used by T2W; please see Figure 17-1.

In both cases, a connection between computers at a process-to-process level allows data to flow in both directions. Windows 98 includes the following inter-process communication (IPC) mechanisms to support distributed computing: Windows Sockets, remote procedure calls (RPCs), NetBIOS, named pipes, mailslots, and the distributed component object model (DCOM).

DLL SERVER THAT SPANS MULTIPLE SERVERS . . . .

Pros

- Scales well when objects require vast amounts of computer resources, like media conversion.
- Excellent infrastructure in place under the Windows NT environment.
- DCOM is an open architecture, since Microsoft gave the code to the open group.

Cons

- DCOM is five to ten times slower at launching objects than local object calls.
- Many single calls are five to ten times slower than a single multiple call when the object requires vast amounts of resources to process.[1]

[1]Grimes, pg. 315.

- Performance is poor for objects that do not require much in terms of computer resources, since they take time to initiate.
- The DCOM infrastructure under UNIX from Software AG was a beta version that was just adequate for understanding how DCOM would work. It was not ready for production; the performance was poor.

EXE SERVER ON ONE PLATFORM . . . .

Pros

- EXE servers call CoInitialize() and CoUninitialize for themselves.
- EXEs have control over their own lifetime. An executable will unload when its code finishes running. In C++, that means that an executable will unload whenever it returns from its main() or WinMain() process.
- EXE servers create their class objects when the process is first loaded and register them with the class table. Clients are given pointers to interfaces on the class objects (indirectly) from the class table.
- EXE servers offer more protection to the client application than DLLs—EXEs have their own memory address space, so they cannot write across the client's memory.
- Multiple clients can connect to the same instance of an EXE server (if the server will allow it).

Cons

- EXE servers are usually less efficient than DLL servers, because communications with an EXE involves a proxystub.

DISTRIBUTED BATCH PROCESSING USING A PROXY . . . .

To distribute processing, the T2W program was split. The first part is basically a stub that takes all of the calls to the speech API and marshals the data over the network to the second part. The server portion continues to perform the synthesis and send digital audio data back to the stub. The engine stub supports all of the interfaces that the full engine supports, although it does almost none of the processing. In order to reduce network usage, the stub might accept a "compressed" audio format from the server and decompress on the host.

The second part of the engine lies on a server. It accepts the marshaled data from the stub and processes it, sending back notifications to the stub as digital audio is synthesized. The engine also supports a custom interface, ImyDistributed. The ImyDistributed interface allows an application that knows about remote processing to control which machine the processing is on, and to finely control what kind of data is transmitted over the LAN (or other communication method), so that unneeded data (such as mouth synchronization information) is not transmitted.

Furthermore, the use of CoInitializeEx(0,COINIT_MULTITHREADED) and a call against CoInitializeSecurity() is required on both sides of a DCOM session.

DISTRIBUTED CLIENT PROCESSING . . . .

The effort involved with making a client that could be distributed in one of several ways is described in this section. Below is a list of the alternatives for distributing the client command program (i.e., T2W):

- Default values are used to connect to a local out-of-process server.
- Command option *-node* <node address> allows the default node address for out-of-process activation to be overwritten.
- Command option *-domain* <domain address> allows the default node address for out-of-process activation on the least-used computer in the domain to be overwritten. This was not tried since it was not available. However, it should be possible with COM+.
- Command option *-inproc* activates an in-process server.
- Command option *-help* presents a help screen.

DCOM SERVER . . . .

Register the out-of-process server by starting the server with the *-regserver* command option (this was typically done automatically with the make -f makefile.make command). This will make all of the necessary entries into the registry to allow an activation of this server by the DCOM run time (namely RPCSS). To unregister the server again, use the *-unregserver* command option.

Start the server (atltest2_s) with the *-embedding* option to have the server pre-started.

DCOM INTERNALS . . . .

Figure 17-2 shows the internal structure of a DCOM client–server architecture. It is good for accessing components like a text-to-wave (T2W) or a wave-to-vox file (H2V) across machines in a secure, reliable, and flexible DCOM (DCE RPC) based manner.

DCOM CONFIGURATION . . . .

Figure 17-3 shows the processor diagram necessary for distributing the media conversion process using DCOM. The engines are on different machines than their clients' for the purpose of application remote activation.

Tech Talk

The proxy–directory server becomes a single point of failure, which is not the case when queues are used (See Figure 17-3.)

Tech Talk

DCOM was used on UNIX as well.

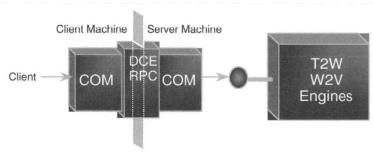

Figure 17-2
DCE–RPC-based DCOM protocol.

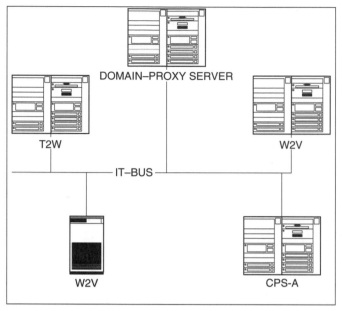

Figure 17-3
DCOM processor diagram.

Pros

Table 17.1 summarizes the problems solved with DCOM.[2]

Cons

- Complexity is the greatest disadvantage of DCOM, since it results in a long learning curve for developers.
- Initial out-of-process remote activation of an application takes time, due to establishing the security connection and searching through a stack of protocols for TCP/IP.
- Not all off-the-shelf products use DCOM.
- The open group maintains the source code, but it has not been well received.

[2]Brockschmidt, 1996.

Table 17.1 *Summary of Solutions to Component Software Problems*

Problem	Solution
Path dependencies, multiple providers of a service	Uses registry to map from abstract class identifiers to absolute server locations as well as to map between categories and class identifiers.
Decentralized definition of identifiers	Uses GUIDs generated by an algorithm to guarantee uniqueness across time and space, eliminating the need for centralized identifier allocation.
Specific management APIs for each service category	Supply a very simple generic and universal management API that accommodates all services categories, called "Implementation Location."
Sharing object instances across both process and machine boundaries	Implement marshalling of interface pointers with local–remote transparency, providing the ability to implement a server as an .EXE or a .DLL.
Different in-process, local, and remote programming models	Design a single model for all types of client–object connections supported through the local–remote transparency interface structure.
Lifetime management of servers and objects	Institute universal reference counting through the *IUNKNOWN* base interface, which all objects support and from which all other interfaces are derived.
Multiple services per server module	Use the CLSID:IID:table_offset syntax instead of module:ordinal to absolutely identify functions.
Versioning	Supports the concept of multiple immutable interfaces as well as interfaces that are strongly typed at both compile time and run time.
Single log in	DCOM allows a developer to create a wireless solution, requiring only one log in.
Management and maintenance	Many tools exist for maintenance and for monitoring transactions, as well as for security.
Open source code	Microsoft made the source code public. It is now available from the open group.

DISTRIBUTED PROCESSING USING QUEUES . . . . . .

This section begins with a simple single-threaded client/server program that uses a simple message pair between queues and finishes with more elaborate multithreaded client/server processing, using a split–join structure between queues.

Tech Talk

Psion Enterprise Computing is the first mobile device manufacturer to provide its customers with a new version of IBM's MQSeries that was developed for embedded devices. MQSeries is the world's best-selling enterprise messaging software from IBM. Having a version of it on a device allows mobile applications to exchange data with back-office systems, helping to ensure that data transactions between the Psion device and the server are made with security and reliability.

In addition, Psion supports IBM's new DB2 Everywhere database application in its new generation of products. This will enable Psion users to synchronize their mobile data with business-critical information that resides on enterprise servers. Psion and IBM also intend to work together to enable the new netBook product to support IBM's 340-megabyte (MB) microdrive, the world's smallest hard disk drive.

UDP and MQSeries

MQSeries for AIX version 5.1 supports the user datagram protocol (UDP), a part of the Internet suite of protocols, as an alternative to TCP. Use UDP instead of TCP for your mobile radio network when you need to reduce the traffic, and therefore the cost, on a packet radio data network.

UDP is supplied as part of the operating system or TCP/IP suite you are using; you do not need to buy and install a separate UDP product.

Client/Server Processing Using a Message Pair

The message pair is the basis for the support of traditional, synchronous client/server processing using message queuing. In this section, program CPS requests some service from program T2W. Program CPS requires a reply from program T2W in order to complete its processing. For example, the request from program CPS was to process a text file; the reply is a notification that the processing is completed. Figure 17-4 illustrates this example. Program CPS sends just the queue to respond on, Windows NT path, and file name (i.e., "Q2 \\SERVERx\R02.TXT") to program T2W through queue Q1, while the replies are returned to it from program T2W by Q2. Because program CPS requires the reply before it can complete its operation, this example is essentially synchronous. Although program CPS may perform processing after it has issued the message-to-program T2W, there will come a point when CPS needs the reply and will have to wait for it if the reply has not already been sent.

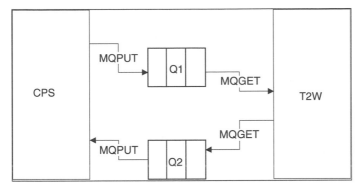

Figure 17-4
Client/server processing using a message pair (single thread).

Independent Message Pairs

Naturally, message pairs can be used to connect multiple client applications to a single server. The arrangement for two clients is shown in Figure 17-5. Though both clients send requests to the single server queue QS, the server correctly distributes replies back to their source. This is achieved in the server using the reply-to-queues command. The server sends replies to the specified queues. Naturally, because MQSeries completely hides the underlying network from the server, the clients might be communicating with the server with different and incompatible forms of networking. For example, one client might be using TCP/IP, while the other uses SNA LU.6.

RPC Equivalent

Because of its synchronous characteristics, the message pair is very similar to the traditional remote procedure call. Both client and server have to be available simultaneously, as does the network connecting them. For client-server arrangements, which must be synchronous, the message pair is the natural choice. However, it does not exploit any of the features of MQSeries, which lead to true time independence. Shortly, it is shown arrangements that do.

CLIENT/SERVER PROCESSING USING A TREE STRUCTURE . . . .

In Figure 17-6, program CPS is a client and there are two server programs—T2W and W2V. The client program CPS requests service from the server T2W by sending a message through queue *qsT2W*. Similarly, the request to server W2V is a message on

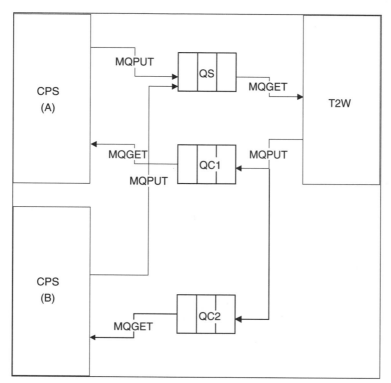

Figure 17-5
Client/server processing with independent message pairs (single thread).

queue *qsW2V*, and the request to server W2V is a message on queue QC1. All messages specify the same reply-to-queue command, namely QC1. Consequently, the client program CPS (A) can read the replies from the servers from this single queue.

TREE STRUCTURE WITH MULTIPLE CLIENTS . . . . . .

The tree arrangement shown in Figure 17-7 introduces additional parallelism into the processing of an application. While the servers are handling requests, additional processing is possible on the client. The servers themselves are operating in parallel on separate machines.

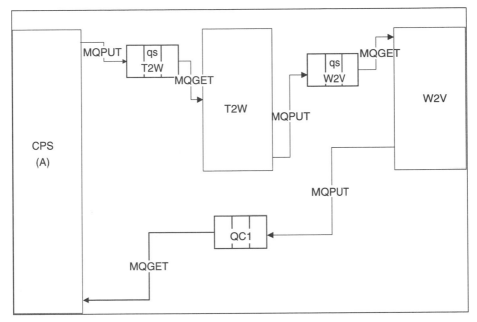

Figure 17-6
Application using a tree structure (single thread).

CLIENT ACCESS TO MULTIPLE SERVERS . . . .

This tree arrangement has the same kind of synchronous processing characteristic that we saw earlier in the example based on a message pair. Consequently, it is eminently suitable for those situations in which synchronous operation is required. The client issues the requests and waits for all of the replies to arrive. As with the message pair, network delays or failures will be apparent to the client. Since the servers may be running on different remote machines, the time taken for their replies to arrive may be very different. The tree is a classic structure for accessing multiple servers from a single client. However, it is a synchronous processing structure. We will see a time-independent version of this type of structure in the next section.

SPLIT-JOIN STRUCTURE . . . .

Figure 17-8 shows a split–join structure, roughly equivalent to the tree structure of Figure 17-7. As in the tree structure, the client program CPS (A) issues requests to the server programs T2W (A), (B), and (C), using their respective queues, QS1, QS2, and

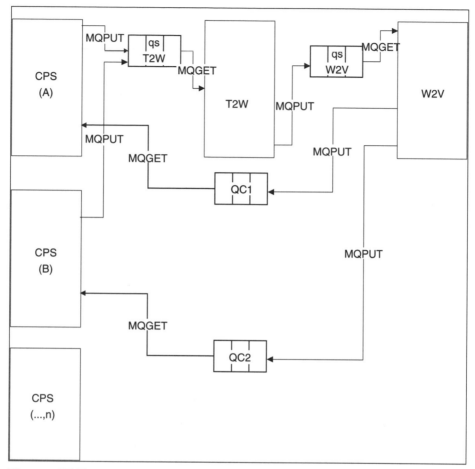

Figure 17-7
Client/server processing using a tree structure to support multiple clients (single thread).

QS3. The servers process the requests in parallel, and each sends its reply to the same reply-to-queue location, namely QS. The difference, then, is that QS is no longer read by client program CPS (A). Indeed, program CPS (A) has probably already terminated, having sent its requests to the servers. The reply-to-queue QS is processed by program CPS (B). The overall processing of the requests from client program CPS (A) is now time independent.

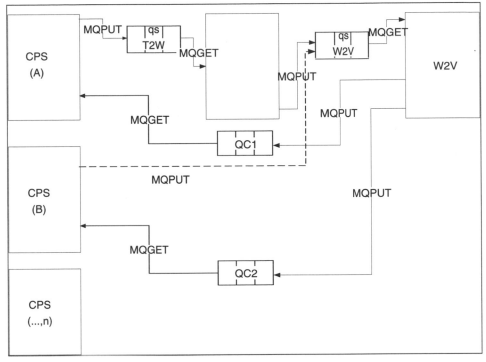

Figure 17-8
Clients accessing multiple servers (single thread).

REDUCING THE PROBLEM
OF THE BATCH WINDOW ....

Two major problems with batch operations are serialization and single threading. The intermediate files are produced in their entirety before the next step is started in part for protection. Should one step in the overall job fail, all of the information required for the job to be rerun is available. This reduces the time it takes to complete the over-all task, and, therefore, it is not necessary to restart the job from the beginning. An obvious consequence of the serial nature of a task is that the total length of time taken to execute the batch operations is the sum of the times needed for the individual steps. In the message-queuing version of a task, the intermediate files have been replaced by MQSeries queues. All of the application programs now execute concurrently, reading data from queues and writing data to queues. Of course, the initial input and the final

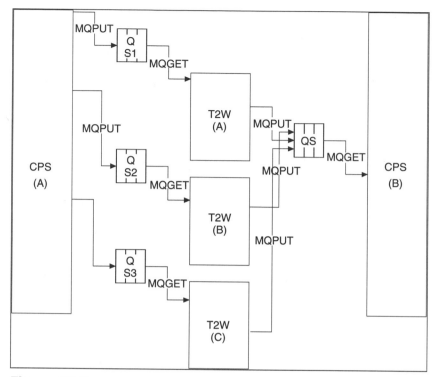

Figure 17-9
Client/server processing using a split–join structure.

output can be files. The overlap of processing made possible by the concurrent execution of the multiple steps provides the possibility for reducing the overall execution time of the batch operation.

In summary, queues can transform some of the serialized processing into parallel processing, so that everything can be accomplished within a fixed-time batch window.

DEVELOPMENT ENVIRONMENT QUANDARY . . . . .

Each supplier of development environments provides the developer different methods for creating distributed software. For example, Microsoft provides COM and DCOM, while Sun Microsystems is moving toward Java and RMI. HP uses RPC and CORBA.

This creates problems for developers, including, but not limited to the following:

- RPC-based applications cannot communicate with COM clients.
- COM clients cannot communicate with Java application servers.
- COM clients cannot communicate with CORBA servers, and so on.

SUMMARY AND CONCLUSION . . . .

Using MQSeries or an equivalent queuing product has its advantages over using DCOM/DCE from an architectural standpoint, since MQSeries is not dependent upon a directory or a proxy server. Furthermore, the complexity of the interface descriptions language is alleviated, and the development environment quandary is solved. However, this is not to say that MQSeries does not have drawbacks. The most glaring problem with queuing is infrastructure maintenance, which is not a trivial task.

However, Candle Corporation and others provide standards-based management software that helps minimize the cost. (See the Wireless Network Management Service section.)

Finally, it was learned that DCOM works well on large audio objects, since the audio objects may be manipulated in place through synchronous object calls. This process is less expensive than moving the file through the queuing infrastructure. The queuing infrastructure is good for short text messages. The MQSeries program writers must understand this too, because in the latest release they have introduced a new infrastructure, called "reference message," in which the sending program sends only the reference to a file, not the file itself. Similarly, the receiving program only receives notification of the arrival of a file through a reference message—it does not receive the actual file.

Therefore, to conclude this report, a discussion of value reference from a development perspective is suitable.

Value vs. Reference

Value implies that

- The object itself gets sent.
- The object must be translated into the receiver's space (i.e., MIME).
- Sending and decoding can be expensive.

- Using the object is inexpensive.
- Each side has its own copy.
- Specifically, performance is good for text messages, but not for large audio objects.

Reference means

- A "pointer" is sent to the object.
- There is no need to translate and build a new object.
- Using the object is much more expensive.
- We can build a value copy using a reference.
- Performance is good for large audio objects, since the objects are not moved like text messages.

In light of this comparison, there are some cases in which using both technologies is advantageous. For example, in a text-to-speech service, a message originates on a multitude of platforms; using a reliable text-messaging infrastructure makes sense for collecting audio objects. But, the actual generation of the audio would be best accomplished with DCOM, in which the central processor orchestrates the audio processing in the originating machines.

Finally, it should be possible to replace DCOM with the open Internet protocol IIOP.

REFERENCES . . . .

- Blakeley, Burnie, *Messaging & Queuing Using the MQI* (McGraw-Hill, Inc, 1995).
- Grimes, Dr. Richard, *DCOM Programming* (Wrox Press, 1997).
- Brockschmidt, Kraig, *What OLE is Really About* (Microsoft Corporation, 1996).

ACRONYMS . . . .

IIOP—Internet Inter-ORB protocol is an object-oriented protocol that makes it possible for distributed programs written in different programming languages to communicate with each other over the Internet.

RPC—Remote procedure call.

QS—Queue for server.

QC—Queue client.

CPS—Call processing service. This program retrieves messages from both the telephone network and the message storage server.

T2W—Text-to-wave program. This program takes a text file as input and returns a wave file.

W2V—Wave-to-VOX program. This program takes a wave file as input and returns a VOX file.

UDP—User datagram protocol. This is a transport layer, connectionless mode protocol, providing a (potentially unreliable, unsequenced, or duplicated) datagram mode of communication for delivery of packets to a remote or a local user.

18 Queuing Theory for Fixed and Wireless Communications

ABSTRACT AND PURPOSE · · · · · · · · · · · · · · · · · · ·

Queuing theory enables us to determine the statistics of the queue, from which such desired performance parameters as the time spent waiting in the queue or the probabilities that a transaction is blocked, or lost, on arrival, may be found.

Hence, Queuing Theory enables us to forecast the performance of a wireless packet network (i.e., CDPD, GPRS). In addition, a connection-oriented fixed network (i.e., sockets, SS7, GSM, and multifrequency network) falls into this category, but is a special case in which there is no waiting room (queue size = 0).

The goal of any queue analysis is to answer the following questions as they relate to the service or application:

Tech Talk

"Transaction," "message," and "packet" are used interchangeably.

- How long does a transaction wait to get serviced (delay)?
- If the queue fills, what happens?
- What should be the queue size?
- What is the average packet length, and what effect does it have on performance?
- How many servers are needed to meet transaction flow?
- How do competing products compare to MQSeries software?

Performance And Sizing

Performance is based on the following:

- Delay.
- Loss probability.

- Units of throughput = packets, messages, or transactions—unit time.

Sizing is based on the following:

- Number of servers required to meet the load.
- The amount of disk space necessary to support a given application to min-imize cost.

Hence, the forth coming sections explain techniques for performance tuning and sizing.

BACKGROUND . . . .

Imagine the following situations:

1. Shoppers waiting in front of checkout stands in a supermarket.
2. Cars waiting at a bridge.
3. Broken machines waiting to be serviced by a repairman.
4. Programs waiting to be processed by a digital computer.
5. E-mail waiting for routing.
6. Transactions waiting to be processed by a server.

What these situations have in common is the phenomenon of waiting. It would be most convenient if we could be offered these services and others like it without the "nuisance" of having to wait.

The waiting phenomenon is the direct result of randomness in the operation of service facilities. In general, the customer's arrival and his or her service time are not known in advance; otherwise the facility operation could be scheduled in a manner that would eliminate waiting completely.

The principal actors in a queuing situation are the customer and the server. The terms "jobs" and "customers" are used rather than "transactions" in more general queuing literature. A special case (i.e., Erlang B) is used for circuit-switched voice and data connections as well as ACD (automatic call distributors), operator pools tend to conform to the Erlang C model.

ELEMENTS OF QUEUING . . . .

Arrival Process

In queuing models, transaction arrival and service times are summarized in terms of probability distributions normally referred to as *arrivals* and *service time distribution*. These distributions may represent situations in which transactions may arrive or be served individually (i.e., the bank scenario). In other situations, transactions may arrive or be served in *batches* (i.e., the restaurant scenario).

Although the patterns of arrivals and departures are the main factors in the analysis of queues, other factors figure prominently in the development of queuing forcasts. The first factor is the manner of choosing customers from the waiting line to start service. This is referred to as the *service discipline*.

Service Discipline

Choosing transactions from the waiting line to start service is referred to as the service discipline. They are as follows:

- LIFO—Last in, first out.
- FIFO—First in, first out.
- SIRO—Service in random order.

In addition, it is possible that transactions may arrive at a facility in which *priority queues* are used. Those with higher priority will receive preference to start service first. However, the specific selection of customers from each priority queue may, follow any service discipline.

Execution of Service

This element of queuing deals with the design of a facility and the execution of a service. The facility may include more than one server, thus allowing as many transactions as the number of servers to be serviced simultaneously (i.e., bank tellers). In this case, all servers offer the same service and the facility is said to have *parallel servers*. On the other hand, the facility may comprise a number of series of stations, or threads of execution, through which the transaction may pass before service is completed (i.e., processing of a product on a sequence of machines). In this case, waiting lines may or may not be allowed between stations. The resulting situations are normally known as *queues in series,* or *tandem queues.*

The most general design of a service facility includes both series and parallel processing stations. These result in what we call *network queues.*

Queue Size

This element of queuing concerns admissible *queue size.* In certain situations, only a limited number of transactions may be allowed, possibly due to space limitation (i.e., MQSeries Version 2.1's capacity is only 1,000,000 messages). Once the queue fills to capacity, newly arriving customers are denied service and may not join the queue.

Calling Source

Another queuing element deals with the nature of the source from which calls for service (arrivals of transactions) are generated. The *calling source* may be capable of generating a finite number of transactions or (theoretically) infinitely many transactions. A finite source exists when an arrival affects the rate of the arrival of new transactions. For example, in a machine shop with a total of M machines, the calling source before any machine breaks down consists of M potential transactions. Once a machine is broken, it becomes a transaction and hence is incapable of generating new transactions until it is repaired. A distinction must be made between the machine shop situation and another scenario in which the "cause" for generating calls is limited, yet capable of generating an infinity of arrivals. For example, in a typing pool, the number of users is finite, yet each user could generate a limitless number of arrivals, since a user generally need not wait for the completion of previously submitted materials before generating new ones.

Human Behavior

Queuing models represent situations in which human beings take the roles of customers or in which servers must be designed to account for the effect of *human behavior.* A "human" server may speed up the rate of service when the waiting line builds up in size. A "human" customer may *jockey* from one waiting line to another in hopes of reducing his or her waiting time. Some "human" customers also may *balk* from joining a waiting line altogether because they anticipate a long delay, or they may *renege or abort* after being in the queue for a while because their wait has been too long.

These same scenarios can occur at the transaction level as well, depending on the implementation details.

There are as many queuing models as there are variations on the elements listed, which is why simulation software, as shown in Figure 18-4, becomes necessary to help define the scope.

Lastly, decision situations have been reported in which the effect of human behavior has so influenced the decision problem that the solution obtained from the mathematical model is deemed impractical. A good illustration of these cases is a version of the widely circulated elevator problem. In response to tenants' complaints about the slow elevator service in a large office building, a solution based on analysis by the waiting-line theory was found unsatisfactory. After studying the system further, it was discovered that the tenants' complaints were more a case of boredom, since, in reality, the actual waiting time was quite small. A solution was proposed whereby full-length mirrors were installed at the entrances of the elevators. The complaints disappeared because the elevator users were kept occupied watching themselves and others while waiting for the elevator.

The elevator illustration underscores the importance of viewing the mathematical aspect of operation research in the wider context of a decision-making process whose elements cannot be represented totally by a mathematical model.

NOTATION REVIEWED ·

Figure 18-1 shows a simple queue consisting of things arriving, things waiting to be served, and a server. Kendal notation is used later in this section.

Tech Talk

The following are interchangeable terms: arrivals = "inserts" or "puts," and departures = "deletes" or "gets."

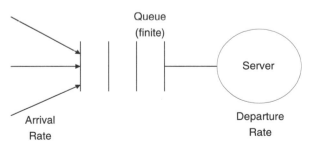

Figure 18-1
Queuing notation.

MIDDLEWARE . . . .

The middleware resides on a stack of queues each performing differently. Therefore, measurements are needed on each layer.

Example Spreadsheet for TCP/IP

Figure 18-3 shows an example output of an FTP application (one layer above the TCP/UDP) that runs on several platforms. It is shown here to illustrate that both network performance and middleware performance differ greatly from one implementation to the next. In addition, it provides insight about some potential problems that might be occurring below the middleware software.

Tech Talk

Another exercise would be the analysis of only UDP.

FORECASTING AND MODELING . . . .

Process

Here is the process for forecasting the performance of the middleware software:

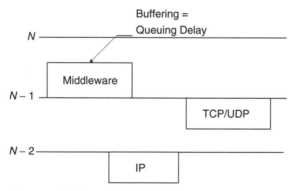

Figure 18-2
Layers of queues.

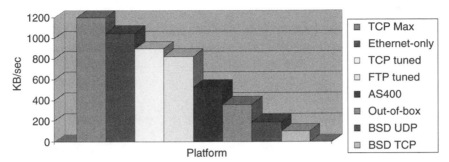

Figure 18-3
Network performance on a 10-Mbps Ethernet.

1. Data collection.
2. Data reduction or condensation.
3. Model building.
4. Model extrapolation (the actual forecast).

Data Collection

Gathering queuing data by benchmarking, among other things, may be done with timing class libraries. Table 18.1 shows the results of a get and a put timing class.

Table 18.1 Data Collection Performance as a Function of Message Size Example

Test Message Size	Iterations	Time (ms)	Num/sec
Calibration	100,000,000	751	133,155,792
PutMQ_01k	100,000	278,481	359
GetMQ_01k	100,000	214,299	466
PutMQ_02k	100,000	279,312	358
GetMQ_02k	100,000	621,114	161
PutMQ_04k	100,000	664,005	150
⋮	⋮	⋮	⋮
PutMQ_512k	100,000	685,426	145
GetMQ_512k	100,000	595,957	167

Tech Talk

PLATFORM: Pentium 266-MHz processor with 128-MB RAM and separate 2-GB SCSI drive.

Data Reduction

Data reduction is often involved in model building, since it is possible to have too much data in the forecasting process, as well as too little, or the granularity might be off.

Furthermore, some data may not be relevant to the problem and may just cloud the issue. It may come from the wrong hardware platform. Other data may be appropriate, but only in certain historical periods—for example, in forecasting the performance only since the last software crash.

Model Building

Model building involves fitting the collected data into a forecasting model that is appropriate in terms of minimizing the forecasting error. Obviously, judgement is involved in this process. It is the intent of this account to provide the reader with a starting point for creating good forecasting models. A simulator is the most useful tool, but spreadsheets come in handy when dealing with disk storage calculations.

Use the data gathered from the benchmarks as input into the simulator. Try different scenarios.

Tweak spreadsheets and programs to match reality.

Model Extrapolation

Model extrapolation deals with a model that matches reality but is extended by "what ifs"; first, run the simulator on the actual data recorded in the previous sections, then try and improve on the results. For example, increase the number of servers to see if the transaction holding time diminishes. The result may be counterintuitive; for example, adding another server may actually increase holding time on a transaction (context switching side effect).

Simulator

The queue simulator is useful in determining whether a queue is transient, whether the size of the queue is adequate, or if increasing the number of servers has any effect on the service rate, among other things. Figure 18-4 shows the user interface to a queue simulator. The back end is an *awk* script with a *Java* front end. Another simulator worth trying is found on the Web site www.erlang.com.

Tech Talk

The equilibrium solutions (averages) do not mean that the queuing system settles down to a set of fixed values. Rather, the queue continues to change as customers enter the system and have their service completed. The formula means that the probabilities or output generated for the queue length at some future time will settle down to these fixed values. Due to the randomness of the arrivals, the actual queue length continues to fluctuate indefinitely.

Output Examined

Table 18.2 provides a description of the output variables.

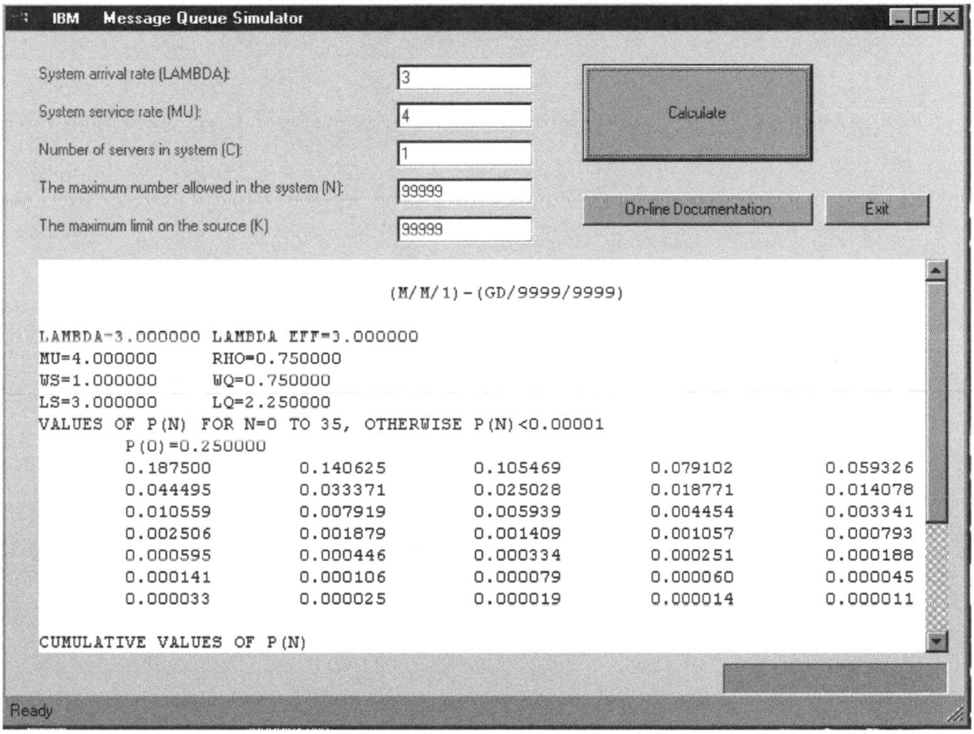

Figure 18-4
Queue simulator.

Table 18.2 Description of Output Variables

Variable	Description
P(N)	Probability of n transactions in the system
LS	Expected number of transactions in system
LQ	Expected number of customers in queue
WS	Expected waiting time in system (in queue + in service)
WQ	Expected waiting time in queue
LAMBDA (a)	Arrival rate of distribution
MU (b)	Departure rate or distribution
RHO	LAMBDA/MU
N (e)	Maximum number allowed in the system (in queue + in service)
K (f)	Size of calling source
C (c)	Number of servers in system
99999	This number or greater is treated as infinity
GD (d)	Service discipline (e.g., FIFO, LIFO, or SIRO)

Program Capabilities

This program is capable of handling the following scenarios (using Kendal notation):

M/M/1:GD/XXX/XXX.
M/M/1:GD/****/**** (* – represents infinity).
M/M/N:GD/***/**** (* – represents infinity).
M/M/99999:GD/99999/99999 is a special case.
M/M/99999:GD/0/9999 is a special case of no waiting room. Erlang B equivalent.
PURE BIRTH MODEL (MU=0).
PURE DEATH MODEL (LAMBDA=0).

Requirements for Queue Simulator

Here are the requirements for using the queue simulator on a service:

- Work-conserving queue ideal scenario: Transactions or messages must be delivered or served once admitted to the server, and the transmission link is never idle, so long as there is at least one message waiting for transmission.
- Observation required, since not all transaction servers behave like the ideal scenario.
- Some applications are SIRO (serviced in random order); therefore, random element queue access is needed.

Criteria for Picking the Simulator Over the Web Site

First, determine whether the connections should be queued or straight socket connections by referring to Table 18.3. If queues are used, so is the simulator. Otherwise, for connections, the Web site (www.erlang.com) is the recommended tool for simulation.

CONCLUSION . . . .

Upon collecting the data, reducing it, modeling it, and using it in forecasts, it shall be possible to predict the following:

- How many servers are needed.
- The disk storage requirements.
- The average transaction delay.

Table 18.3 Queues vs. Connections

WHEN Message or Transaction	THEN Use queues	ELSE Use connections
Duration of message exchange	Short (fewer than 10 messages)	Long (10 messages or more)
Criticality of network restart time	High, need fastest restart possible	Low, delayed restart tolerated
Importance of parallel operations	High	Low
Variety of information flow patterns	All information flow patterns	Most closed trees and chains
Dependence upon serialization	Very low	High or medium

Furthermore, the analysis results in the following benefits:

- Performance comparison knowledge (platforms or products).
- Ability to dimension system without waste.
- Gained understanding of system equates to fewer surprises in the field.
- Bottlenecks uncovered (i.e., context switching).

ACRONYMS . . . .

Table 18.4 shows computer scientists' most frequently used terms in queuing theory and operations research.

Table 18.4 *Acronyms*

Term	Description
Arrivals	The arrival process is single or bulk, random or stochastic.
Blocking probability	The blocking probability determines the grade of service. It varies from almost zero (best case, but most expensive) to one (worst case, all transactions blocked). The grade of service is written as P.05 (five percent blocking).
Design of service facility	The designs of service facility include • Series. • Parallel. • Network station.
Engset ($M > N$)	Used in tandem switching where M is an incoming trunk and is outgoing. The blocking probability is not straightforward Erlang C.
Erlang B	A probability distribution developed by A.K. Erlang to estimate the number of telephone trunks needed to carry a given amount of traffic. Erlang B assumes that, when a call arriving at random finds all trunks busy, it vanishes (the blocked calls cleared condition). Erlang B is also known as "lost calls cleared." *Erlang B is issued when traffic is random and there is no queuing.* Calls that cannot get through go away and do not return. This is the primary assumption behind Erlang B. Erlang B is easier to program than Poisson or Erlang C. This convenience is one of its main recommendations. Using Erlang B will produce a phone network with fewer trunks than one using Poisson formulae.

Table 18.4 Acronyms (continued)

Term	Description
Erlang C	A formula for designing operator pools, ACDs, and telephone traffic handling. Used when traffic is random and there is queuing. It assumes that all callers will wait indefinitely to get through. Therefore, offered traffic cannot be bigger than the number of trunks available (if it is, more traffic will come in than goes out, and queue delay will become infinite.). For a forecasting tool, please see www.erlang.com.
Filled, empty	Filled is one of the many states a queue may be in, but more importantly, when a queue is full, it blocks oncoming transactions.
Finite size	Queues are finite in size. Processor, memory, and disk space, in the case of MQSeries software, bind them.
Human behavior	Certain aspects of human behavior affect a queue's performance. They are as follows: • Jockeying, balking. • Reneging, perception.
Kendal notation	D.G. Kendal (1953) initially devised the standard queuing notation in the form (a/b/c). Later, A.M. Lee (1966) added the symbols (d) and (e). Lastly, it was augmented by H. A. Taha (a/b/c):(d/e/f).
Link utilization (load vs. capacity)	The ratio of load to capacity is defined as link utilization.
Little's formula	This formula relates the delay directly to the average queue occupancy. This theorem says that, for any work-conserving queuing system, the average occupancy of the system must equal the average delay for the system multiplied by the average arrival rate.
Loss probability	This is measured by the fraction of packet arrivals that are lost over a specified interval of time. The buffer is full at a packet arrival.
Poisson distribution	A mathematical formula, named after the French mathematician S. D. Poisson, that indicates the probability of certain events occurring. The formula assumes no blocking. It is not to be confused with the Poisson process.

(continued)

Table 18.4 Acronyms (continued)

Term	Description
Poisson process (equally spaced in time)	A kind of random process, based on simplified mathematical assumptions, that makes the development of complex probability function easier. In queuing theory, the arrival of transactions for service is considered a Poisson process if they arrive at random, individually and collectively. In addition, the probability of a new transaction arriving in any time interval is independent of the number of transactions already present.
Priority service	Priority service may follow one of two rules: 1. Preemptive rule—the service of a lower priority customer may be interrupted in favor of an arriving customer with higher priority. 2. Nonpreemptive rule— a customer, once in service, will leave the facility only after his service is completed and regardless of the priority of the arriving customer.
Queue states (pure death, steady, transient, pure birth)	Since any queuing system operates as a function of time, one must decide in advance whether the interest is in the analysis of the system in the transient or steady-state condition. Transient conditions prevail when the behavior of the system continues to depend on time. Thus, the pure birth and death processes always operate under transient conditions. On the other hand, queues with combined arrivals and departures start under transient conditions and gradually reach steady state after a sufficient amount of time has elapsed.
Server states (busy, idle)	A server has two states—busy and idle.
Service time	The time it takes for a request to be served, not including the time spent on queue. It is related to the server characteristics. Transactions are served in a statistically varying manner, because of the server characteristics.
Simulation	Simulation models can be physical models (either exact replicas or scaled-down versions), simple mathematical models, linear statistical models, complex mathematical models, or nonlinear statistical models.

Table 18.4 Acronyms (continued)

Term	Description
Statistic dependencies	The dependencies are as follows: • Message arrival process (Poisson). • Packet-length distribution (fixed, random). • Number of servers. • Service discipline (LIFO, FIFO, SIRO).
Throughput	This is defined by an expression. The expression differs by queue and by queue size (finite). State-dependent queues have another expression.

REFERENCES . . . .

- Blakeley, *Messaging and Queuing Using the MQI.* (McGraw-Hill, 1995).
- Lewis, *Wireless PC-Based Services: How to Design, Build, and Program Systems Using the Latest Internet Standards and Organizational Techniques.* (Intellectual Capital, 1999).
- Schwartz, *Telecommunications Networks Protocols, Modeling and Analysis.* (Addison-Wesley, 1987).
- Stevens, W. Richard, *UNIX Network Programming.* (Prentice Hall, 1990).
- Stevens, W. Richard, *Advanced Programming in the UNIX Environment.* (Addison-Wesley, 1992).
- Taha, *Operations Researc,* 4th Ed. (Macmillan, 1987).

19 The Future of Wireless Services

THE ULTIMATE WIRELESS COMMUNICATIONS . . . .

Origin

In the early 1990s, IBM Fellow Charles H. Bennet of the Thomas J. Watson Research Center and five other scientist proposed the theory of quantum teleportation. In their scheme, information about a specific property of a particle, such as a proton of light, could be transferred along both a classical and a quantum mechanical channel. As a result, a proton with exactly the same property would be produced at a remote location a galaxy apart!

First Demonstration

Experimenters at Austria's University of Innsbruck have provided the first demonstration of quantum teleportation. Anton Zeilinger's group transferred a property of a single proton—its angle of polarization—to another, independent remote proton. Another scientific team in Rome has reportedly confirmed the result.

Research Goals

The ultimate goal of the various efforts in quantum information theory include

- Teleportation.
- Quantum error-correction procedures.
- Quantum computer.
- Quantum security encryption.

Theoretically, the quantum computer should work much faster than conventional computers. Bennett says, "quantum computers, like fusion power, prove possible in principle, but not practical for a long time."[1]

Quantum Computer

A 10-bit quantum computer will probably be built in two years, and the number of bits should double every four years, according to Seth Lloyd, MIT.[2]

Qubit

Quantum mechanics enables the encoding of information in quantum bits (qubits). Unlike a classical bit, which stores only a single value (0 or 1), a qubit can store both 0 and 1 at the same time.

Quantum Registers

A 64-qubit quantum register can hold 2^{64} values at once, unlike the classical register, which holds a 64-bit value.

Entanglement Particles

At the foundation of quantum parallelism lies the fact that quantum superposition of multiple particles admits strange correlation with no classical equivalent.

How It Works Metaphor

When Scott and Nathalie play with their coins individually, the coins appear to behave normally—tossing each coin gives perfectly random results. However, we soon notice that every time Nathalie's coin lands on heads, so does Scott's, and vice versa. Since there is no possible means of communications between the two coins, this must be magic, right? No, it is quantum mechanics.

---

[1]*Demonstrating Teleportation*, IBM Research Number 1 & 2, p. 4 (International Business Machines Corporation, 1998).

[2]Lloyd, Seth, *Millennium Speculation.* **33** (2000) 1:40. IEEE.

Although physicists have not seen such correlations between large, separate objects like coins, they have created such correlations between individual atoms.

EPR

Objects correlated in this way are said to be quantum mechanically entangled, and pairs of objects exhibiting such correlations are called EPR (Einstein, Podolsky, and Rosen) pairs.

Einstein's Law Violated?

The remaining question is, "Does this violate Einstein's Special Theory of Relativity, which postulates the speed of light as the fastest speed at which we can transmit information?" The answer is no—there is no information sent. The process is completely random, and randomness is precisely not information. Both the sender and the receiver of the message simultaneously access the identical random decisions of the entangled object (i.e., proton), which are used to encode and decode a message at speeds far greater than the speed of light. The only way to convert the random decisions of the protons into information is to edit the random sequence of proton decisions. But editing this random sequence would require observing the proton decision, which in turn would cause quantum decoherence, which would destroy the quantum entanglement. So, Einstein's theory is preserved.

Even though we cannot instantly transmit information using quantum entanglement, transmitting randomness is still very useful in the process of encryption. If the sender and the receiver of a message are at the two ends of a microwave shot, they can use the precisely matched random decisions of a stream of quantum entangled protons to respectively encode and decode a message. Since the encryption is fundamentally random and nonrepeating, it cannot be broken. Eavesdropping would also be impossible, as this would cause quantum decoherence that could be detected at both ends. Privacy would be preserved.

Tech Talk

The quantum encryption is transmitting the code instantaneously. The actual wireless message will arrive much more slowly—at only the speed of light.

VOLTAGE CONTROL OSCILLATORS . . . .

Origin

A group headed by Mehmet Soyuer at IBM Research has taken a significant step toward creating a wireless technology that can support the high data rates needed to bring the Internet and multimedia to the mobile user.

The team designed and tested integrated circuits, known as voltage control oscillators (VCOs), that help generate carrier frequencies in four frequencies and in four frequency ranges. This technology could become the heartbeat of a wireless device; it generates the carrier frequency in a wireless system on which the signal carrying the data is impressed.

Frequencies

Frequencies of 17.1 GHz have been reached and are the basis for a new European microwave communications band. The technology also applies to frequencies at 5 GHz, a band that the US FCC has dedicated to short-range, high-speed wireless data communications, as well as to frequencies around 9 GHz and 4.4 GHz.

The new VCOs are fully monolithic and contain no external components, such as inductors or capacitors. Equally as important is their fully differential architecture, which minimizes noise coupling between the digital parts of a highly integrated chip and a sensitive analog VCO. The added circuitry of such architecture normally requires high power levels. However, the silicon germanium (SiGe) technology that the team used succeeds with an increase in power consumption.

KURZWEIL APPLIED INTELLIGENCE . . . .

Prediction

Mr. Ray Kurzweil, author of *When Computers Exceed Human Intelligence—The Age of Spiritual Machines*, predicted the following:

The three technologies for a translating telephone (a device that allows you speak and listen in one language, such as English, and your caller hears you and replies in another language, such as German) are as follows:

1. Speaker independent, continuous, large-vocabulary speech recognition.
2. Language translation.
3. Speech synthesis.

Will each exist in sufficient quality for a first-generation system soon? We can expect "translating telephones with reasonable levels of performance for at least the more popular languages early in the first decade of the twenty-first century."

What Happened

Effective, speaker-independent speech recognition capable of handling continuous speech and a large vocabulary has been introduced with little success in the wireless space. Third-generation wireless may address the voice sampling issues associated with this technology. However, deployment of these systems will not begin until the year 2002. Speaker-dependent recognition works well, today.

Automatic language translation, which rapidly translates Web-site text from one language to another, is available directly from Web browsers. As discussed, applying this technology to the microbrowser phone is possible now.

Text-to-speech synthesis for a wide variety of languages has been available for many years. Kurweil predicted systems to be available commercially early in the first decade of the twenty-first century. The truth is that this technology is available now.

Glossary

Table G.1   Acronyms

CGI	Common Gateway Interface
LDAP	Lightweight Directory Access Protocol
HTML	Hypertext Markup Language
IMAP	Internet Message Access Protocol
SMTP	Simple Mail Transfer Protocol
UDP	User Datagram Protocol
WAE	Wireless Application Environment
WAP	Wireless Application Protocol
WDP	Wireless Datagram Protocol
WML	Wireless Markup Language
WSP	Wireless Session Protocol
WTLS	Wireless Transport Layer Security
WTP	Wireless Transaction Protocol
TDMA	Time Division Multiple Access—A technique in which each frequency channel is divided into several time slots, each corresponding to a voice channel.
GSM 900	Includes variants of DCS 1800 and PCS 1900, D-AMPS and PDC, are all of which TDMA systems, as are DECT, PHS, and several other digital systems.
GPRS	General Packet Radio System
WCDMA	Wideband CDMA
EDGE	Enhanced Data Rates for GSM Evolution
UMTS	Universal Mobile Telecommunications System

(continued)

Table G.1   Acronyms (continued)

ITU	The International Telecommunications Union, headquartered in Geneva, Switzerland, is an international organization through which governments and the private sector coordinate global telecom networks and services. ITU activities include the coordination, development, regulation, and standardization of telecommunications, as well as organization of regional and world telecom events.
IETF	The Internet Engineering Task Force is the protocol engineering and development arm of the Internet. The IETF is a large, open, international community of network designers, operators, vendors, and researchers concerned with the evolution of the Internet architecture and the smooth operation of the Internet.
IMTC	The International Multimedia Telecommunications Consortium, Inc. is a nonprofit corporation founded to promote the creation and adoption of international standards for multipoint document and video teleconferencing. The IMTC and its members promote a "standards first" initiative to guarantee interworking for all aspects of multimedia teleconferencing.
PCI	The Peripheral Component Interconnect hosts controllers and peripherals.
AAC	Aeronautical Administrative Communications
ACARS	Aeronautical Communication Addressing and Reporting System
ADS	Automated Dependent Surveillance
AEEC	Airline Electronic Engineering Committee
AGS	Aeronautical Gateway Subsystem
AMCP	Aeronautical Mobile Communication Panel
AMPS	Advanced Mobile Phone System
AMS(R)S	Aeronautical Mobile Satellite (Route) Service—a safety-related service
AMSS	Aeronautical Mobile Satellite Service
ANC	Air Navigation Commission
AOC	Aeronautical Operational Control
APC	Aeronautical Passenger Communications
ASOC	Allied Signal Operations Center
ATC	Air Traffic Control
ATM	Air Traffic Management
ATN	Aeronautical Telecommunications Network
ATS	Air Traffic Services

BER	Bit Error Rate
BPSK	Binary Phase Shift Keying
CDR	Call Detail Record
CEPT	Conference Européenne des Postes et Telecommunications
CNS	Control, Navigation & Surveillance
EIRP	Effective Isotropic Radiated Power
ETSI	European Telecommunications Standards Institute
FANS	Future Air Navigation System
FDMA	Frequency Division Multiple Access
GATM	Government Air Traffic Management
GTA	Ground-to-Air
GW	Gateway
HFDL	High-Frequency Data Link
HLR	Home Location Register
HPA	High-Power Amplifier
IAV	Iridium Avionics
ICAO	International Civil Aviation Organization
IFE	In-flight Entertainment
ISU	Individual Subscriber Unit
ITU-R	International Telecommunication Union—Radio Communication Bureau
Kbps	Kilobits per second
Ksps	Kilosymbols per second
LBT	L-band Transceiver
LEO	Low Earth Orbit
LLA	Latitude, Longitude, Altitude
MASPS	Minimum Avionics System Performance Standards
MDA	Message Delivery Area
MOC	Message Origination Center
MOPS	Minimum Operational Performance Standards
MOS	Mean Opinion Score
NATS	North American Air Traffic Service

(continued)

Table G.1   Acronyms (continued)

OEM	Original Equipment Manufacturer
OOOI	Out, Off, On, In
QPSK	Quaternary Phase Shift Keying
RCU	Radio Channel Unit
RTCA	Radio Tele communication Association
SARP	Standard and Recommended Practices—An RTCA standard
SIM	Subscriber Identification Module
SNOC	System Network Operational Control
STU	Satellite Terminal Unit
SV	Space Vehicle
TDMA	Time Division Multiple Access
TFTS	Terrestrial Flight Telephony System

Reference

FOR MORE INFORMATION . . . .

Please contact me for more information, with any corrections, or if you have any suggestions for future editions of this book, at

- R.Scott.Lewis@excite.com

or

- Intellectual Capital
  PO Box 904
  Floral Park, NY 11002.

Portal

The information and source-code portal (a.k.a., URL) for Intellectual Capital is http://www.go2intelllectualcapital.com.

REFERENCES . . . .

- Angel, Jonathan, "Satellite-Based Networking: Set for Takeoff?," *Network Magazine—A Miller Freeman Publication* **14** (1999) 6:44.
- Booch, Grady, *Object Solutions Managing the Object-Oriented Project* (Addison-Wesley, 1996).
- RFC1733-M. Crispin [1 DEC 94] *Distributed Electronic Mail Models in IMAP4.*
- Dutta-Roy, Amitava, *Fixed Wireless Routes for Internet Access* (*IEEE Spectrum,* 1999, **36,** 9:61.

- Johnston, Stuart, [1998] "Microsoft Invests in the Millennium" (*Information Week* 1998).

- Meurling, John and Richard Jeans, *The Mobile Phone Book: The invention of the mobile phone industry* (Ericsson Radio System AB, 1994).

- Newman, David, "Cellular Modems: Hurry Up and Wait," *Data Communications Magazine* (1996) 69.

- Oliphant, Malcom W., "The Mobile Phone Meets the Internet," *IEEE Spectrum* **36** (1999) 8:20.

- Robinson, Sara, "Researchers Crack Code in Cell Phone," *The New York Times,* December 1999, C1. Section 1.

- Royce, Walker, *Software Project Management: A Unified Framework* (Addison-Wesley, 1998).

- Thompson, Tom, [1998] "I$_2$O Beats I/O Bottlenecks, *Byte Magazine,* pg. 85.

Index

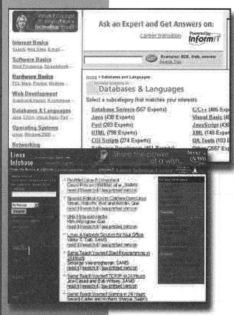

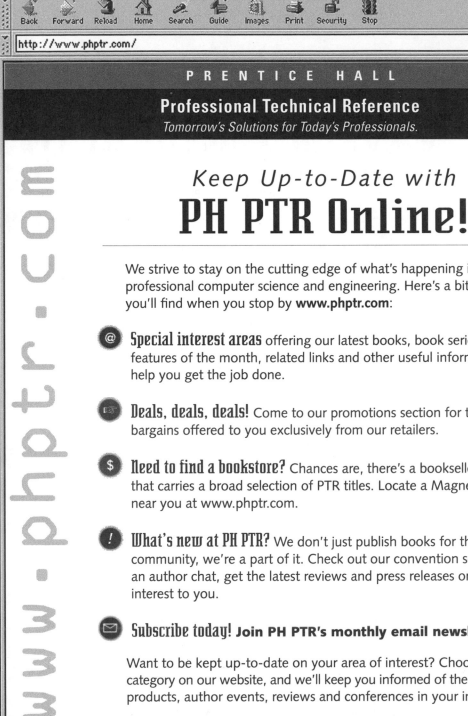